PSYCHOLOGY AND WESTERN RELIGION

from

The Collected Works of C. G. Jung

VOLUMES 11, 18

BOLLINGEN SERIES XX

PSYCHOLOGY AND WESTERN RELIGION

C. G. JUNG

TRANSLATED BY R.F.C. HULL

BOLLINGEN SERIES

PRINCETON UNIVERSITY PRESS

41 WILLIAM STREET, PRINCETON, NEW JERSEY 08540

"Letter to Père Lachat" was translated from the French by A.S.B. Glover; the last two articles were written by Jung in English.

All the volumes comprising the Collected Works constitute number XX in Bollingen Series, under the editorship of Herbert Read (d. 1968), Michael Fordham, and Gerhard Adler; executive editor, William McGuire.

LIBRARY OF CONGRESS CATALOG CARD NUMBER: 84-42548
ISBN 0-691-01862-6
PRINTED IN THE UNITED STATES OF AMERICA

First Princeton/Bollingen Paperback Edition, 1984

9 8 7 6 5

EDITORIAL NOTE

Jung's principal interest was in the psychology of Western man and so in his religious life and development. Religion, Jung stated, is "a careful and scrupulous observation of what Rudolf Otto aptly termed the *numinosum*, that is, a dynamic agency or effect not caused by an arbitrary act of will." He was struck by the contrasting methods of observation employed in the religions of the East and in those of the predominantly Christian West. In his view, the two are radically different. An entire volume of the Collected Works, some 600 pages, is devoted to "Psychology and Religion: West and East," but for a full understanding of Jung's thesis on religion a thorough grasp of his theory of the archetypes is essential, as well as a knowledge of several other of the volumes, of which *Aion* and *Psychology and Alchemy* may be singled out.

The present selection opens with two of Jung's weightier essays on Christian religion, devoted respectively to the Dogma of the Trinity and Transformation Symbolism in the Mass. Both originated as lectures at the Eranos Conference in Ascona, Switzerland, during the dark early years of World War II, when the country was isolated and the future doubtful. Jung subsequently expanded both essays into the versions here published.[1]

Several shorter works, both earlier and later, are grouped in the third section: a study of the Swiss patron saint, Brother Klaus; two essays on the relation between psychotherapy and religious healing; the two documents that originated as communications—to a French priest, on the subject of the Holy Spirit, and to a group of American women, on Resurrection. The selection closes with a lengthy and rather unclassifiable work which the Editors entitled "Jung and

[1] A third and equally weighty essay is *Psychology and Religion*, originally given as The Terry Lectures at Yale University in 1937, and available in its original form from the Yale University Press. The revised and augmented version, 1940, is in Collected Works 11, which also contains Jung's most mature and challenging brief on Western religion, *Answer to Job*, also available in a separate paperback (Princeton).

Religious Belief," consisting of questions put to Jung by two English clergymen and his often extensive replies.

The last three works are taken from Volume 18, *The Symbolic Life*, which contains a number of other shorter writings on aspects of religion. The reader is directed, furthermore, to the two-volume edition of Jung's *Letters*, selected and edited by Gerhard Adler and Aniela Jaffé, for numerous statements on religion particularly in the late years.[2] Jung's *earliest* formulations on Christian belief are found in a recently published work, *The Zofingia Lectures* (Supplementary Volume A, 1983), being Jung's addresses to an undergraduate society during his years at Basel University, 1896-1899.

The essential writings on Eastern religion and philosophy are collected in a paperback entitled *Psychology and the East.*

W. M.

[2] Some of these are found in the paperback volume *Selected Letters*, edited by Gerhard Adler (Princeton, 1984).

TABLE OF CONTENTS

Editorial Note v

I

A Psychological Approach to the Dogma of the Trinity 3

II

Transformation Symbolism in the Mass 97

III

Shorter Essays

Psychotherapists or the Clergy 195

Psychoanalysis and the Cure of Souls 217

Brother Klaus 225

Letter to Père Lachat 233

On Resurrection 247

IV

Jung and Religious Belief 253

Contents of the Collected Works 299

PSYCHOLOGY AND WESTERN RELIGION

I

A PSYCHOLOGICAL APPROACH TO THE DOGMA OF THE TRINITY

Noli foras ire, in teipsum redi;
in interiore homine habitat veritas.

(Go not outside, return into thyself:
Truth dwells in the inward man.)

—St. Augustine,
Liber de vera religione, xxix (72)

INTRODUCTION

169 The present study grew up out of a lecture I gave at the Eranos meeting in 1940, under the title "On the Psychology of the Idea of the Trinity." The lecture, though subsequently published,[1] was no more than a sketch, and it was clear to me from the beginning that it needed improving. Hence I felt under a kind of moral obligation to return to this theme in order to treat it in a manner befitting its dignity and importance.

170 From the reactions the lecture provoked, it was plain that some of my readers found a psychological discussion of Christian symbols objectionable even when it carefully avoided any infringement of their religious value. Presumably my critics would have found less to object to had the same psychological treatment been accorded to Buddhist symbols, whose sacredness is just as indubitable. Yet, what is sauce for the goose is sauce for the gander. I have to ask myself also, in all seriousness, whether it might not be far more dangerous if Christian symbols were made inaccessible to thoughtful understanding by being banished to a sphere of sacrosanct unintelligibility. They can easily become so remote from us that their irrationality turns

[1] "Zur Psychologie der Trinitätsidee," *Eranos-Jahrbuch 1940–41* (Zurich, 1942). [Later revised and expanded as "Versuch zu einer psychologischen Deutung des Trinitätsdogmas," *Symbolik des Geistes* (Zurich, 1948), pp. 321–446, from which version the present translation is made.—Editors.]

into preposterous nonsense. Faith is a charisma not granted to all; instead, man has the gift of thought, which can strive after the highest things. The timid defensiveness certain moderns display when it comes to thinking about symbols was certainly not shared by St. Paul or by many of the venerable Church Fathers.[2] This timidity and anxiety about Christian symbols is not a good sign. If these symbols stand for a higher truth—which, presumably, my critics do not doubt—then science can only make a fool of itself if it proceeds incautiously in its efforts to understand them. Besides, it has never been my intention to invalidate the meaning of symbols; I concern myself with them precisely because I am convinced of their psychological validity. People who merely believe and don't think always forget that they continually expose themselves to their own worst enemy: doubt. Wherever belief reigns, doubt lurks in the background. But thinking people welcome doubt: it serves them as a valuable stepping-stone to better knowledge. People who can believe should be a little more tolerant with those of their fellows who are only capable of thinking. Belief has already conquered the summit which thinking tries to win by toilsome climbing. The believer ought not to project his habitual enemy, doubt, upon the thinker, thereby suspecting him of destructive designs. If the ancients had not done a bit of thinking we would not possess any dogma about the Trinity at all. The fact that a dogma is on the one hand believed and on the other hand is an object of thought is proof of its vitality. Therefore let the believer rejoice that others, too, seek to climb the mountain on whose peak he sits.

171 My attempt to make the most sacred of all dogmatic symbols, the Trinity, an object of psychological study is an undertaking of whose audacity I am very well aware. Not having any theological knowledge worth mentioning, I must rely in this respect on the texts available to every layman. But since I have no intention of involving myself in the metaphysics of the Trinity, I am free to accept the Church's own formulation of the dogma, without having to enter into all the complicated metaphysical speculations that have gathered round it in the course of history. For the purposes of psychological discussion the elaborate ver-

2 Of the older ones I refer chiefly to Clement of Alexandria (d. *c.* 216), Origen (d. 253), and Pseudo-Dionysus the Areopagite (d. end of 5th cent.).

sion contained in the Athanasian Creed would be sufficient, as this shows very clearly what Church doctrine understands by the Trinity. Nevertheless, a certain amount of historical explanation has proved unavoidable for the sake of psychological understanding. My chief object, however, is to give a detailed exposition of those psychological views which seem to me necessary if we are to understand the dogma as a symbol in the psychological sense. Yet my purpose would be radically misunderstood if it were conceived as an attempt to "psychologize" the dogma. Symbols that have an archetypal foundation can never be reduced to anything else, as must be obvious to anybody who possesses the slightest knowledge of my writings. To many people it may seem strange that a doctor with a scientific training should interest himself in the Trinity at all. But anyone who has experienced how closely and meaningfully these *représentations collectives* are bound up with the weal and woe of the human soul will readily understand that the central symbol of Christianity must have, above all else, a psychological meaning, for without this it could never have acquired any universal meaning whatever, but would have been relegated long ago to the dusty cabinet of spiritual monstrosities and shared the fate of the many-armed and many-headed gods of India and Greece. But since the dogma stands in a relationship of living reciprocity to the psyche, whence it originated in the first place, it expresses many of the things I am endeavouring to say over again, even though with the uncomfortable feeling that there is much in my exposition that still needs improvement.

1. PRE-CHRISTIAN PARALLELS

I. BABYLONIA

172 In proposing to approach this central symbol of Christianity, the Trinity, from the psychological point of view, I realize that I am trespassing on territory that must seem very far removed from psychology. Everything to do with religion, everything it is and asserts, touches the human soul so closely that psychology least of all can afford to overlook it. A conception like the Trinity pertains so much to the realm of theology that the only one of the profane sciences to pay any attention to it nowadays is history. Indeed, most people have ceased even to think about dogma, especially about a concept as hard to visualize as the Trinity. Even among professing Christians there are very few who think seriously about the Trinity as a matter of dogma and would consider it a possible subject for reflection—not to mention the educated public. A recent exception is Georg Koepgen's very important book, *Die Gnosis des Christentums,*[1] which, unfortunately, soon found its way onto the Index despite the episcopal "Placet." For all those who are seriously concerned to understand dogmatic ideas, this book of Koepgen's is a perfect example of thinking which has fallen under the spell of trinitarian symbolism.

1 Salzburg, 1939.

173 Triads of gods appear very early, at a primitive level. The archaic triads in the religions of antiquity and of the East are too numerous to be mentioned here. Arrangement in triads is an archetype in the history of religion, which in all probability formed the basis of the Christian Trinity. Often these triads do not consist of three different deities independent of one another; instead, there is a distinct tendency for certain family relationships to arise within the triads. I would mention as an example the Babylonian triads, of which the most important is Anu, Bel, and Ea. Ea, personifying knowledge, is the father of Bel ("Lord"), who personifies practical activity.[2] A secondary, rather later triad is the one made up of Sin (moon), Shamash (sun), and Adad (storm). Here Adad is the son of the supreme god, Anu.[3] Under Nebuchadnezzar, Adad was the "Lord of heaven and earth." This suggestion of a father-son relationship comes out more clearly at the time of Hammurabi: Marduk, the son of Ea, was entrusted with Bel's power and thrust him into the background.[4] Ea was a "loving, proud father, who willingly transferred his power and rights to his son." [5] Marduk was originally a sun-god, with the cognomen "Lord" (Bel); [6] he was the mediator between his father Ea and mankind. Ea declared that he knew nothing that his son did not know.[7] Marduk, as his fight with Tiamat shows, is a redeemer. He is "the compassionate one, who loves to awaken the dead"; the "Great-eared," who hears the pleadings of men. He is a helper and healer, a true saviour. This teaching about a redeemer flourished on Babylonian soil all through the Christian era and goes on living today in the religion of the Mandaeans (who still exist in Mesopotamia), especially in their redeemer figure Manda d' Hayya or Hibil Ziwa.[8] Among the Mandaeans he appears also as a light-bringer and at the same time as a world-creator.[9] Just as, in the Babylonian epic, Marduk fashions the universe out of Tiamat, so Mani, the Original Man, makes heaven and earth from the skin, bones, and excrement of the children of darkness.[10] "The all-round influence which the myth of Marduk

2 Jastrow, *Die Religion Babyloniens und Assyriens,* I, p. 61.

3 Ibid., pp. 102, 143f. 4 P. 112. 5 P. 130. 6 P. 112.

7 P. 130. Cf. John 16:15.

8 Jeremias, *The Old Testament in the Light of the Ancient East,* I, p. 137.

9 Cf. John 1:3. 10 Kessler, *Mani,* pp. 267ff.

had on the religious ideas of the Israelites is surprising." [11]

174 It appears that Hammurabi worshipped only a dyad, Anu and Bel; but, as a divine ruler himself, he associated himself with them as the "proclaimer of Anu and Bel," [12] and this at a time when the worship of Marduk was nearing its height. Hammurabi felt himself the god of a new aeon [13]—the aeon of Aries, which was then beginning—and the suspicion is probably justified that tacit recognition was given to the triad Anu-Bel-Hammurabi.[14]

175 The fact that there is a secondary triad, Sin-Shamash-Ishtar, is indicative of another intra-triadic relationship. Ishtar [15] appears here in the place of Adad, the storm god. She is the mother of the gods, and at the same time the daughter [16] of Anu as well as of Sin.

176 Invocation of the ancient triads soon takes on a purely formal character. The triads prove to be "more a theological tenet than a living force." [17] They represent, in fact, the earliest beginnings of theology. Anu is the Lord of heaven, Bel is the Lord of the lower realm, earth, and Ea too is the god of an "underworld," but in his case it is the watery deep.[18] The knowledge that Ea personifies comes from the "depths of the waters." According to one Babylonian legend, Ea created Uddushunamir, a creature of light, who was the messenger of the gods on Ishtar's journey to hell. The name means: "His light (or rising) shines." [19] Jeremias connects him with Gilgamesh, the hero who was more than half a god.[20] The messenger of the gods was usually called Girru (Sumerian "Gibil"), the god of fire. As such he has an ethical aspect, for with his purifying fire he destroys evil. He too is a son of Ea, but on the other hand he is also described as a son of Anu. In this connection it is worth mentioning that Marduk as well has a dual nature, since in one

11 Roscher, *Lexikon,* II, 2, cols. 2371f., s.v. "Marduk."

12 Jastrow, p 139. Cf. John 1 : 18.

13 Cf. the Christian fish-symbol.

14 "Anu and Bel called me, Hammurabi, the exalted prince, the worshipper of the Gods, to go forth like the sun . . . to enlighten the land." Harper, *The Code of Hammurabi,* p. 3.

15 Cf. the invocation of the Holy Ghost as "Mother" in the Acts of Thomas (James, *The Apocryphal New Testament,* p. 376). Also the feminine nature of Sophia, who frequently represents the Holy Ghost.

16 Cf. Mary as creature and as Θεοτόκος.

17 Jastrow, p. 141.

18 P. 61.

19 P. 133.

20 Jeremias, I, pp. 247ff.

hymn he is called Mar Mummi, 'son of chaos.' In the same hymn his consort Sarpanitu is invoked along with Ea's wife, the mother of Marduk, as the "Silver-shining One." This is probably a reference to Venus, the *femina alba*. In alchemy the *albedo* changes into the moon, which, in Babylonia, was still masculine.[21] Marduk's companions were four dogs.[22] Here the number four may signify totality, just as it does in the case of the four sons of Horus, the four seraphim in the vision of Ezekiel, and the four symbols of the evangelists, consisting of three animals and one angel.

II. EGYPT

177 The ideas which are present only as intimations in Babylonian tradition are developed to full clarity in Egypt. I shall pass lightly over this subject here, as I have dealt with the Egyptian prefigurations of the Trinity at greater length elsewhere, in an as yet unfinished study of the symbolical bases of alchemy.[1] I shall only emphasize that Egyptian theology asserts, first and foremost, the essential unity (homoousia) of God as father and son, both represented by the king.[2] The third person appears in the form of Ka-mutef ("the bull of his mother"), who is none other than the *ka*, the procreative power of the deity. In it and through it father and son are combined not in a triad but in a triunity. To the extent that Ka-mutef is a special manifestation of the divine *ka*, we can "actually speak of a triunity of God, king, and *ka*, in the sense that God is the father, the king is the son, and *ka* the connecting-link between them." [3] In his concluding chapter Jacobsohn draws a parallel between this Egyptian idea and the Christian credo. Apropos the passage "qui conceptus est de Spiritu Sancto, natus ex Maria virgine," he

21 Cf. Mary's connections with the moon in Rahner, *Griechische Mythen in christlicher Deutung*, pp. 200ff., and "Mysterium Lunae," p. 80.

22 A possible reference to the realm of the dead on the one hand and to Nimrod the mighty hunter on the other. See Roscher, *Lexikon*, II, cols. 2371f., s.v. "Marduk."

1 [*Mysterium Coniunctionis*, ch. IV, 1–3.]

2 Jacobsohn, "Die dogmatische Stellung des Königs in der Theologie der alten Aegypter," p. 17.

3 Ibid., p. 58.

cites Karl Barth's formulation: "There is indeed a unity of God and man; God himself creates it. . . . It is no other unity than his own eternal unity as father and son. This unity is the Holy Ghost." [4] As procreator the Holy Ghost would correspond to Ka-mutef, who connotes and guarantees the unity of father and son. In this connection Jacobsohn cites Barth's comment on Luke 1:35 ("The Holy Ghost shall come upon thee, and the power of the Highest shall overshadow thee: therefore also that holy thing which shall be born of thee shall be called the Son of God"): "When the Bible speaks of the Holy Ghost, it is speaking of God as the combination of father and son, of the *vinculum caritatis.*" [5] The divine procreation of Pharaoh takes place through Ka-mutef, in the human mother of the king. But, like Mary, she remains outside the Trinity. As Preisigke points out, the early Christian Egyptians simply transferred their traditional ideas about the *ka* to the Holy Ghost.[6] This explains the curious fact that in the Coptic version of *Pistis Sophia,* dating from the third century, Jesus has the Holy Ghost as his double, just like a proper *ka.*[7] The Egyptian mythologem of the unity of substance of father and son, and of procreation in the king's mother, lasted until the Vth dynasty (about 2500 B.C.). Speaking of the birth of the divine boy in whom Horus manifests himself, God the Father says: "He will exercise a kingship of grace in this land, for my soul is in him," and to the child he says: "You are the son of my body, begotten by me." [8] "The sun he bears within him from his father's seed rises anew in him." His eyes are the sun and moon, the eyes of Horus.[9] We know that the passage in Luke 1:78f.: "Through the tender mercy of our God, whereby the dayspring from on high hath visited us, to give light to them that sit in darkness and in the shadow of death," refers to Malachi 4:2: "But unto you that fear my name shall the sun of righteousness arise with healing in his wings." Who does not think here of the winged sun-disc of Egypt?

4 P. 64. Barth, *Credo,* p. 70.

5 Barth, *Bibelstunden über Luk I,* p. 26.

6 Preisigke, *Die Gotteskraft der frühchristlichen Zeit;* also *Vom göttlichen Fluidum nach ägyptischer Anschauung.*

7 *Pistis Sophia* (trans. by Mead), p. 118.

8 Cf. Hebrews 1:5: "Thou art my Son, this day have I begotten thee."

9 A. Moret, "Du caractère religieux de la royauté pharaonique."

178 These ideas[10] passed over into Hellenistic syncretism and were transmitted to Christianity through Philo and Plutarch.[11] So it is not true, as is sometimes asserted even by modern theologians, that Egypt had little if any influence on the formation of Christian ideas. Quite the contrary. It is, indeed, highly improbable that only Babylonian ideas should have penetrated into Palestine, considering that this small buffer state had long been under Egyptian hegemony and had, moreover, the closest cultural ties with its powerful neighbour, especially after a flourishing Jewish colony established itself in Alexandria, several centuries before the birth of Christ. It is difficult to understand what could have induced Protestant theologians, whenever possible, to make it appear that the world of Christian ideas dropped straight out of heaven. The Catholic Church is liberal enough to look upon the Osiris-Horus-Isis myth, or at any rate suitable portions of it, as a prefiguration of the Christian legend of salvation. The numinous power of a mythologem and its value as truth are considerably enhanced if its archetypal character can be proved. The archetype is "that which is believed always, everywhere, and by everybody," and if it is not recognized consciously, then it appears from behind in its "wrathful" form, as the dark "son of chaos," the evil-doer, as Antichrist instead of Saviour—a fact which is all too clearly demonstrated by contemporary history.

III. GREECE

179 In enumerating the pre-Christian sources of the Trinity concept, we should not omit the mathematical speculations of the Greek philosophers. As we know, the philosophizing temper of the Greek mind is discernible even in St. John's gospel, a work that is, very obviously, of Gnostic inspiration. Later, at the time of the Greek Fathers, this spirit begins to amplify the archetypal content of the Revelation, interpreting it in Gnostic terms. Pythagoras and his school probably had the most to do with the moulding of Greek thought, and as one aspect of the Trinity is based on number symbolism, it would be worth our while to

10 Further material concerning pagan sources in Nielsen, *Der dreieinige Gott,* I.
11 Cf. Norden, *Die Geburt des Kindes,* pp. 77ff.

examine the Pythagorean system of numbers and see what it has to say about the three basic numbers with which we are concerned here. Zeller [1] says: "One is the first from which all other numbers arise, and in which the opposite qualities of numbers, the odd and the even, must therefore be united; two is the first even number; three the first that is uneven and perfect, because in it we first find beginning, middle, and end." [2] The views of the Pythagoreans influenced Plato, as is evident from his *Timaeus;* and, as this had an incalculable influence on the philosophical speculations of posterity, we shall have to go rather deeply into the psychology of number speculation.

180 The number one claims an exceptional position, which we meet again in the natural philosophy of the Middle Ages. According to this, one is not a number at all; the first number is two.[3] Two is the first number because, with it, separation and multiplication begin, which alone make counting possible. With the appearance of the number two, *another* appears alongside the one, a happening which is so striking that in many languages "the other" and "the second" are expressed by the same word. Also associated with the number two is the idea of right and left,[4] and remarkably enough, of favourable and unfavourable, good and bad. The "other" can have a "sinister" significance—or one feels it, at least, as something opposite and alien. Therefore, argues a medieval alchemist, God did not praise the second day of creation, because on this day (Monday, the day of the moon) the *binarius,* alias the devil,[5] came into existence. Two implies a one which is different and distinct from the "numberless" One. In other words, as soon as the number two appears, a unit is produced out of the original unity, and this unit is none other than that same unity split into two and turned into a "number." The "One" and the "Other" form an opposition, but there is no opposition between one and two, for these are simple numbers which are distinguished only by their arithmetical

1 *A History of Greek Philosophy,* I, p. 429.

2 Authority for the latter remark in Aristotle, *De coelo,* I, i, 268a.

3 The source for this appears to be Macrobius, *Commentarius in Somnium Scipionis,* I, 6, 8.

4 Cf. "the movement of the Different to the left" in the *Timaeus* 36C (trans. by Cornford, p. 73).

5 Cf. the etymological relations between G. *zwei,* 'two,' and *Zweifler,* 'doubter.' [In Eng., cf. *duplicity, double-dealer, double-cross, two-faced.*—TRANS.]

value and by nothing else. The "One," however, seeks to hold to its one-and-alone existence, while the "Other" evei strives to be another opposed to the One. The One will not let go of the Other because, if it did, it would lose its character; and the Other pushes itself away from the One in order to exist at all. Thus there arises a tension of opposites between the One and the Other. But every tension of opposites culminates in a release, out of which comes the "third." In the third, the tension is resolved and the lost unity is restored. Unity, the absolute One, cannot be numbered, it is indefinable and unknowable; only when it appears as a unit, the number one, is it knowable, for the "Other" which is required for this act of knowing is lacking in the condition of the One. Three is an unfolding of the One to a condition where it can be known—unity become recognizable; had it not been resolved into the polarity of the One and the Other, it would have remained fixed in a condition devoid of every quality. Three therefore appears as a suitable synonym for a process of development in time, and thus forms a parallel to the self-revelation of the Deity as the absolute One unfolded into Three. The relation of Threeness to Oneness can be expressed by an equilateral triangle,[6] $A = B = C$, that is, by the identity of the three, threeness being contained in its entirety in each of the three angles. This intellectual idea of the equilateral triangle is a conceptual model for the logical image of the Trinity.

181 In addition to the Pythagorean interpretation of numbers, we have to consider, as a more direct source of trinitarian ideas in Greek philosophy, the mystery-laden *Timaeus* of Plato. I shall quote, first of all, the classical argument in sections 31B–32A:

Hence the god, when he began to put together the body of the universe, set about making it of fire and earth. But two things alone cannot be satisfactorily united without a third; for there must be some bond between them drawing them together. And of all bonds the best is that which makes itself and the terms it connects a unity in the fullest sense; and it is of the nature of a continued geometrical proportion to effect this most perfectly. For whenever, of three numbers, the middle one between any two that are either solids or planes

[6] Harnack (*Dogmengeschichte,* II, p. 303) compares the scholastic conception of the Trinity to an equilateral triangle.

[i.e., cubes or squares] is such that, as the first is to it, so is it to the last, and conversely as the last is to the middle, so is the middle to the first, then since the middle becomes first and last, and again the last and first become middle, in that way all will necessarily come to play the same part towards one another, and by so doing they will all make a unity.[7]

In a geometrical progression, the quotient (q) of a series of terms remains the same, e.g.: $2:1 = 4:2 = 8:4 = 2$, or, algebraically expressed: a, aq, aq^2. The proportion is therefore as follows: 2 is to 4 as 4 is to 8, or a is to aq as aq is to aq^2.

182 This argument is now followed by a reflection which has far-reaching psychological implications: if a simple pair of opposites, say fire and earth, are bound together by a mean (μέσον), and if this bond is a geometrical proportion, then *one* mean can only connect plane figures, since two means are required to connect solids:

Now if it had been required that the body of the universe should be a plane surface with no depth, a single mean would have been enough to connect its companions and itself; but in fact the world was to be solid in form, and solids are always conjoined, not by one mean, but by two.[8]

Accordingly, the two-dimensional connection is not yet a physical reality, for a plane without extension in the third dimension is only an *abstract thought*. If it is to become a physical reality, three dimensions and therefore two means are required. Sir Thomas Heath[9] puts the problem in the following algebraic formulae:

Union in two dimensions of earth (p^2) and fire (q^2):

$$p^2 : pq = pq : q^2$$

Obviously the mean is pq.

Physical union of earth and fire, represented by p^3 and q^3 respectively:

$$p^3 : p^2q = p^2q : pq^2 = pq^2 : q^3$$

The two means are p^2q and pq^2, corresponding to the physical elements water and air.

7 Trans. by Cornford, p. 44. 8 Ibid., p. 44.

9 *A History of Greek Mathematics*, I, p. 89; Cornford, p. 47.

Accordingly, the god set water and air between fire and earth, and made them, so far as was possible, proportional to one another, so that as fire is to air, so is air to water, and as air is to water, so is water to earth, and thus he bound together the frame of a world visible and tangible. For these reasons and from such constituents, four in number, the body of the universe was brought into being, coming into concord by means of proportion, and from these it acquired Amity, so that united with itself it became indissoluble by any other power save him who bound it together.[10]

183 The union of one pair of opposites only produces a two-dimensional triad: $p^2 + pq + q^2$. This, being a plane figure, is not a reality but a thought. Hence two pairs of opposites, making a *quaternio* ($p^3 + p^2q + pq^2 + q^3$), are needed to represent physical reality. Here we meet, at any rate in veiled form, the dilemma of three and four alluded to in the opening words of the *Timaeus*. Goethe intuitively grasped the significance of this allusion when he says of the fourth Cabir in *Faust:* "He was the right one / Who thought for them all," and that "You might ask on Olympus" about the eighth "whom nobody thought of." [11]

184 It is interesting to note that Plato begins by representing the union of opposites two-dimensionally, as an intellectual problem to be solved by thinking, but then comes to see that its solution does not add up to reality. In the former case we have to do with a self-subsistent triad, and in the latter with a quaternity. This was the dilemma that perplexed the alchemists for more than a thousand years, and, as the "axiom of Maria Prophetissa" (the Jewess or Copt), it appears in modern dreams,[12] and is also found in psychology as the opposition between the functions of consciousness, three of which are fairly well differentiated, while the fourth, undifferentiated, "inferior" function is undomesticated, unadapted, uncontrolled, and primitive. Because of its contamination with the collective unconscious, it possesses archaic and mystical qualities, and is the complete opposite of the most differentiated function. For instance, if the most differentiated is thinking, or the intellect, then the inferior,[13] fourth

10 Cornford, pp. 44–45, slightly modified.

11 For a detailed account see *Psychology and Alchemy,* pars. 204ff.

12 As the dream in *Psychology and Alchemy,* par. 200, shows.

13 Judging, of course, from the standpoint of the most differentiated function.

function[14] will be feeling. Hence the opening words of the *Timaeus*—"One, two, three—but where, my dear Timaeus, is the fourth . . . ?"—fall familiarly upon the ears of the psychologist and alchemist, and for him as for Goethe there can be no doubt that Plato is alluding to something of mysterious import. We can now see that it was nothing less than the dilemma as to whether something we think about is a mere thought or a reality, or at least capable of becoming real. And this, for any philosopher who is not just an empty babbler, is a problem of the first order and no whit less important than the moral problems inseparably connected with it. In this matter Plato knew from personal experience how difficult is the step from two-dimensional thinking to its realization in three-dimensional fact.[15] Already with his friend Dionysius the Elder, tyrant of Syracuse, he had so many disagreements that the philosopher-politician contrived to sell him as a slave, from which fate he was preserved only because he had the good fortune to be ransomed by friends. His attempts to realize his political theories under Dionysius the Younger also ended in failure, and from then on Plato abandoned politics for good. Metaphysics seemed to him to offer more prospects than this ungovernable world. So, for him personally, the main emphasis lay on the two-dimensional world of thought; and this is especially true of the *Timaeus,* which was written after his political disappointments. It is generally reckoned as belonging to Plato's late works.

185 In these circumstances the opening words, not being attributable either to the jocosity of the author or to pure chance, take on a rather mournful significance: one of the four is absent because he is "unwell." If we regard the introductory scene as symbolical, this means that of the four elements out of which reality is composed, either air or water is missing. If air is missing, then there is no connecting link with spirit (fire), and if water is missing, there is no link with concrete reality (earth). Plato certainly did not lack spirit; the missing element he so much desired was the concrete realization of ideas. He had to

14 Cf. *Psychological Types,* Def. 30.

15 "The world is narrow and the brain is wide;
Thoughts in the head dwell lightly side by side,
Yet things in space run counter and fall foul."
—Schiller, *Wallensteins Tod,* II, 2.

content himself with the harmony of airy thought-structures that lacked weight, and with a paper surface that lacked depth. The step from three to four brought him sharply up against something unexpected and alien to his thought, something heavy, inert, and limited, which no "μὴ ὄν"[16] and no "privatio boni" can conjure away or diminish. Even God's fairest creation is corrupted by it, and idleness, stupidity, malice, discontent, sickness, old age and death fill the glorious body of the "blessed god." Truly a grievous spectacle, this sick world-soul, and unfortunately not at all as Plato's inner eye envisaged it when he wrote:

All this, then, was the plan of the everlasting god for the god who was going to be. According to this plan he made the body of the world smooth and uniform, everywhere equidistant from its centre, a body whole and complete, with complete bodies for its parts. And in the centre he set the soul and caused it to extend throughout the whole body, and he further wrapped the body round with soul on the outside. So he established one world alone, round and revolving in a circle, solitary but able by reason of its excellence to bear itself company, needing no other acquaintance or friend but sufficient unto itself. On all these accounts the world which he brought into being was a blessed god.[17]

186 This world, created by a god, is itself a god, a son of the self-manifesting father. Further, the demiurge furnished it with a soul which is "prior" to the body (34B). The world-soul was fashioned by the demiurge as follows: he made a mixture of the indivisible (ἀμερές) and the divisible (μεριστόν), thus producing a third form of existence. This third form had a nature independent of the "Same" (τὸ αὐτον) and the "Different" (τὸ ἕτερον). At first sight the "Same" seems to coincide with the indivisible and the "Different" with the divisible.[18] The text says: [19] "From

16 "Not being." 17 Cornford, p. 58, slightly modified.

18 Theodor Gomperz (*Greek Thinkers,* III, p. 215) mentions two primary substances which are designated as follows in Plato's *Philebus:* limit, unlimited; the same, the other; the divisible, the indivisible. He adds that Plato's pupils would have spoken of "unity" and of "the great and the small" or of "duality." From this it is clear that Gomperz regards the "Same" and the "indivisible" as synonymous, thus overlooking the resistance of the "Other," and the fundamentally fourfold nature of the world soul. (See below.)

19 [The version here given is translated from the German text of Otto Apelt (*Plato: Timaios und Kritias,* p. 52) cited by the author.—TRANS.]

the indivisible and ever the same substance [Cornford's "Sameness"], and that which is physically divisible, he mixed an intermediate, third form of existence which had its own being beside the Same and the Different, and this form he fashioned accordingly [κατὰ ταὐτά] as a mean between the indivisible and the physically divisible. Then taking these three existences, he mixed them again, forcing the nature of the Different, though it resisted the mixture, into union with the Same. Thus, with the admixture of being (οὐσία), the three became one." [20]

187 The world-soul, representing the governing principle of the whole physical world, therefore possesses a triune nature. And since, for Plato, the world is a δεύτερος θεός (second god), the world-soul is a revelation or unfolding of the God-image.[21]

188 Plato's account of the actual process of creation is very curious and calls for some elucidation. The first thing that strikes us is the twice-repeated συνεκεράσατο ('he mixed'). Why should the mixture be repeated, since it consists of three elements in the first place and contains no more than three at the end, and, in the second place, Same and Different appear to correspond with indivisible and divisible? Appearances, however, are deceptive. During the first mixture there is nothing to suggest that the divisible was recalcitrant and had to be forcibly united with the indivisible. In both mixtures it is rather a question of combining two separate pairs of opposites,[22] which, because they

20 Τῆς ἀμερίστου καὶ ἀεὶ κατὰ ταὐτὰ ἐχούσης οὐσίας καὶ τῆς αὖ περὶ τὰ σώματα γιγνομένης μεριστῆς, τρίτον ἐξ ἀμφοῖν ἐν μέσῳ συνεκεράσατο οὐσίας εἶδος· τῆς τὲ ταὐτοῦ φύσεως αὖ πέρι καὶ τῆς τοῦ ἑτέρου, καὶ κατὰ ταὐτὰ συνέστησεν ἐν μέσῳ τοῦ τε ἀμεροῦς αὐτῶν καὶ τοῦ κατὰ τὰ σώματα μεριστοῦ· καὶ τρία λαβὼν αὐτὰ ὄντα συνεκεράσατο εἰς μίαν πάντα ἰδέαν, τὴν θατέρου φύσιν δύσμεικτον οὖσαν εἰς ταὐτὸν συναρμόττων βίᾳ, μειγνὺς δὲ μετὰ τῆς οὐσίας.

Cornford (pp. 59–60) translates as follows: "Between the indivisible Existence that is ever in the same state and the divisible Existence that becomes in bodies, he compounded a third form of Existence composed of both. Again, in the case of Sameness and in that of Difference, he also on the same principle made a compound intermediate between that kind of them which is indivisible and the kind that is divisible in bodies. Then, taking the three, he blended them all into a unity, forcing the nature of Difference, hard as it was to mingle, into union with Sameness, and mixing them together with Existence" (35A).

21 Cf. *Timaeus* 37C, where the first God is described as the "father" and his creation as the copy of an original "pattern," which is himself (Cornford, p. 97).

are called upon to make a unity, may be thought of as arranged in a *quaternio:*

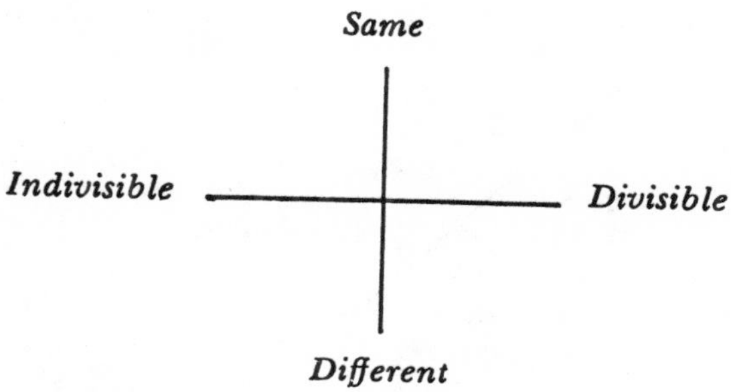

Indivisible and divisible, together with their mean, form a simple triad which has "its own being" beside the Same and the Different. This triad corresponds to the condition of "thought" not yet become "reality." For this a second mixture is needed, in which the Different (i.e., the "Other") is incorporated by force. The "Other" is therefore the "fourth" element, whose nature it is to be the "adversary" and to resist harmony. But the fourth, as the text says, is intimately connected with Plato's desire for "being." One thinks, not unnaturally, of the impatience the philosopher must have felt when reality proved so intractable to his ideas. That reasonableness might, under certain circumstances, have to be imposed by force is a notion that must sometimes have crossed his mind.

189 The passage as a whole, however, is far from simple. It can be translated in many ways and interpreted in many more. The critical point for us is *συνέστησεν ἐν μέσῳ τοῦ τε ἀμεροῦς*, literally, 'he compounded (a form of the nature of sameness and difference) *in the middle* (*ἐν μέσῳ*) of the indivisible (and the divisible).' Consequently the middle term of the second pair of opposites would coincide with the middle term of the first pair. The resultant figure is a quincunx, since the two pairs of opposites have a common mean or "third form" (*τρίτον εἶδος*):

22 This seems borne out by the fact that the first pair of opposites is correlated with *οὐσία* (being), and the second with *φύσις* (nature). If one had to choose between *οὐσία* and *φύσις*, the latter would probably be considered the more concrete of the two.

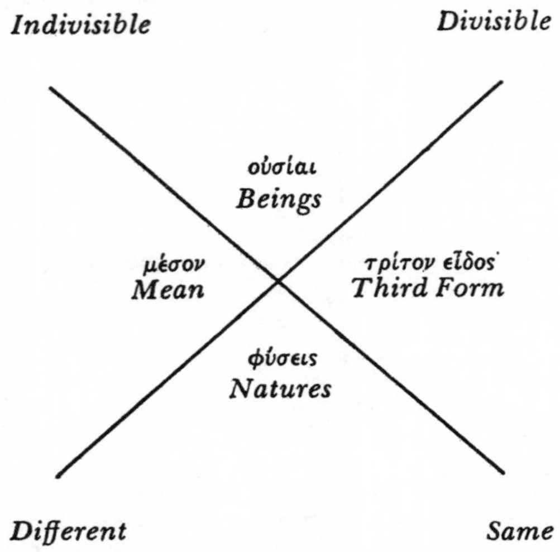

190 I have placed the pairs of opposites side by side, instead of facing one another (as in the previous diagram), in order to illustrate their union in a single mean. Three elements are to be distinguished in our diagram: the two pairs of opposites and their common mean, and I understand the text as referring to these three elements when it says: "Then, taking these three existences . . ." Since the mean is called the "third form," each pair of opposites can presumably be taken as representing the first and second forms: Indivisible = first form, Divisible = second form, mean = third form, and so on. Their union in a quincunx signifies union of the four elements in a world-body. Thomas Taylor, who was strongly influenced by Proclus, says in his commentary to the *Timaeus:* "For those which are connected with her essence in a following order, proceed from her [the *anima mundi*] according to the power of the fourth term (4), which possesses generative powers; but return to her according to the fifth (9) which reduces them to one." [23] Further confirmation of the quaternary nature of the world-soul and world-body may be found in the passage where the demiurge splits this whole fabric lengthwise into two halves and joins them up again in the form of a X.[24] According to Porphyry, a X in a circle

23 Reprinted as Bollingen Series III, *Plato: Timaeus and Critias,* p. 71.

24 *Timaeus* 36B (Cornford, p. 73).

signified the world-soul for the Egyptians.[25] It is, in fact, the hieroglyph for 'city.' [26] Perhaps Plato was trying, in this passage, to bring forth the mandala structure that later appeared as the capital of Atlantis in his *Critias.*

191 The two mixtures could be regarded as a parallel to the two means of the physical elements. Cornford, on the other hand, considers that Plato is referring to three intermedia, which he calls "Intermediate Existence," "Intermediate Sameness," "Intermediate Difference." [27] His main insistence is on the threefold procedure and not on the four substances. The Middle Ages were also familiar with the *quatuor elementa* (A B C D) and the *tria regimina* (three procedures) which united them as follows: AB, BC, CD. From this point of view, Cornford fails to catch Plato's subtle allusion to the recalcitrant fourth.

192 We do not wish it to be supposed that the thought-processes we have deduced from the text of the *Timaeus* represent Plato's conscious reflections. However extraordinary his genius may have been, it by no means follows that his thoughts were all conscious ones. The problem of the fourth, for instance, which is an absolutely essential ingredient of totality, can hardly have reached his consciousness in complete form. If it had, he would have been repelled by the violence with which the elements were to be forced into a harmonious system. Nor would he have been so illogical as to insist on the threefoldness of his world-soul. Again, I would not venture to assert that the opening words of the *Timaeus* are a conscious reference to the underlying problem of the recalcitrant fourth. Everything suggests that the same unconscious *spiritus rector* was at work which twice impelled the master to try to write a tetralogy, the fourth part remaining unfinished on both occasions.[28] This factor also ensured that Plato would remain a bachelor to the end of his life, as if affirming the masculinity of his triadic God-image.

25 Taylor, p. 75.

26 Griffith, *A Collection of Hieroglyphs,* p. 34 B. Fig. 142: 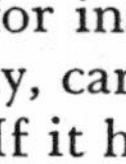 = Plan of a village with cross-streets.

27 P. 61. The intermedia are constructed on the assumption that Indivisible and Divisible are opposite attributes of each of the three principles, Existence, Sameness, Difference. I do not know whether the text permits of such an operation.

28 Gomperz, III, p. 200 [The two unfinished tetralogies are (a) *Republic, Timaeus, Critias* (left incomplete), (*Hermocrates,* never written); (b) *Theaetetus, Sophist, Statesman,* (*Philosopher,* never written).—Trans.]

193 As history draws nearer to the beginning of our era, the gods become more and more abstract and spiritualized. Even Yahweh had to submit to this transformation. In the Alexandrian philosophy that arose in the last century B.C., we witness not only an alteration of his nature but an emergence of two other divinities in his immediate vicinity: the Logos and Sophia. Together with him they form a triad,[29] and this is a clear prefiguration of the post-Christian Trinity.

29 Leisegang, *Pneuma Hagion*, p. 86.

2. FATHER, SON, AND SPIRIT

194 I have dwelt at some length on the views of the Babylonians and Egyptians, and on Platonist philosophy, in order to give the reader some conception of the trinitarian and unitarian ideas that were in existence many centuries before the birth of Christianity. Whether these ideas were handed down to posterity as a result of migration and tradition or whether they arose spontaneously in each case is a question of little importance. The important thing is that they occurred because, once having sprung forth from the unconscious of the human race (and not just in Asia Minor!), they could rearise anywhere at any time. It is, for instance, more than doubtful whether the Church Fathers who devised the *homoousios* formula were even remotely acquainted with the ancient Egyptian theology of kingship. Nevertheless, they neither paused in their labours nor rested until they had finally reconstructed the ancient Egyptian archetype. Much the same sort of thing happened when, in A.D. 431, at the Council of Ephesus, whose streets had once rung with hymns of praise to many-breasted Diana, the Virgin Mary was declared the θεοτόκος, 'birth-giver of the god.' [1] As we know from Epiphanius,[2] there was even a sect, the Collyridians,

[1] Here one might recall the legend that, after the death of Christ, Mary betook herself with John to Ephesus, where she is said to have lived until her death.

[2] *Panarium* (*Contra octoginta haereses*) LXXIX. See Migne, *P.G.*, vol. 41, cols. 739ff.

who worshipped Mary after the manner of an antique goddess. Her cult had its chief centres in Arabia, Thrace, and Upper Scythia, the most enthusiastic devotees being women. Their provocations moved Epiphanius to the rebuke that "the whole female sex is slippery and prone to error, with a mind that is very petty and narrow." [3] It is clear from this chastening sermon that there were priestesses who on certain feast days decorated a wagon or four-cornered seat and covered it with linen, on which they placed offerings of bakemeats "in the name of Mary" (εἰς ὄνομα τῆς Μαρίας), afterwards partaking of the sacrificial meal. This plainly amounted to a Eucharistic feast in honour of Mary, at which wheaten bread was eaten. The orthodox standpoint of the time is aptly expressed in the words of Epiphanius: "Let Mary be held in honour, and let the Father and the Son and the Holy Ghost be adored, but let no one adore Mary."

195 Thus the archetype reasserted itself, since, as I have tried to show, archetypal ideas are part of the indestructible foundations of the human mind. However long they are forgotten and buried, always they return, sometimes in the strangest guise, with a personal twist to them or intellectually distorted, as in the case of the Arian heresy, but continually reproducing themselves in new forms representing the timeless truths that are innate in man's nature.[4]

196 Even though Plato's influence on the thinkers of the next few centuries can hardly be overestimated, his philosophically formulated triad cannot be held responsible for the origins of the Christian dogma of the Trinity. For we are concerned here not with any philosophical, that is conscious, assumptions but with unconscious, archetypal forms. The Platonic formula for the triad contradicts the Christian Trinity in one essential point: the triad is built on opposition, whereas the Trinity contains no opposition of any kind, but is, on the contrary, a complete harmony in itself. The three Persons are characterized in such a manner that they cannot possibly be derived from Pla-

3 "Quod genus lubricum et in errorem proclive, ac pusilli admodum et angusti animi esse solet."

4 The special emphasis I lay on archetypal predispositions does not mean that mythologems are of exclusively psychic origin. I am not overlooking the social conditions that are just as necessary for their production.

tonic premises, while the terms Father, Son, and Holy Ghost do not proceed in any sense from the number three. At most, the Platonic formula supplies the intellectual scaffolding for contents that come from quite other sources. The Trinity may be conceived platonically as to its form, but for its content we have to rely on psychic factors, on irrational data that cannot be logically determined beforehand. In other words, we have to distinguish between the *logical idea* of the Trinity and its *psychological reality*. The latter brings us back to the very much more ancient Egyptian ideas and hence to the archetype, which provides the authentic and eternal justification for the existence of any trinitarian idea at all.

197 The psychological datum consists of Father, Son, and Holy Ghost. If we posit "Father," then "Son" logically follows; but "Holy Ghost" does not follow logically from either "Father" or "Son." So we must be dealing here with a special factor that rests on a different presupposition. According to the old doctrine, the Holy Ghost is "vera persona, quae a filio et patre missa est" (a real person who is sent by the Son and the Father). The "processio a patre filioque" (procession from the Father and the Son) is a "spiration" and not a "begetting." This somewhat peculiar idea corresponds to the separation, which still existed in the Middle Ages, of "corpus" and "spiramen," the latter being understood as something more than mere "breath." What it really denoted was the *anima,* which, as its name shows, is a breath-being (*anemos* = wind). Although an activity of the body, it was thought of as an independent substance (or hypostasis) existing alongside the body. The underlying idea is that the body "lives," and that "life" is something superadded and autonomous, conceived as a soul unattached to the body. Applying this idea to the Trinity formula, we would have to say: Father, Son, and Life—the life proceeding from both or lived by both. The Holy Ghost as "life" is a concept that cannot be derived logically from the identity of Father and Son, but is, rather, a psychological idea, a datum based on an irrational, primordial image. This primordial image is the archetype, and we find it expressed most clearly in the Egyptian theology of kingship. There, as we have seen, the archetype takes the form of God the father, Ka-mutef (the begetter), and the son. The *ka* is the life-spirit, the animating principle of men and gods, and therefore

can be legitimately interpreted as the soul or spiritual double. He is the "life" of the dead man, and thus corresponds on the one hand to the living man's soul, and on the other to his "spirit" or "genius." We have seen that Ka-mutef is a hypostatization of procreative power.[5] In the same way, the Holy Ghost is hypostatized procreative power and life-force.[6] Hence, in the Christian Trinity, we are confronted with a distinctly archaic idea, whose extraordinary value lies precisely in the fact that it is a supreme, hypostatic representation of an abstract thought (two-dimensional triad). The form is still concretistic, in that the archetype is represented by the relationship "Father" and "Son." Were it nothing but that, it would only be a dyad. The third element, however, the connecting link between "Father" and "Son," is spirit and not a human figure. The masculine father-son relationship is thus lifted out of the natural order (which includes mothers and daughters) and translated to a sphere from which the feminine element is excluded: in ancient Egypt as in Christianity the Theotokos stands outside the Trinity. One has only to think of Jesus's brusque rejection of his mother at the marriage in Cana: "Woman, what have I to do with thee?" (John 2:4), and also earlier, when she sought the twelve-year-old child in the temple: "How is it that ye sought me? wist ye not that I must be about my Father's business?" (Luke 2:49). We shall probably not be wrong in assuming that this special sphere to which the father-son relationship is removed is the sphere of primitive mysteries and masculine initiations. Among certain tribes, women are forbidden to look at the mysteries on pain of death. Through the initiations the young men are systematically alienated from their mothers and are reborn as spirits. The celibacy of the priesthood is a continuation of this archetypal idea.[7]

198 The intellectual operation that lies concealed in the higher father-son relationship consists in the extrapolation of an invisi-

[5] The *ka* of the king even has an individual name. Thus "the living *ka* of the Lord of the Two Lands," Thutmosis III, was called the "victorious bull which shines in Thebes." Erman, *Life in Ancient Egypt,* p. 307.

[6] The "doubling" of the spirit occurs also in the Old Testament, though more as a "potency" emanating from God than as an hypostasis. Nevertheless, Isaiah 48:16 looks very like a hypostasis in the Septuagint text: Κύριος Κύριος ἀπεστειλέν με καὶ τὸ πνεῦμα αὐτοῦ (The Lord the Lord sent me and his spirit).

[7] For an instructive account of the Greek background see Harrison, *Themis,* ch. 1.

ble figure, a "spirit" that is the very essence of masculine life. The life of the body or of a man is posited as something different from the man himself. This led to the idea of a *ka* or immortal soul, able to detach itself from the body and not dependent on it for its existence. In this respect, primitives have extraordinarily well developed ideas about a plurality of souls. Some are immortal, others are only loosely attached to the body and can wander off and get lost in the night, or they lose their way and get caught in a dream. There are even souls that belong to a person without being lodged in his body, like the bush-soul, which dwells outside in the forest, in the body of an animal. The juxtaposition of a person and his "life" has its psychological basis in the fact that a mind which is not very well differentiated cannot think abstractly and is incapable of putting things into categories. It can only take the qualities it perceives and place them side by side: man and his life, or his sickness (visualized as a sort of demon), or his health or prestige (mana, etc.). This is obviously the case with the Egyptian *ka.* Father-son-life (or procreative power), together with rigorous exclusion of the Theotokos, constitute the patriarchal formula that was "in the air" long before the advent of Christianity.

199 The Father is, by definition, the prime cause, the creator, the *auctor rerum,* who, on a level of culture where reflection is still unknown, can only be One. The Other follows from the One by splitting off from it. This split need not occur so long as there is no criticism of the *auctor rerum*—so long, that is to say, as a culture refrains from all reflection about the One and does not start criticizing the Creator's handiwork. A feeling of oneness, far removed from critical judgment and moral conflict, leaves the Father's authority unimpaired.

200 I had occasion to observe this original oneness of the father-world when I was with a tribe of Negroes on Mount Elgon. These people professed to believe that the Creator had made everything good and beautiful. "But what about the bad animals that kill your cattle?" I asked. They replied: "The lion is good and beautiful." "And your horrible diseases?" "You lie in the sun, and it is beautiful." I was impressed by their optimism. But at six o'clock in the evening this philosophy came to a sudden stop, as I was soon to discover. After sunset, another world took over—the dark world of the Ayik, who is everything evil,

dangerous, and terrifying. The optimistic philosophy ends and a philosophy of fear, ghosts, and magical spells for averting the Evil One begins. Then, at sunrise, the optimism starts off again without any trace of inner contradiction.

201 Here man, world, and God form a whole, a unity unclouded by criticism. It is the world of the Father, and of man in his childhood state. Despite the fact that twelve hours out of every twenty-four are spent in the world of darkness, and in agonizing belief in this darkness, the doubt never arises as to whether God might not also be the Other. The famous question about the origin of evil does not yet exist in a patriarchal age. Only with the coming of Christianity did it present itself as the principal problem of morality. The world of the Father typifies an age which is characterized by a pristine oneness with the whole of Nature, no matter whether this oneness be beautiful or ugly or awe-inspiring. But once the question is asked: "Whence comes the evil, why is the world so bad and imperfect, why are there diseases and other horrors, why must man suffer?"—then reflection has already begun to judge the Father by his manifest works, and straightway one is conscious of a doubt, which is itself the symptom of a split in the original unity. One comes to the conclusion that creation is imperfect—nay more, that the Creator has not done his job properly, that the goodness and almightiness of the Father cannot be the sole principle of the cosmos. Hence the One has to be supplemented by the Other, with the result that the world of the Father is fundamentally altered and is superseded by the world of the Son.

202 This was the time when the Greeks started criticizing the world, the time of "gnosis" in its widest sense, which ultimately gave birth to Christianity. The archetype of the redeemer-god and Original Man is age-old—we simply do not know how old. The Son, the revealed god, who voluntarily or involuntarily offers himself for sacrifice as a man, in order to create the world or redeem it from evil, can be traced back to the Purusha of Indian philosophy, and is also found in the Persian conception of the Original Man, Gayomart. Gayomart, son of the god of light, falls victim to the darkness, from which he must be set free in order to redeem the world. He is the prototype of the Gnostic redeemer-figures and of the teachings concerning Christ, redeemer of mankind.

203 It is not hard to see that a critique which raised the question of the origin of evil and of suffering had in mind another world—a world filled with longing for redemption and for that state of perfection in which man was still one with the Father. Longingly he looked back to the world of the Father, but it was lost forever, because an irreversible increase in man's consciousness had taken place in the meantime and made it independent. With this mutation he broke away from the world of the Father and entered upon the world of the Son, with its divine drama of redemption and the ritualistic retelling of those things which the God-man had accomplished during his earthly sojourn.[8] The life of the God-man revealed things that could not possibly have been known at the time when the Father ruled as the One. For the Father, as the original unity, was not a defined or definable object; nor could he, strictly speaking, either be called the "Father" or be one. He only became a "Father" by incarnating in the Son, and by so doing became defined and definable. By becoming a father and a man he revealed to man the secret of his divinity.

204 One of these revelations is the Holy Ghost. As a being who existed before the world was, he is eternal, but he appears empirically in this world only when Christ had left the earthly stage. He will be for the disciples what Christ was for them. He will invest them with the power to do works greater, perhaps, than those of the Son (John 14:12). The Holy Ghost is a figure who deputizes for Christ and who corresponds to what Christ received from the Father. From the Father comes the Son, and common to both is the living activity of the Holy Ghost, who, according to Christian doctrine, is breathed forth ("spirated") by both. As he is the third term common to Father and Son, he puts an end to the duality, to the "doubt" in the Son. He is, in fact, the third element that rounds out the Three and restores the One. The point is that the unfolding of the One reaches its climax in the Holy Ghost after polarizing itself as Father and Son. Its descent into a human body is sufficient in itself to make it become another, to set it in opposition to itself. Thenceforward there are two: the "One" and the "Other,"

8 Cf. the detailed exposition of the death and rebirth of the divine κοῦρος in Harrison, *Themis.*

which results in a certain tension.[9] This tension works itself out in the suffering and fate of the Son [10] and, finally, in Christ's admission of abandonment by God (Matthew 27:46).

205 Although the Holy Ghost is the progenitor of the Son (Matthew 1:18), he is also, as the Paraclete, a legacy from him. He continues the work of redemption in mankind at large, by descending upon those who merit divine election. Consequently, the Paraclete is, at least by implication, the crowning figure in the work of redemption on the one hand and in God's revelation of himself on the other. It could, in fact, be said that the Holy Ghost represents the final, complete stage in the evolution of God and the divine drama. For the Trinity is undoubtedly a higher form of God-concept than mere unity, since it corresponds to a level of reflection on which man has become more conscious.

206 The trinitarian conception of a life-process within the Deity, which I have outlined here, was, as we have seen, already in existence in pre-Christian times, its essential features being a continuation and differentiation of the primitive rites of renewal and the cult-legends associated with them. Just as the gods of these mysteries become extinct, so, too, do the mysteries themselves, only to take on new forms in the course of history. A large-scale extinction of the old gods was once more in progress at the beginning of our era, and the birth of a new god, with new mysteries and new emotions, was an occurrence that healed the wound in men's souls. It goes without saying that any conscious borrowing from the existing mystery traditions would have hampered the god's renewal and rebirth. It had to be an entirely unprejudiced revelation which, quite unrelated to anything else, and if possible without preconceptions of any kind, would usher into the world a new *δρώμενον* and a new cult-legend. Only at a comparatively late date did people notice the striking parallels with the legend of Dionysus, which they then declared to be the work of the devil. This attitude on the part of the early Christians can easily be understood, for Christianity

9 The relation of Father to Son is not arithmetical, since both the One and the Other are still united in the original Unity and are, so to speak, eternally on the point of becoming two. Hence the Son is eternally being begotten by the Father, and Christ's sacrificial death is an eternally present act.

10 The *πάθη* of Dionysus would be the Greek parallels.

did indeed develop in this unconscious fashion, and furthermore its seeming lack of antecedents proved to be the indispensable condition for its existence as an effective force. Nobody can doubt the manifold superiority of the Christian revelation over its pagan precursors, for which reason it is distinctly superfluous today to insist on the unheralded and unhistorical character of the gospels, seeing that they swarm with historical and psychological assumptions of very ancient origin.

3. THE SYMBOLA

207 The trinitarian drama of redemption (as distinct from the intellectual conception of it) burst upon the world scene at the beginning of a new era, amid complete unconsciousness of its resuscitation from the past. Leaving aside the so-called prefigurations in the Old Testament, there is not a single passage in the New Testament where the Trinity is formulated in an intellectually comprehensible manner.[1] Generally speaking, it is more a question of formulae for triple benediction, such as the end of the second epistle to the Corinthians: "The grace of the Lord Jesus Christ, and the love of God, and the communion of the Holy Ghost, be with you all,"[2] or the beginning of the first

1 The so-called "Comma Johanneum," which would seem to be an exception, is a demonstrably late interpolation of doubtful origin. Regarded as a dogmatic and revealed text *per se,* it would afford the strongest evidence for the occurrence of the Trinity in the New Testament. The passage reads (I John 5:8: "And there are three that bear witness: the Spirit, and the water, and the blood; and these three are one" (DV). That is to say, they agree in their testimony that Christ "came in water and in blood" (verse 6, DV). [In verse 8, AV has "and these three agree in one"; RSV: "and these three agree."—TRANS.] The Vulgate has the late interpolation in verse 7: "Quoniam tres sunt, qui testimonium dant *in caelo: Pater, Verbum et Spiritus Sanctus:* et hi tres unum sunt." Note that in the Greek text the three neuter nouns *πνεῦμα, ὕδωρ,* and *αἷμα* are followed by a masculine plural: *οἱ τρεῖς εἰς τὸ ἕν εἰσιν.*

2 II Cor. 13:14 (AV). The baptismal formula "In the name of the Father and the Son and the Holy Ghost" comes into this category, though its authenticity is

epistle of Peter: ". . . chosen and destined by God the Father and sanctified by the Spirit for obedience to Jesus Christ and for sprinkling with his blood," [3] or Jude 20–21. Another passage cited in favour of the Trinity is I Corinthians 12:4–6, but this only gives the emphatic assurance that the Spirit is one (repeated in Ephesians 4:4–6), and may be taken more as an incantation against polytheism and polydemonism than an assertion of the Trinity. Triadic formulae were also current in the post-apostolic epoch. Thus Clement says in his first letter (46:6): ". . . Have we not one God, and one Christ, and one Spirit . . ." [4] Epiphanius even reports that Christ taught his disciples that "the Father and the Son and the Holy Ghost are the same." [5]

208 Epiphanius took this passage from the apocryphal "Gospel according to the Egyptians," [6] of which unfortunately only fragments are preserved. The formula is significant insofar as it provides a definite starting-point for a "modalistic" concept of the Trinity.

209 Now the important point is not that the New Testament contains no trinitarian formulae, but that we find in it three figures who are reciprocally related to one another: the Father, the Son, begotten through the Holy Ghost, and the Holy Ghost. Since olden times, formulae for benediction, all solemn agreements, occasions, attributes, etc. have had a magical, threefold character (e.g., the Trishagion).[7] Although they are no evidence for the Trinity in the New Testament, they nevertheless occur and, like the three divine Persons, are clear indications of an active archetype operating beneath the surface and throwing up triadic formations. This proves that the trinitarian archetype is

doubted. It seems that originally people were baptized only in the name of Jesus Christ. The formula does not occur in Mark and Luke. Cf. Krueger, *Das Dogma von der Dreieinigkeit und Gottmenschheit in seiner geschichtlichen Entwicklung,* p. 11.

3 I Peter 1:2 (RSV).

4 *Apostolic Fathers,* trans. by Lake, I, p. 89. Clement was the third bishop of Rome after Peter, according to Irenaeus. His dating is unsure, but he seems to have been born in the second half of the 2nd cent.

5 *Panarium,* LXII, II, in Migne, *P.G.,* vol. 41, cols. 1052–53.

6 Cf. James, *The Apocryphal New Testament,* pp. 10f.

7 We might also mention the division of Christ's forbears into 3 × 14 generations in Matthew 1:17. Cf. the role of the 14 royal ancestors in ancient Egypt: Jacobsohn, "Die dogmatische Stellung des Königs in der Theologie der alten Aegypter," pp. 66ff.

already at work in the New Testament, for what comes after is largely the result of what has gone before, a proposition which is especially apposite when, as in the case of the Trinity, we are confronted with the effects of an unconscious content or archetype. From the creeds to be discussed later, we shall see that at the synods of the Fathers the New Testament allusions to the divine trio were developed in a thoroughly consistent manner until the homoousia was restored, which again happened unconsciously, since the Fathers knew nothing of the ancient Egyptian model that had already reached the homoousian level. The after-effects on posterity were inevitable consequences of the trinitarian anticipations that were abroad in the early days of Christianity, and are nothing but amplifications of the constellated archetype. These amplifications, so far as they were naïve and unprejudiced, are direct proof that what the New Testament is alluding to is in fact the Trinity, as the Church also believes.

210 Since people did not actually *know* what it was that had so suddenly revealed itself in the "Son of Man," but only *believed* the current interpretations, the effects it had over the centuries signify nothing less than the gradual unfolding of the archetype in man's consciousness, or rather, its absorption into the pattern of ideas transmitted by the cultures of antiquity.[8] From this historical echo it is possible to recognize what had revealed itself in a sudden flash of illumination and seized upon men's minds, even though the event, when it happened, was so far beyond their comprehension that they were unable to put it into a clear formula. Before "revealed" contents can be sorted out and properly formulated, time and distance are needed. The results of this intellectual activity were deposited in a series of tenets, the dogmata, which were then summed up in the "symbolum" or creed. This breviary of belief well deserves the name "symbolum," for, from a psychological point of view, it gives symbolical expression to, and paints an anthropomorphic picture of, a transcendent fact that cannot be demonstrated or explained rationally, the word "transcendent" being used here in a strictly psychological sense.[9]

8 As we know, St. John's gospel marks the beginning of this process.

9 Cf. *Psychological Types*, Def. 51.

I. THE SYMBOLUM APOSTOLICUM

211 The first of these summaries was attempted fairly early, if tradition may be relied on. St. Ambrose, for instance, reports that the confession used at baptism in the church of Milan originated with the twelve apostles.[10] This creed of the old Church is therefore known as the Apostles' Creed. As established in the fourth century, it ran:

I believe in God the Father Almighty, and in Jesus Christ his only begotten Son our Lord, who was born of the Holy Ghost and the Virgin Mary, was crucified under Pontius Pilate, buried, and on the third day rose again from the dead, ascended into heaven, and sitteth on the right hand of the Father, whence he shall come to judge the quick and the dead. And [I believe] in the Holy Ghost, the holy Church, the forgiveness of sins, the resurrection of the flesh.

212 This creed is still entirely on the level of the gospels and epistles: there are three divine figures, and they do not in any way contradict the one God. Here the Trinity is not explicit, but exists latently, just as Clement's second letter says of the pre-existent Church: "It was spiritually there." Even in the very early days of Christianity it was accepted that Christ as Logos was God himself (John 1:1). For Paul he is pre-existent in God's form, as is clear from the famous "kenosis" passage in Philippians 2:6 (AV): "Who, being in the form of God, thought it not robbery to be equal with God" (τὸ εἶναι ἴσα θεῷ = *esse se aequalem Deo*). There are also passages in the letters where the author confuses Christ with the Holy Ghost, or where the three are seen as one, as in II Corinthians 3:17 (DV): "Now the Lord is the spirit" (ὁ δὲ κύριος τὸ πνεῦμα ἐστιν = *Dominus autem spiritus est*). When the next verse speaks of the "glory of the Lord" (δόξα κυρίου = *gloria Domini*), "Lord" seems to refer to Christ. But if you read the whole passage, from verses 7 to 18, it is evident that the "glory" refers equally to God, thus proving the promiscuity of the three figures and their latent Trinity.

10 *Explanatio symboli ad initiandos.*

II. THE SYMBOLUM OF GREGORY THAUMATURGUS

213 Although the Apostles' Creed does not stipulate the Trinity in so many words, it was nevertheless "spiritually there" at a very early date, and it is nothing but a quibble to insist, as many people do, that the Trinity was "invented only long afterwards." In this connection, therefore, I must mention the vision of Gregory Thaumaturgus (210–70), in which the Blessed Virgin and St. John appeared to him and enunciated a creed which he wrote down on the spot.[11] It runs:

One God, Father of the living Word, [of his] self-subsistent wisdom and power, [of his] eternal likeness, perfect Begetter of what is perfect, Father of the only begotten Son. One Lord, Alone of the Alone, God of God, veritable likeness of Godhead, effectual Word, comprehensive Wisdom by which all things subsist, Power that creates all Creation, true Son of the true Father, unseen [Son] of the unseen [Father], incorruptible of the incorruptible, deathless of the deathless, everlasting of the everlasting. And one Holy Spirit, having existence from God and appearing through the Son, Image of the Son and perfect [Image] of the perfect [Father], Life and cause of life, holy Fount, Ringleader [Χορηγός] of holiness: in whom is manifest God the Father, who is above all and in all, and God the Son, who pervades all. Perfect Trinity, whose glory and eternity and dominion is not divided and not separate.[12]

214 This trinitarian creed had already established itself in a position of authority long before the appearance of the Apostles' Creed, which is far less explicit. Gregory had been a pupil of Origen until about 238. Origen (182–251) employed the concept of the Trinity [13] in his writings and gave it considerable thought, concerning himself more particularly with its internal economy (οἰκονομία, *oeconomia*) and the management of its power: "I am of the opinion, then, that the God and Father, who holds the universe together, is superior to every being that exists, for he imparts to each one from his own existence that which each one is. The Son, being less than the Father, is superior to

11 Gregory of Nyssa, *De Vita S. Gregorii Thaumaturgi,* in Migne, *P.G.*, vol. 46, cols. 911–14.

12 Caspari, *Alte und neue Quellen zur Geschichte des Taufsymbols,* pp. 10–17.

13 First mentioned in Tertullian (d. 220).

rational creatures alone (for he is second to the Father). The Holy Spirit is still less, and dwells within the saints alone. So that in this way the power of the Father is greater than that of the Son and of the Holy Spirit, and in turn the power of the Holy Spirit exceeds that of every other holy being." [14] He is not very clear about the nature of the Holy Spirit, for he says: "The Spirit of God, therefore, who, as it is written, moved upon the waters in the beginning of the creation of the world, I reckon to be none other than the Holy Spirit, so far as I can understand." [15] Earlier he says: "But up to the present we have been able to find no passage in the holy scriptures which would warrant us in saying that the Holy Spirit was a being made or created." [16]

III. THE NICAENUM

215 Trinitarian speculation had long passed its peak when the Council of Nicaea, in 325, created a new creed, known as the "Nicene." It runs:

We believe in one God, the Father Almighty, Creator of all things visible and invisible, and in one Lord Jesus Christ, Son of God, the only begotten of the Father, being of the substance [οὐσία] of the Father, God of God, Light of Light, very God of very God, begotten not made, consubstantial [ὁμοούσιος] with the Father, through whom all things have been made which are in heaven and on earth. Who for us men and for our salvation descended and was made flesh, became man, suffered, rose again the third day, ascended into heaven, and will come to judge the living and the dead. And in the Holy Spirit. As for those who say, "There was a time when He was not," or "Before He was begotten He was not," or "He was made from that which was not, or from another subsistence [ὑπόστασις], or substance," or "The Son of God is created, changeable, or subject to change," these the Catholic Church anathematizes.[17]

216 It was, apparently, a Spanish bishop, Hosius of Cordoba, who proposed to the emperor the crucial word ὁμοούσιος. It did

14 Origen, *On First Principles*, trans. by Butterworth, pp. 33f.

15 Ibid., p. 31. 16 Ibid.

17 Cf. J. R. Palanque and others, *The Church in the Christian Roman Empire*, I: *The Church and the Arian Crisis*, p. 96.

not occur then for the first time, for it can be found in Tertullian, as the "unitas substantiae." The concept of homoousia can also be found in Gnostic usage, as for instance in Irenaeus' references to the Valentinians (140–*c.* 200), where the Aeons are said to be of one substance with their creator, Bythos.[18] The Nicene Creed concentrates on the father-son relationship, while the Holy Ghost receives scant mention.

IV. THE NICAENO-CONSTANTINOPOLITANUM, THE ATHANASIANUM, AND THE LATERANENSE

217 The next formulation in the Nicene-Constantinopolitan Creed of 381 brings an important advance. It runs:

We believe in one God the Father Almighty, Maker of heaven and earth, and of all things visible and invisible. And in one Lord Jesus Christ, the only begotten Son of God, begotten of his Father before all worlds, God of God, Light of Light, very God of very God, begotten, not made, being of one substance with the Father, by whom all things were made; who for us men and for our salvation came down from heaven and was made flesh by the Holy Ghost and the Virgin Mary and became man, and was crucified for us under Pontius Pilate, suffered and was buried, and on the third day rose again according to the Scriptures, and ascended into heaven, and sitteth on the right hand of God the Father, whence he shall come again in glory to judge the quick and the dead, and whose kingdom shall have no end. And [we believe] in the Holy Ghost, the Lord and Giver of life, who proceedeth from the Father,[19] who with the Father and the Son together is worshipped and glorified, who spake through the prophets. And [we believe] in one holy Catholic and Apostolic Church. We acknowledge one baptism for the remission of sins. And we await the resurrection of the dead and the life of the world to come. Amen.

18 More accurately, the unity of substance consists in the fact that the Aeons are descended from the Logos, which proceeds from Nous, the direct emanation of Bythos. Cf. Irenaeus, *Adversus haereses,* II, 17, 4, in Migne, *P.G.,* vol. 7, cols. 762–63 (trans. by Roberts and Rambaut, p. 174).

19 [The addition at this point of the words "and from the Son" (*Filioque*), which, though never accepted by the Eastern Churches, has been universal in the West, both Catholic and Protestant, since the beginning of the eleventh century, is still one of the principal points of contention between the two main sections of the Christian body.—EDITORS.]

218 Here the Holy Ghost is given due consideration: he is called "Lord" and is worshipped together with Father and Son. But he proceeds from the Father only. It was this point that caused the tremendous controversy over the "filioque" question, as to whether the Holy Ghost proceeds from the Father only, or from the Son as well. In order to make the Trinity a complete unity, the *filioque* was just as essential as the *homoousia.* The (falsely so-called) Athanasian Creed [20] insisted in the strongest possible terms on the equality of all three Persons. Its peculiarities have given much offence to rationalistic and liberal-minded theologians. I quote, as a sample, a passage from the beginning:

Now the Catholic Faith is this: That we worship one God in Trinity, and Trinity in Unity, neither confounding the Persons nor dividing the substance. For there is one Person of the Father, another of the Son, another of the Holy Ghost. But the Godhead of the Father and of the Son and of the Holy Ghost is all one; the glory equal, the majesty co-eternal. Such as the Father is, such is the Son, and such is the Holy Ghost. The Father uncreated, the Son uncreated, the Holy Ghost uncreated. The Father infinite, the Son infinite, the Holy Ghost infinite. The Father eternal, the Son eternal, the Holy Ghost eternal. And yet not three Eternals, but one Eternal. As also there are not three Uncreated, nor three Infinites, but one Infinite and one Uncreated. So likewise is the Father almighty, the Son almighty, the Holy Ghost almighty; and yet there are not three Almighties, but one Almighty. So the Father is God, the Son is God, the Holy Ghost is God; and yet there are not three Gods, but one God. Likewise the Father is Lord, the Son is Lord, the Holy Ghost is Lord; and yet there are not three Lords, but one Lord. For just as we are compelled by the Christian verity to acknowledge each Person by himself to be both God and Lord, so we are forbidden by the Catholic religion to say there are three Gods or three Lords. The Father is made of none, neither created nor begotten. The Son is of the Father alone, not made, nor created, but begotten. The Holy Ghost is of the Father and the Son, not made, nor created, nor begotten, but proceeding. So there is one Father, not three Fathers; one Son, not three Sons; one Holy Ghost, not three Holy Ghosts. And in this Trinity none is before or after, none is greater or less; but all three Persons are coeternal together and coequal. So that in

20 It is also known as the "Symbolum Quicumque," on account of the opening words: "Quicumque vult salvus esse" (Whosoever would be saved). It does not go back to Athanasius.

all ways, as is aforesaid, both the Trinity is to be worshipped in Unity, and the Unity in Trinity. He, therefore, that would be saved, let him think thus of the Trinity.[21]

219 Here the Trinity is a fully developed conceptual schema in which everything balances, the *homoousia* binding all three Persons equally. The Creed of the Lateran Council, 1215, brings a further differentiation. I shall quote only the beginning:

We firmly believe and wholeheartedly confess that there is only one true God, eternal, infinite, and unchanging; incomprehensible, almighty, and ineffable; Father and Son and Holy Ghost; three Persons, but one essence; entirely simple in substance and nature. The Father is of none, the Son is of the Father alone, and the Holy Ghost is of both equally; for ever without beginning and without end; the Father begetting, the Son being born, and the Holy Ghost proceeding; consubstantial and coequal and coalmighty and coeternal.[22]

220 The "filioque" is expressly taken up into this creed, thus assigning the Holy Ghost a special activity and significance. So far as I can judge, the later Creed of the Council of Trent adds nothing further that would be of interest for our theme.

221 Before concluding this section, I would like to call attention to a book well known in the Middle Ages, the *Liber de Spiritu et Anima*,[23] which attempts a psychological interpretation of the Trinity. The argument starts with the assumption that by self-knowledge a man may attain to a knowledge of God.[24] The *mens rationalis* is closest to God, for it is "excellently made, and expressly after his likeness." If it recognizes its own likeness to God it will the more easily recognize its creator. And thus knowledge of the Trinity begins. For the intellect sees how wisdom (*sapientia*) proceeds from it and how it loves this wisdom. But, from intellect and wisdom, there proceeds love, and thus all three, intellect, wisdom, and love, appear in one. The origin of all wisdom, however, is God. Therefore intellect (*νοῦς*) corresponds to the Father, the wisdom it begets corresponds to the

21 [Official version from the Revised Book of Common Prayer (1928), with alternative readings.—TRANS.]

22 [From the Decrees of the Lateran Council, ch. 1.—TRANS.]

23 Erroneously ascribed to St. Augustine. Cf. *Opera,* VI.

24 Ibid., p. 1194, B.

Son (λόγος), and love corresponds to the Spirit (πνεῦμα) breathed forth between them.[25] The wisdom of God was often identified with the cosmogonic Logos and hence with Christ. The medieval mind finds it natural to derive the structure of the psyche from the Trinity, whereas the modern mind reverses the procedure.

25 "The begetter is the Father, the begotten is the Son, and that which proceeds from both is the Holy Spirit." Ibid., p. 1195, D.

4. THE THREE PERSONS IN THE LIGHT OF PSYCHOLOGY

I. THE HYPOTHESIS OF THE ARCHETYPE

222 The sequence of creeds illustrates the evolution of the Trinity idea through the centuries. In the course of its development it either consistently avoided, or successfully combated, all rationalistic deviations, such as, for instance, the so-plausible-looking Arian heresy. The creeds superimposed on the trinitarian allusions in the Holy Scriptures a structure of ideas that is a perpetual stumbling-block to the liberal-minded rationalist. Religious statements are, however, never rational in the ordinary sense of the word, for they always take into consideration that other world, the world of the archetype, of which reason in the ordinary sense is unconscious, being occupied only with externals. Thus the development of the Christian idea of the Trinity unconsciously reproduced the archetype of the homoousia of Father, Son, and Ka-mutef which first appeared in Egyptian theology. Not that the Egyptian model could be considered the archetype of the Christian idea. The archetype *an sich,* as I have explained elsewhere,[1] is an "irrepresentable" factor, a "disposition" which starts functioning at a given moment in the de-

1 Cf. my "On the Nature of the Psyche," pp. 200ff.

velopment of the human mind and arranges the material of consciousness into definite patterns.[2] That is to say, man's conceptions of God are organized into triads and trinities, and a whole host of ritualistic and magical practices take on a triple or trichotomous character, as in the case of thrice-repeated apotropaic spells, formulae for blessing, cursing, praising, giving thanks, etc. Wherever we find it, the archetype has a compelling force which it derives from the unconscious, and whenever its effect becomes conscious it has a distinctly numinous quality. There is never any conscious invention or cogitation, though speculations about the Trinity have often been accused of this. All the controversies, sophistries, quibbles, intrigues, and dissensions that are such an odious blot on the history of this dogma owe their existence to the compelling numinosity of the archetype and to the unexampled difficulty of incorporating it in the world of rational thought. Although the emperors may have made political capital out of the quarrels that ensued, this singular chapter in the history of the human mind cannot possibly be traced back to politics, any more than social and economic causes can be held responsible for it. The sole reason for the dogma lies in the Christian "message," which caused a psychic revolution in Western man. On the evidence of the gospels, and of Paul's letters in particular, it announced the real and veracious appearance of the God-man in this humdrum human world, accompanied by all the marvellous portents worthy of the son of God. However obscure the historical core of this phenomenon may seem to us moderns, with our hankering for factual accuracy, it is quite certain that those tremendous psychic effects, lasting for centuries, were not causelessly called

2 I have often been asked where the archetype comes from and whether it is acquired or not. This question cannot be answered directly. Archetypes are, by definition, factors and motifs that arrange the psychic elements into certain images, characterized as archetypal, but in such a way that they can be recognized only from the effects they produce. They exist preconsciously, and presumably they form the structural dominants of the psyche in general. They may be compared to the invisible presence of the crystal lattice in a saturated solution. As *a priori* conditioning factors they represent a special, psychological instance of the biological "pattern of behaviour," which gives all living organisms their specific qualities. Just as the manifestations of this biological ground plan may change in the course of development, so also can those of the archetype. Empirically considered, however, the archetype did not ever come into existence as a phenomenon of organic life, but entered into the picture with life itself.

forth, by just nothing at all. Unfortunately the gospel reports, originating in missionary zeal, form the meagrest source imaginable for attempts at historical reconstruction. But, for that very reason, they tell us all the more about the psychological reactions of the civilized world at that time. These reactions and assertions are continued in the history of dogma, where they are still conceived as the workings of the Holy Ghost. This interpretation, though the psychologist has nothing to say in regard to its metaphysical validity, is of the greatest moment, for it proves the existence of an overwhelming opinion or conviction that the operative factor in the formation of ideas is not man's intellect but an authority above and beyond consciousness. This psychological fact should on no account be overlooked, for any theoretical reasons whatsoever. Rationalistic arguments to the effect that the Holy Ghost is an hypothesis that cannot be proved are not commensurable with the statements of the psyche. A delusional idea is real, even though its content is, factually considered, nonsense. Psychology's concern is with psychic phenomena and with nothing else. These may be mere aspects of phenomena which, in themselves, could be subjected to a number of quite different modes of observation. Thus the statement that dogmas are inspired by the Holy Ghost indicates that they are not the product of conscious cogitation and speculation but are motivated from sources outside consciousness and possibly even outside man. Statements of this kind are the rule in archetypal experiences and are constantly associated with the sensed presence of a numen. An archetypal dream, for instance, can so fascinate the dreamer that he is very apt to see in it some kind of illumination, warning, or supernatural help. Nowadays most people are afraid of surrendering to such experiences, and their fear proves the existence of a "holy dread" of the numinous. Whatever the nature of these numinous experiences may be, they all have one thing in common: they relegate their source to a region outside consciousness. Psychology uses instead the concept of the unconscious, and specially that of the collective unconscious as opposed to the personal unconscious. People who reject the former and give credence only to the latter are forced into personalistic explanations. But collective and, above all, manifestly archetypal ideas can never be derived from the personal sphere. If Communism, for instance, refers to Engels,

Marx, Lenin, and so on as the "fathers" of the movement, it does not know that it is reviving an archetypal order of society that existed even in primitive times, thereby explaining, incidentally, the "religious" and "numinous" (i.e., fanatical) character of Communism. Neither did the Church Fathers know that their Trinity had a prehistory dating back several thousand years.

223 There can be no doubt that the doctrine of the Trinity originally corresponded with a patriarchal order of society. But we cannot tell whether social conditions produced the idea or, conversely, the idea revolutionized the existing social order. The phenomenon of early Christianity and the rise of Islam, to take only these two examples, show what ideas can do. The layman, having no opportunity to observe the behaviour of autonomous complexes, is usually inclined, in conformity with the general trend, to trace the origin of psychic contents back to the environment. This expectation is certainly justified so far as the ideational contents of consciousness are concerned. In addition to these, however, there are irrational, affective reactions and impulses, emanating from the unconscious, which organize the conscious material in an archetypal way. The more clearly the archetype is constellated, the more powerful will be its fascination, and the resultant religious statements will formulate it accordingly, as something "daemonic" or "divine." Such statements indicate possession by an archetype. The ideas underlying them are necessarily anthropomorphic and are thereby distinguished from the organizing archetype, which in itself is irrepresentable because unconscious.[3] They prove, however, that an archetype has been activated.[4]

224 Thus the history of the Trinity presents itself as the gradual crystallization of an archetype that moulds the anthropomorphic conceptions of father and son, of life, and of different persons into an archetypal and numinous figure, the "Most Holy Three-in-One." The contemporary witnesses of these events apprehended it as something that modern psychology would call a psychic presence outside consciousness. If there is a consensus of

[3] Cf. the detailed argument which I have put forward in "On the Nature of the Psyche," pp. 200ff.

[4] It is very probable that the activation of an archetype depends on an alteration of the conscious situation, which requires a new form of compensation.

opinion in respect of an idea, as there is here and always has been, then we are entitled to speak of a collective presence. Similar "presences" today are the Fascist and Communist ideologies, the one emphasizing the power of the chief, and the other communal ownership of goods in a primitive society.

225 "Holiness" means that an idea or thing possesses the highest value, and that in the presence of this value men are, so to speak, struck dumb. Holiness is also revelatory: it is the illuminative power emanating from an archetypal figure. Nobody ever feels himself as the subject of such a process, but always as its object.[5] *He* does not perceive holiness, *it* takes him captive and overwhelms him; nor does *he* behold it in a revelation, *it* reveals itself to him, and he cannot even boast that he has understood it properly. Everything happens apparently outside the sphere of his will, and these happenings are contents of the unconscious. Science is unable to say anything more than this, for it cannot, by an act of faith, overstep the limits appropriate to its nature.

II. CHRIST AS ARCHETYPE

226 The Trinity and its inner life process appear as a closed circle, a self-contained divine drama in which man plays, at most, a passive part. It seizes on him and, for a period of several centuries, forced him to occupy his mind passionately with all sorts of queer problems which today seem incredibly abstruse, if not downright absurd. It is, in the first place, difficult to see what the Trinity could possibly mean for us, either practically, morally, or symbolically. Even theologians often feel that speculation on this subject is a more or less otiose juggling with ideas, and there are not a few who could get along quite comfortably without the divinity of Christ, and for whom the role of the Holy Ghost, both inside and outside the Trinity, is an embarrassment of the first order. Writing of the Athanasian Creed, D. F. Strauss remarks: "The truth is that anyone who has sworn

5 Koepgen makes the following trenchant remark in his *Gnosis des Christentums*, p. 198: "If there is such a thing as a history of the Western mind . . . it would have to be viewed from the standpoint of the personality of Western man, which grew up under the influence of trinitarian dogma."

to the Symbolum Quicumque has abjured the laws of human thought." Naturally, the only person who can talk like that is one who is no longer impressed by the revelation of holiness and has fallen back on his own mental activity. This, so far as the revealed archetype is concerned, is an inevitably retrograde step: the liberalistic humanization of Christ goes back to the rival doctrine of homoiousia and to Arianism, while modern anti-trinitarianism has a conception of God that is more Old Testament or Islamic in character than Christian.

227 Obviously, anyone who approaches this problem with rationalistic and intellectualistic assumptions, like D. F. Strauss, is bound to find the patristic discussions and arguments completely nonsensical. But that anyone, and especially a theologian, should fall back on such manifestly incommensurable criteria as reason, logic, and the like, shows that, despite all the mental exertions of the Councils and of scholastic theology, they failed to bequeath to posterity an intellectual understanding of the dogma that would lend the slightest support to belief in it. There remained only submission to faith and renunciation of one's own desire to understand. Faith, as we know from experience, often comes off second best and has to give in to criticism which may not be at all qualified to deal with the object of faith. Criticism of this kind always puts on an air of great enlightenment—that is to say, it spreads round itself that thick darkness which the Word once tried to penetrate with its light: "And the light shineth in the darkness, and the darkness comprehended it not."

228 Naturally, it never occurs to these critics that their way of approach is incommensurable with their object. They think they have to do with rational facts, whereas it entirely escapes them that it is and always has been primarily a question of irrational psychic phenomena. That this is so can be seen plainly enough from the unhistorical character of the gospels, whose only concern was to represent the miraculous figure of Christ as graphically and impressively as possible. Further evidence of this is supplied by the earliest literary witness, Paul, who was closer to the events in question than the apostles. It is frankly disappointing to see how Paul hardly ever allows the real Jesus of Nazareth to get a word in. Even at this early date (and not only in John) he is completely overlaid, or rather smothered,

by metaphysical conceptions: he is the ruler over all daemonic forces, the cosmic saviour, the mediating God-man. The whole pre-Christian and Gnostic theology of the Near East (some of whose roots go still further back) wraps itself about him and turns him before our eyes into a dogmatic figure who has no more need of historicity. At a very early stage, therefore, the real Christ vanished behind the emotions and projections that swarmed about him from far and near; immediately and almost without trace he was absorbed into the surrounding religious systems and moulded into their archetypal exponent. He became the collective figure whom the unconscious of his contemporaries expected to appear, and for this reason it is pointless to ask who he "really" was. Were he human and nothing else, and in this sense historically true, he would probably be no more enlightening a figure than, say, Pythagoras, or Socrates, or Apollonius of Tyana. He opened men's eyes to revelation precisely because he was, from everlasting, God, and therefore unhistorical; and he functioned as such only by virtue of the consensus of unconscious expectation. If nobody had remarked that there was something special about the wonder-working Rabbi from Galilee, the darkness would never have noticed that a light was shining. Whether he lit the light with his own strength, or whether he was the victim of the universal longing for light and broke down under it, are questions which, for lack of reliable information, only faith can decide. At any rate the documentary reports relating to the general projection and assimilation of the Christ-figure are unequivocal. There is plenty of evidence for the co-operation of the collective unconscious in view of the abundance of parallels from the history of religion. In these circumstances we must ask ourselves what it was in man that was stirred by the Christian message, and what was the answer he gave.

229 If we are to answer this psychological question, we must first of all examine the Christ-symbolism contained in the New Testament, together with the patristic allegories and medieval iconography, and compare this material with the archetypal content of the unconscious psyche in order to find out what archetypes have been constellated. The most important of the symbolical statements about Christ are those which reveal the attributes of the hero's life: improbable origin, divine father,

hazardous birth, rescue in the nick of time, precocious development, conquest of the mother and of death, miraculous deeds, a tragic, early end, symbolically significant manner of death, post-mortem effects (reappearances, signs and marvels, etc.). As the Logos, Son of the Father, *Rex gloriae, Judex mundi,* Redeemer, and Saviour, Christ is himself God, an all-embracing totality, which, like the definition of Godhead, is expressed iconographically by the circle or mandala.[6] Here I would mention only the traditional representation of the *Rex gloriae* in a mandala, accompanied by a quaternity composed of the four symbols of the evangelists (including the four seasons, four winds, four rivers, and so on). Another symbolism of the same kind is the choir of saints, angels, and elders grouped round Christ (or God) in the centre. Here Christ symbolizes the integration of the kings and prophets of the Old Testament. As a shepherd he is the leader and centre of the flock. He is the vine, and those that hang on him are the branches. His body is bread to be eaten, and his blood wine to be drunk; he is also the mystical body formed by the congregation. In his human manifestation he is the hero and God-man, born without sin, more complete and more perfect than the natural man, who is to him what a child is to an adult, or an animal (sheep) to a human being.

230 These mythological statements, coming from within the Christian sphere as well as from outside it, adumbrate an archetype that expresses itself in essentially the same symbolism and also occurs in individual dreams or in fantasy-like projections upon living people (transference phenomena, hero-worship, etc.). The content of all such symbolic products is the idea of an overpowering, all-embracing, complete or perfect being, represented either by a man of heroic proportions, or by an animal with magical attributes, or by a magical vessel or some other "treasure hard to attain," such as a jewel, ring, crown, or,

6 "Deus est circulus cuius centrum est ubique, circumferentia vero nusquam" (God is a circle whose centre is everywhere and the circumference nowhere). This definition occurs in the later literature. In the form "Deus est sphaera infinita" (God is an infinite sphere) it is supposed to have come from the *Liber Hermetis, Liber Termegisti,* Cod. Paris. 6319 (14th cent.); Cod. Vat. 3060 (1315). Cf. Baumgartner, *Die Philosophie des Alanus de Insulis,* p. 118. In this connection, mention should be made of the tendency of Gnostic thought to move in a circle, e.g.: "In the beginning was the Word, and the Word was with God, and God was the Word." Cf. Leisegang, *Denkformen,* pp. 60ff.

geometrically, by a mandala. This archetypal idea is a reflection of the individual's wholeness, i.e., of the self, which is present in him as an unconscious image. The conscious mind can form absolutely no conception of this totality, because it includes not only the conscious but also the unconscious psyche, which is, as such, inconceivable and irrepresentable.

231 It was this archetype of the self in the soul of every man that responded to the Christian message, with the result that the concrete Rabbi Jesus was rapidly assimilated by the constellated archetype. In this way Christ realized the idea of the self.[7] But as one can never distinguish empirically between a symbol of the self and a God-image, the two ideas, however much we try to differentiate them, always appear blended together, so that the self appears synonymous with the inner Christ of the Johannine and Pauline writings, and Christ with God ("of one substance with the Father"), just as the atman appears as the individualized self and at the same time as the animating principle of the cosmos, and Tao as a condition of mind and at the same time as the correct behaviour of cosmic events. Psychologically speaking, the domain of "gods" begins where consciousness leaves off, for at that point man is already at the mercy of the natural order, whether he thrive or perish. To the symbols of wholeness that come to him from there he attaches names which vary according to time and place.

232 The self is defined psychologically as the psychic totality of the individual. Anything that a man postulates as being a greater totality than himself can become a symbol of the self. For this reason the symbol of the self is not always as total as the definition would require. Even the Christ-figure is not a totality, for it lacks the nocturnal side of the psyche's nature, the darkness of the spirit, and is also without sin. Without the integration of evil there is no totality, nor can evil be "added to the mixture by force." One could compare Christ as a symbol to the mean of the first mixture: he would then be the middle term of a triad, in which the One and Indivisible is represented by the Father, and the Divisible by the Holy Ghost, who, as we know, can divide himself into tongues of fire. But

7 Koepgen (p. 307) puts it very aptly: "Jesus relates everything to his ego, but this ego is not the subjective ego, it is a cosmic ego."

this triad, according to the *Timaeus,* is not yet a reality. Consequently a second mixture is needed.

233 The goal of psychological, as of biological, development is self-realization, or individuation. But since man knows himself only as an ego, and the self, as a totality, is indescribable and indistinguishable from a God-image, self-realization—to put it in religious or metaphysical terms—amounts to God's incarnation. That is already expressed in the fact that Christ is the son of God. And because individuation is an heroic and often tragic task, the most difficult of all, it involves suffering, a passion of the ego: the ordinary, empirical man we once were is burdened with the fate of losing himself in a greater dimension and being robbed of his fancied freedom of will. He suffers, so to speak, from the violence done to him by the self.[8] The analogous passion of Christ signifies God's suffering on account of the injustice of the world and the darkness of man. The human and the divine suffering set up a relationship of complementarity with compensating effects. Through the Christ-symbol, man can get to know the real meaning of his suffering: he is on the way towards realizing his wholeness. As a result of the integration of conscious and unconscious, his ego enters the "divine" realm, where it participates in "God's suffering." The cause of the suffering is in both cases the same, namely "incarnation," which on the human level appears as "individuation." The divine hero born of man is already threatened with murder; he has nowhere to lay his head, and his death is a gruesome tragedy. The self is no mere concept or logical postulate; it is a psychic reality, only part of it conscious, while for the rest it embraces the life of the unconscious and is therefore inconceivable except in the form of symbols. The drama of the archetypal life of Christ describes in symbolic images the events in the conscious life—as well as in the life that transcends consciousness—of a man who has been transformed by his higher destiny.

III. THE HOLY GHOST

234 The psychological relationship between man and the trinitarian life process is illustrated first by the human nature of

[8] Cf. Jacob's struggle with the angel at the ford.

Christ, and second by the descent of the Holy Ghost and his indwelling in man, as predicted and promised by the Christian message. The life of Christ is on the one hand only a short, historical interlude for proclaiming the message, but on the other hand it is an exemplary demonstration of the psychic experiences connected with God's manifestation of himself (or the realization of the self). The important thing for man is not the *δεικνύμενον* and the *δρώμενον* (what is "shown" and "done"), but what happens afterwards: the seizure of the individual by the Holy Ghost.

235 Here, however, we run into a great difficulty. For if we follow up the theory of the Holy Ghost and carry it a step further (which the Church has not done, for obvious reasons), we come inevitably to the conclusion that if the Father appears in the Son and breathes together with the Son, and the Son leaves the Holy Ghost behind for man, then the Holy Ghost breathes in man, too, and thus is the breath common to man, the Son, and the Father. Man is therefore included in God's sonship, and the words of Christ—"Ye are gods" (John 10:34)—appear in a significant light. The doctrine that the Paraclete was expressly left behind for man raises an enormous problem. The triadic formula of Plato would surely be the last word in the matter of logic, but psychologically it is not so at all, because the psychological factor keeps on intruding in the most disturbing way. Why, in the name of all that's wonderful, wasn't it "Father, Mother, and Son?" That would be much more "reasonable" and "natural" than "Father, Son, and Holy Ghost." To this we must answer: it is not just a question of a natural situation, but of a product of human reflection [9] added on to the natural sequence of father and son. Through reflection, "life" and its "soul" are abstracted from Nature and endowed with a separate existence. Father and son are united in the same soul, or, according to the ancient Egyptian view, in the same procreative force,

9 "Reflection" should be understood not simply as an act of thought, but rather as an attitude. [Cf. *Psychological Types,* Def. 8.—EDITORS.] It is a privilege born of human freedom in contradistinction to the compulsion of natural law. As the word itself testifies ("reflection" means literally "bending back"), reflection is a spiritual act that runs counter to the natural process; an act whereby we stop, call something to mind, form a picture, and take up a relation to and come to terms with what we have seen. It should, therefore, be understood as an act of *becoming conscious.*

Ka-mutef. Ka-mutef is exactly the same hypostatization of an attribute as the breath or "spiration" of the Godhead.[10]

236 This psychological fact spoils the abstract perfection of the triadic formula and makes it a logically incomprehensible construction, since, in some mysterious and unexpected way, an important mental process peculiar to man has been imported into it. If the Holy Ghost is, at one and the same time, the breath of life and a loving spirit and the Third Person in whom the whole trinitarian process culminates, then he is essentially a product of reflection, an hypostatized noumenon tacked on to the natural family-picture of father and son. It is significant that early Christian Gnosticism tried to get round this difficulty by interpreting the Holy Ghost as the Mother.[11] But that would merely have kept him within the archaic family-picture, within the tritheism and polytheism of the patriarchal world. It is, after all, perfectly natural that the father should have a family and that the son should embody the father. This train of thought is quite consistent with the father-world. On the other hand, the mother-interpretation would reduce the specific meaning of the Holy Ghost to a primitive image and destroy the most essential of the qualities attributed to him: not only is he the life common to Father and Son, he is also the Paraclete whom the Son left behind him, to procreate in man and bring forth works of divine parentage. It is of paramount importance that the idea of the Holy Ghost is not a natural image, but a recognition of the living quality of Father and Son, abstractly conceived as the "third" term between the One and the Other. Out of the tension of duality life always produces a "third" that seems somehow incommensurable or paradoxical. Hence, as the "third," the Holy Ghost is bound to be incommensurable and paradoxical too. Unlike Father and Son, he has no name and no character. He is a *function,* but that function is the Third Person of the Godhead.

10 "Active spiration" is a manifestation of life, an immanent act of Father and Son; "passive spiration," on the other hand, is a quality of the Holy Ghost. According to St. Thomas, spiration does not proceed from the intellect but from the will of the Father and Son. In relation to the Son the Holy Ghost is not a spiration, but a procreative act of the Father.

11 Cf. the Acts of Thomas (trans. by James, p. 388): "Come, O communion of the male; come, she that knoweth the mysteries of him that is chosen. . . . Come, holy dove that beareth the twin young; come, hidden mother."

237 He is psychologically heterogeneous in that he cannot be logically derived from the father-son relationship and can only be understood as an idea introduced by a process of human reflection. The Holy Ghost is an exceedingly "abstract" conception, since a "breath" shared by two figures characterized as distinct and not mutually interchangeable can hardly be conceived at all. Hence one feels it to be an artificial construction of the mind, even though, as the Egyptian Ka-mutef concept shows, it seems somehow to belong to the very essence of the Trinity. Despite the fact that we cannot help seeing in the positing of such a concept a product of human reflection, this reflection need not necessarily have been a conscious act. It could equally well owe its existence to a "revelation," i.e., to an unconscious reflection,[12] and hence to an autonomous functioning of the unconscious, or rather of the self, whose symbols, as we have already said, cannot be distinguished from God-images. A religious interpretation will therefore insist that this hypostasis was a divine revelation. While it cannot raise any objections to such a notion, psychology must hold fast to the conceptual nature of the hypostasis, for in the last analysis the Trinity, too, is an anthropomorphic configuration, gradually taking shape through strenuous mental and spiritual effort, even though already preformed by the timeless archetype.

238 This separating, recognizing, and assigning of qualities is a mental activity which, although unconscious at first, gradually filters through to consciousness as the work proceeds. What started off by merely happening to consciousness later becomes integrated in it as its own activity. So long as a mental or indeed any psychic process at all is unconscious, it is subject to the law governing archetypal dispositions, which are organized and arranged round the self. And since the self cannot be distinguished from an archetypal God-image, it would be equally true to say of any such arrangement that it conforms to natural law and that it is an act of God's will. (Every metaphysical statement is, *ipso facto,* unprovable). Inasmuch, then, as acts of cognition and judgment are essential qualities of consciousness, any accumulation of unconscious acts of this sort [13] will have the

12 For this seeming *contradictio in adjecto* see "On the Nature of the Psyche," p. 172.

13 The existence of such process is evidenced by the content of dreams.

effect of strengthening and widening consciousness, as one can see for oneself in any thorough analysis of the unconscious. Consequently, man's achievement of consciousness appears as the result of prefigurative archetypal processes or—to put it metaphysically—as part of the divine life-process. In other words, God becomes manifest in the human act of reflection.

239 The nature of this conception (i.e., the hypostatizing of a quality) meets the need evinced by primitive thought to form a more or less abstract idea by endowing each individual quality with a concrete existence of its own. Just as the Holy Ghost is a legacy left to man, so, conversely, the concept of the Holy Ghost is something begotten by man and bears the stamp of its human progenitor. And just as Christ took on man's bodily nature, so through the Holy Ghost man as a spiritual force is surreptitiously included in the mystery of the Trinity, thereby raising it far above the naturalistic level of the triad and thus beyond the Platonic triunity. The Trinity, therefore, discloses itself as a symbol that comprehends the essence of the divine *and* the human. It is, as Koepgen [14] says, "a revelation not only of God but at the same time of man."

240 The Gnostic interpretation of the Holy Ghost as the Mother contains a core of truth in that Mary was the instrument of God's birth and so became involved in the trinitarian drama as a human being. The Mother of God can, therefore, be regarded as a symbol of mankind's essential participation in the Trinity. The psychological justification for this assumption lies in the fact that thinking, which originally had its source in the self-revelations of the unconscious, was felt to be the manifestation of a power external to consciousness. The primitive does not think; the thoughts come to him. We ourselves still feel certain particularly enlightening ideas as "in-fluences," "in-spirations," etc. Where judgments and flashes of insight are transmitted by unconscious activity, they are often attributed to an archetypal feminine figure, the anima or mother-beloved. It then seems as if the inspiration came from the mother or from the beloved, the "femme inspiratrice." In view of this, the Holy Ghost would have a tendency to exchange his neuter designation (τὸ πνεῦμα) for a feminine one. (It may be noted that the Hebrew word for spirit—*ruach*—is predominantly feminine.) Holy Ghost

14 *Die Gnosis des Christentums*, p. 194.

and Logos merge in the Gnostic idea of Sophia, and again in the Sapientia of the medieval natural philosophers, who said of her: "In gremio matris sedet sapientia patris" (the wisdom of the father lies in the lap of the mother). These psychological relationships do something to explain why the Holy Ghost was interpreted as the mother, but they add nothing to our understanding of the Holy Ghost as such, because it is impossible to see how the mother could come third when her natural place would be second.

241 Since the Holy Ghost is an hypostasis of "life," posited by an act of reflection, he appears, on account of his peculiar nature, as a separate and incommensurable "third," whose very peculiarities testify that it is neither a compromise nor a mere triadic appendage, but rather the logically unexpected resolution of tension between Father and Son. The fact that it is precisely a process of human reflection that irrationally creates the uniting "third" is itself connected with the nature of the drama of redemption, whereby God descends into the human realm and man mounts up to the realm of divinity.

242 Thinking in the magic circle of the Trinity, or trinitarian thinking, is in truth motivated by the "Holy Spirit" in so far as it is never a question of mere cogitation but of giving expression to imponderable psychic events. The driving forces that work themselves out in this thinking are not conscious motives; they spring from an historical occurrence rooted, in its turn, in those obscure psychic conditions for which one could hardly find a better or more succinct formula than the "change from father to son," from unity to duality, from non-reflection to criticism. To the extent that personal motives are lacking in trinitarian thinking, and the forces motivating it derive from impersonal and collective psychic conditions, it expresses a need of the unconscious psyche far surpassing all personal needs. This need, aided by human thought, produced the symbol of the Trinity, which was destined to serve as a saving formula of wholeness in an epoch of change and psychic transformation. Manifestations of a psychic activity not caused or consciously willed by man himself have always been felt to be daemonic, divine, or "holy," in the sense that they heal and make whole. His ideas of God behave as do all images arising out of the unconscious: they compensate or complete the general mood or attitude of the mo-

ment, and it is only through the integration of these unconscious images that a man becomes a psychic whole. The "merely conscious" man who is all ego is a mere fragment, in so far as he seems to exist apart from the unconscious. But the more the unconscious is split off, the more formidable the shape in which it appears to the conscious mind—if not in divine form, then in the more unfavourable form of obsessions and outbursts of affect.[15] Gods are personifications of unconscious contents, for they reveal themselves to us through the unconscious activity of the psyche.[16] Trinitarian thinking had something of the same quality, and its passionate profundity rouses in us latecomers a naïve astonishment. We no longer know, or have not yet discovered, what depths in the soul were stirred by that great turning-point in human history. The Holy Ghost seems to have faded away without having found the answer to the question he set humanity.

15 In the *Rituale Romanum* ("On the Exorcism of Persons Possessed by the Devil": 1952 edn., pp. 839ff.), states of possession are expressly distinguished from diseases. We are told that the exorcist must learn to know the signs by which the possessed person may be distinguished from "those suffering from melancholy or any morbid condition." The criteria of possession are: ". . . speaking fluently in unknown tongues or understanding those who speak them; revealing things that take place at a distance or in secret; giving evidence of greater strength than is natural in view of one's age or condition; and other things of the same kind." The Church's idea of possession, therefore, is limited to extremely rare cases, whereas I would use it in a much wider sense as designating a frequently occurring psychic phenomenon: any autonomous complex not subject to the conscious will exerts a possessive effect on consciousness proportional to its strength and limits the latter's freedom. On the question of the Church's distinction between disease and possession, see Tonquédec, *Les Maladies nerveuses ou mentales et les manifestations diaboliques.*

16 I am always coming up against the misunderstanding that a psychological treatment or explanation reduces God to "nothing but" psychology. It is not a question of God at all, but of man's ideas of God, as I have repeatedly emphasized. There are people who do have such ideas and who form such conceptions, and these things are the proper study of psychology.

5. THE PROBLEM OF THE FOURTH

I. THE CONCEPT OF QUATERNITY

243 The *Timaeus,* which was the first to propound a triadic formula for the God-image in philosophical terms, starts off with the ominous question: "One, two, three—but . . . where is the fourth?" This question is, as we know, taken up again in the Cabiri scene in *Faust:*

> Three we brought with us,
> The fourth would not come.
> He was the right one
> Who thought for them all.

244 When Goethe says that the fourth was the one "who thought for them all," we rather suspect that the fourth was Goethe's own thinking function.[1] The Cabiri are, in fact, the mysterious creative powers, the gnomes who work under the earth, i.e., below the threshold of consciousness, in order to supply us with lucky ideas. As imps and hobgoblins, however, they also play all sorts of nasty tricks, keeping back names and dates that were

1 "Feeling is all; / Names are sound and smoke." [This problem of the "fourth" in *Faust* is also discussed in *Psychology and Alchemy,* pars. 201ff.—EDITORS.]

"on the tip of the tongue," making us say the wrong thing, etc. They give an eye to everything that has not already been anticipated by the conscious mind and the functions at its disposal. As these functions can be used consciously only because they are adapted, it follows that the unconscious, autonomous function is not or cannot be used consciously because it is unadapted. The differentiated and differentiable functions are much easier to cope with, and, for understandable reasons, we prefer to leave the "inferior" function round the corner, or to repress it altogether, because it is such an awkward customer. And it is a fact that it has the strongest tendency to be infantile, banal, primitive, and archaic. Anybody who has a high opinion of himself will do well to guard against letting it make a fool of him. On the other hand, deeper insight will show that the primitive and archaic qualities of the inferior function conceal all sorts of significant relationships and symbolical meanings, and instead of laughing off the Cabiri as ridiculous Tom Thumbs he may begin to suspect that they are a treasure-house of hidden wisdom. Just as, in *Faust,* the fourth thinks for them all, so the whereabouts of the eighth should be asked "on Olympus." Goethe showed great insight in not underestimating his inferior function, thinking, although it was in the hands of the Cabiri and was undoubtedly mythological and archaic. He characterizes it perfectly in the line: "The fourth would not come." Exactly! It wanted for some reason to stay behind or below.[2]

245 Three of the four orienting functions are available to consciousness. This is confirmed by the psychological experience that a rational type, for instance, whose superior function is thinking, has at his disposal one, or possibly two, auxiliary functions of an irrational nature, namely sensation (the "fonction du réel") and intuition (perception via the unconscious). His inferior function will be feeling (valuation), which remains in a retarded state and is contaminated with the unconscious. It refuses to come along with the others and often goes wildly off on its own. This peculiar dissociation is, it seems, a product of civilization, and it denotes a freeing of consciousness from any excessive attachment to the "spirit of gravity." If that function, which is still bound indissolubly to the past and whose roots

2 Cf. *Psychological Types,* Def. 30.

reach back as far as the animal kingdom,[3] can be left behind and even forgotten, then consciousness has won for itself a new and not entirely illusory freedom. It can leap over abysses on winged feet; it can free itself from bondage to sense-impressions, emotions, fascinating thoughts, and presentiments by soaring into abstraction. Certain primitive initiations stress the idea of transformation into ghosts and invisible spirits and thereby testify to the relative emancipation of consciousness from the fetters of non-differentiation. Although there is a tendency, characteristic not only of primitive religions, to speak rather exaggeratedly of complete transformation, complete renewal and rebirth, it is, of course, only a relative change, continuity with the earlier state being in large measure preserved. Were it otherwise, every religious transformation would bring about a complete splitting of the personality or a loss of memory, which is obviously not so. The connection with the earlier attitude is maintained because part of the personality remains behind in the previous situation; that is to say it lapses into unconsciousness and starts building up the shadow.[4] The loss makes itself felt in consciousness through the absence of at least one of the four orienting functions, and the missing function is always the opposite of the superior function. The loss need not necessarily take the form of complete absence; in other words, the inferior function may be either unconscious or conscious, but in both cases it is autonomous and obsessive and not influenceable by the will. It has the "all-or-none" character of an instinct. Although emancipation from the instincts brings a differentiation and enhancement of consciousness, it can only come about at the expense of the unconscious function, so that conscious orientation lacks that element which the inferior function could have supplied. Thus it often happens that people who have an amazing range of consciousness know less about themselves than the veriest infant, and all because "the fourth would not come"—

[3] Cf. the Hymn of Valentinus (Mead, *Fragments of a Faith Forgotten,* p. 307): "All things depending in spirit I see; all things supported in spirit I view; flesh from soul depending; soul by air supported; air from aether hanging; fruits born of the deep; babe born of the womb." Cf. also the προσφυὴς ψυχή of Isidorus, who supposed that all manner of animal qualities attached to the human soul in the form of "outgrowths." [Cf. *Aion,* par. 370.]

[4] Cf. the alchemical symbol of the *umbra solis* and the Gnostic idea that Christ was born "not without some shadow."

it remained down below—or up above—in the unconscious realm.

246 As compared with the trinitarian thinking of Plato, ancient Greek philosophy favoured thinking of a quaternary type. In Pythagoras the great role was played not by three but by four; the Pythagorean oath, for instance, says that the tetraktys "contains the roots of eternal nature." [5] The Pythagorean school was dominated by the idea that the soul was a square and not a triangle. The origin of these ideas lies far back in the dark prehistory of Greek thought. The quaternity is an archetype of almost universal occurrence. It forms the logical basis for any whole judgment. If one wishes to pass such a judgment, it must have this fourfold aspect. For instance, if you want to describe the horizon as a whole, you name the four quarters of heaven. Three is not a natural coefficient of order, but an artificial one. There are four elements, four prime qualities, four colours, four castes, four ways of spiritual development in Buddhism, etc. So, too, there are four aspects of psychological orientation, beyond which nothing fundamental remains to be said. In order to orient ourselves, we must have a function which ascertains that something is there (sensation); a second function which establishes *what* it is (thinking); a third function which states whether it suits us or not, whether we wish to accept it or not (feeling); and a fourth function which indicates where it came from and where it is going (intuition). When this has been done, there is nothing more to say. Schopenhauer proves that the "Principle of Sufficient Reason" has a fourfold root.[6] This is so because the fourfold aspect is the minimum requirement for a complete judgment. The ideal of completeness is the circle or sphere, but its natural minimal division is a quaternity.

247 Now if Plato had had the idea of the Christian Trinity [7]—which of course he did not—and had on that account placed his triad above everything, one would be bound to object that this cannot be a whole judgment. A necessary fourth would be left

5 The four ῥιζώματα of Empedocles.

6 "On the Fourfold Root of the Principle of Sufficient Reason," in *Two Essays by Arthur Schopenhauer.*

7 In Plato the quaternity takes the form of a cube, which he correlates with earth. Lü Pu-wei (*Frühling und Herbst,* trans. into German by Wilhelm, p. 38) says: "Heaven's way is round, earth's way is square."

out; or, if Plato took the three-sided figure as symbolic of the Beautiful and the Good and endowed it with all positive qualities, he would have had to deny evil and imperfection to it. In that case, what has become of them? The Christian answer is that evil is a *privatio boni.* This classic formula robs evil of absolute existence and makes it a shadow that has only a relative existence dependent on light. Good, on the other hand, is credited with a positive substantiality. But, as psychological experience shows, "good" and "evil" are opposite poles of a moral judgment which, as such, originates in man. A judgment can be made about a thing only if its opposite is equally real and possible. The opposite of a seeming evil can only be a seeming good, and an evil that lacks substance can only be contrasted with a good that is equally non-substantial. Although the opposite of "existence" is "non-existence," the opposite of an existing good can never be a non-existing evil, for the latter is a contradiction in terms and opposes to an existing good something incommensurable with it; the opposite of a non-existing (negative) evil can only be a non-existing (negative) good. If, therefore, evil is said to be a mere privation of good, the opposition of good and evil is denied outright. How can one speak of "good" at all if there is no "evil"? Or of "light" if there is no "darkness," or of "above" if there is no "below"? There is no getting round the fact that if you allow substantiality to good, you must also allow it to evil. If evil has no substance, good must remain shadowy, for there is no substantial opponent for it to defend itself against, but only a shadow, a mere privation of good. Such a view can hardly be squared with observed reality. It is difficult to avoid the impression that apotropaic tendencies have had a hand in creating this notion, with the understandable intention of settling the painful problem of evil as optimistically as possible. Often it is just as well that we do not know the danger we escape when we rush in where angels fear to tread.

248 Christianity also deals with the problem in another way, by asserting that evil has substance and personality as the devil, or Lucifer. There is one view which allows the devil a malicious, goblin-like existence only, thus making him the insignificant head of an insignificant tribe of wood-imps and poltergeists. Another view grants him a more dignified status, depending on the

degree to which it identifies him with "ills" in general. How far "ills" may be identified with "evil" is a controversial question. The Church distinguishes between physical ills and moral ills. The former may be willed by divine Providence (e.g., for man's improvement), the latter not, because sin cannot be willed by God even as a means to an end. It would be difficult to verify the Church's view in concrete instances, for psychic and somatic disorders are "ills," and, as illnesses, they are moral as well as physical. At all events there is a view which holds that the devil, though created, is autonomous and eternal. In addition, he is the adversary of Christ: by infecting our first parents with original sin he corrupted creation and made the Incarnation necessary for God's work of salvation. In so doing he acted according to his own judgment, as in the Job episode, where he was even able to talk God round. The devil's prowess on these occasions hardly squares with his alleged shadow-existence as the *privatio boni,* which, as we have said, looks very like a euphemism. The devil as an autonomous and eternal personality is much more in keeping with his role as the adversary of Christ and with the psychological reality of evil.

249 But if the devil has the power to put a spoke in God's Creation, or even corrupt it, and God does nothing to stop this nefarious activity and leaves it all to man (who is notoriously stupid, unconscious, and easily led astray), then, despite all assurances to the contrary, the evil spirit must be a factor of quite incalculable potency. In this respect, anyhow, the dualism of the Gnostic systems makes sense, because they at least try to do justice to the real meaning of evil. They have also done us the supreme service of having gone very thoroughly into the question of where evil comes from. Biblical tradition leaves us very much in the dark on this point, and it is only too obvious why the old theologians were in no particular hurry to enlighten us. In a monotheistic religion everything that goes against God can only be traced back to God himself. This thought is objectionable, to say the least of it, and has therefore to be circumvented. That is the deeper reason why a highly influential personage like the devil cannot be accommodated properly in a trinitarian cosmos. It is difficult to make out in what relation he stands to the Trinity. As the adversary of Christ, he would have to take up an

equivalent counterposition and be, like him, a "son of God." [8] But that would lead straight back to certain Gnostic views according to which the devil, as Satanaël,[9] is God's first son, Christ being the second.[9a] A further logical inference would be the abolition of the Trinity formula and its replacement by a quaternity.

250 The idea of a quaternity of divine principles was violently attacked by the Church Fathers when an attempt was made to add a fourth—God's "essence"—to the Three Persons of the Trinity. This resistance to the quaternity is very odd, considering that the central Christian symbol, the Cross, is unmistakably a quaternity. The Cross, however, symbolizes God's suffering in his immediate encounter with the world.[10] The "prince of this world," the devil (John 12:31, 14:30), vanquishes the God-man at this point, although by so doing he is presumably preparing his own defeat and digging his own grave. According to an old view, Christ is the "bait on the hook" (the Cross), with which he catches "Leviathan" (the devil).[11] It is therefore significant that the Cross, set up midway between heaven and hell as a symbol of Christ's struggle with the devil, corresponds to the quaternity.

251 Medieval iconology, embroidering on the old speculations about the Theotokos, evolved a quaternity symbol in its representations of the coronation of the Virgin [12] and surreptitiously put it in place of the Trinity. The Assumption of the Blessed Virgin Mary, i.e., the taking up of Mary's soul into heaven *with her body,* is admitted as ecclesiastical doctrine but has not yet become dogma.[13] Although Christ, too, rose up with his body,

8 In her "Die Gestalt des Satans im Alten Testament" (*Symbolik des Geistes,* pp. 153ff.), Riwkah Schärf shows that Satan is in fact one of God's sons, at any rate in the Old Testament sense.

9 The suffix *-el* means god, so Satanaël = Satan-God.

9a Michael Psellus, "De Daemonibus," 1497, fol. NVv, ed. M. Ficino. Cf. also Epiphanius, *Panarium,* Haer. XXX, in Migne, *P.G.,* vol. 41, cols. 406ff.

10 Cf. Przywara's meditations on the Cross and its relation to God in *Deus Semper Major,* I. Also the early Christian interpretation of the Cross in the Acts of John, trans. by James, pp. 228ff.

11 See *Psychology and Alchemy,* fig. 28.

12 Cf. *Psychology and Alchemy,* pars. 315ff., and the first paper in this volume, pars. 122ff.

13 As this doctrine has already got beyond the stage of "conclusio probabilis" and has reached that of "conclusio certa," the "definitio sollemnis" is now only a matter of time. The Assumption is, doctrinally speaking, a "revelatum im-

this has a rather different meaning, since Christ was a divinity in the first place and Mary was not. In her case the body would have been a much more material one than Christ's, much more an element of space-time reality.[14] Ever since the *Timaeus* the "fourth" has signified "realization," i.e., entry into an essentially different condition, that of worldly materiality, which, it is authoritatively stated, is ruled by the Prince of this world—for matter is the diametrical opposite of spirit. It is the true abode of the devil, whose hellish hearth-fire burns deep in the interior of the earth, while the shining spirit soars in the aether, freed from the shackles of gravity.

252 The *Assumptio Mariae* paves the way not only for the divinity of the Theotokos (i.e., her ultimate recognition as a goddess),[15] but also for the quaternity. At the same time, matter is included in the metaphysical realm, together with the corrupting principle of the cosmos, evil. One can explain that matter was originally pure, or at least capable of purity, but this does not do away with the fact that matter represents the *concreteness* of God's thoughts and is, therefore, the very thing that makes individuation possible, with all its consequences. The adversary is, quite logically, conceived to be the soul of matter, because they both constitute a point of resistance without which

plicitum"; that is to say, it has never been revealed explicitly, but, in the gradual course of development, it became clear as an original content of the Revelation. (Cf. Wiederkehr, *Die leibliche Aufnahme der allerseligsten Jungfrau Maria in den Himmel.*) From the psychological standpoint, however, and in terms of the history of symbols, this view is a consistent and logical restoration of the archetypal situation, in which the exalted status of Mary is revealed implicitly and must therefore become a "conclusio certa" in the course of time.

[This note was written in 1948, two years before the promulgation of the dogma. The bodily assumption of Mary into heaven was defined as a dogma of the Catholic faith by Pope Pius XII in November 1950 by the Apostolic Constitution *Munificentissimus Deus* (*Acta Apostolicae Sedis,* Rome, XLII, pp. 753ff.), and in an Encyclical Letter, *Ad Caeli Reginam,* of October 11, 1954, the same Pope instituted a feast to be observed yearly in honour of Mary's "regalis dignitas" as Queen of Heaven and Earth (*Acta Apostolicae Sedis,* XLVI, pp. 625ff.). —EDITORS.]

14 Although the assumption of Mary is of fundamental significance, it was not the first case of this kind. Enoch and Elijah were taken up to heaven with their bodies, and many holy men rose from their graves when Christ died.

15 Her divinity may be regarded as a tacit *conclusio probabilis,* and so too may the worship or adoration (προσκύνησις) to which she is entitled.

the relative autonomy of individual existence would be simply unthinkable. The will to be different and contrary is characteristic of the devil, just as disobedience was the hallmark of original sin. These, as we have said, are the necessary conditions for the Creation and ought, therefore, to be included in the divine plan and—ultimately—in the divine realm.[16] But the Christian definition of God as the *summum bonum* excludes the Evil One right from the start, despite the fact that in the Old Testament he was still one of the "sons of God." Hence the devil remained outside the Trinity as the "ape of God" and in opposition to it. Medieval representations of the triune God as having three heads are based on the three-headedness of Satan, as we find it, for instance, in Dante. This would point to an infernal Antitrinity, a true "umbra trinitatis" analogous to the Antichrist.[17] The devil is, undoubtedly, an awkward figure: he is the "odd man out" in the Christian cosmos. That is why people would like to minimize his importance by euphemistic ridicule or by ignoring his existence altogether; or, better still, to lay the blame for him at man's door. This is in fact done by the very people who would protest mightily if sinful man should credit himself, equally, with the origin of all good. A glance at the Scriptures, however, is enough to show us the importance of the devil in the divine drama of redemption.[18] If the power of the Evil One had been as feeble as certain persons would wish it to appear, either the world would not have needed God himself to come down to it or it would have lain within the power of man to set the world to rights, which has certainly not happened so far.

16 Koepgen (p. 185) expresses himself in similar terms: "The essence of the devil is his hatred for God; and God allows this hatred. There are two things which Divine Omnipotence alone makes possible: Satan's hatred and the existence of the human individual. Both are by nature completely inexplicable. But so, too, is their relationship to God."

17 Just how alive and ingrained such conceptions are can be seen from the title of a modern book by Sosnosky, *Die rote Dreifaltigkeit: Jakobiner und Bolschewiken* ["The Red Trinity: Jacobins and Bolsheviks"].

18 Koepgen's views are not so far from my own in certain respects. For instance, he says that "Satan acts, in a sense, as God's power. . . . The mystery of one God in Three Persons opens out a new freedom in the depths of God's being, and this even makes possible the thought of a personal devil existing alongside God and in opposition to him" (p. 186).

253 Whatever the metaphysical position of the devil may be, in psychological reality evil is an effective, not to say menacing, limitation of goodness, so that it is no exaggeration to assume that in this world good and evil more or less balance each other, like day and night, and that this is the reason why the victory of the good is always a special act of grace.

254 If we disregard the specifically Persian system of dualism, it appears that no real devil is to be found anywhere in the early period of man's spiritual development. In the Old Testament, he is vaguely foreshadowed in the figure of Satan. But the real devil first appears as the adversary of Christ,[19] and with him we gaze for the first time into the luminous realm of divinity on the one hand and into the abyss of hell on the other. The devil is autonomous; he cannot be brought under God's rule, for if he could he would not have the power to be the adversary of Christ, but would only be God's instrument. Once the indefinable One unfolds into two, it becomes something definite: the man Jesus, the Son and Logos. This statement is possible only by virtue of something else that is *not* Jesus, not Son or Logos. The act of love embodied in the Son is counterbalanced by Lucifer's denial.

255 Inasmuch as the devil was an angel created by God and "fell like lightning from heaven," he too is a divine "procession" that became Lord of this world. It is significant that the Gnostics thought of him sometimes as the imperfect demiurge and sometimes as the Saturnine archon, Ialdabaoth. Pictorial representations of this archon correspond in every detail with those of a diabolical demon. He symbolized the power of darkness from which Christ came to rescue humanity. The archons issued from the womb of the unfathomable abyss, i.e., from the same source that produced the Gnostic Christ.

256 A medieval thinker observed that when God separated the upper waters from the lower on the second day of Creation, he did not say in the evening, as he did on all the other days, that it was good. And he did not say it because on that day he had

19 Since Satan, like Christ, is a son of God, it is evident that we have here the archetype of the hostile brothers. The Old Testament prefiguration would therefore be Cain and Abel and their sacrifice. Cain has a Luciferian nature because of his rebellious progressiveness, but Abel is the pious shepherd. At all events, the vegetarian trend got no encouragement from Yahweh [Gen. 4:5].

created the *binarius,* the origin of all evil.[20] We come across a similar idea in Persian literature, where the origin of Ahriman is attributed to a *doubting thought* in Ahura-Mazda's mind. If we think in non-trinitarian terms, the logic of the following schema seems inescapable:

257 So it is not strange that we should meet the idea of Antichrist so early. It was probably connected on the one hand with the astrological synchronicity of the dawning aeon of Pisces,[21] and on the other hand with the increasing realization of the duality postulated by the Son, which in turn is prefigured in the fish symbol:)–(, showing two fishes, joined by a commissure, moving in opposite directions.[22] It would be absurd to put any kind of causal construction on these events. Rather, it is a question of preconscious, prefigurative connections between the archetypes themselves, suggestions of which can be traced in other constellations as well and above all in the formation of myths.

258 In our diagram, Christ and the devil appear as equal and opposite, thus conforming to the idea of the "adversary." This opposition means conflict to the last, and it is the task of humanity to endure this conflict until the time or turning-point is reached where good and evil begin to relativize themselves, to doubt themselves, and the cry is raised for a morality "beyond good and evil." In the age of Christianity and in the domain of trinitarian thinking such an idea is simply out of the question, because the conflict is too violent for evil to be assigned any other logical relation to the Trinity than that of an absolute opposite. In an emotional opposition, i.e., in a conflict situation,

20 See the first paper in this volume, par. 104.

21 In antiquity, regard for astrology was nothing at all extraordinary. [Cf. "Synchronicity: An Acausal Connecting Principle," pars. 872ff., and *Aion,* pars. 127ff.—EDITORS.]

22 This applies to the zodion of the Fishes. In the astronomical constellation itself, the fish that corresponds approximately to the first 1,000 years of our era is vertical, but the other fish is horizontal.

thesis and antithesis cannot be viewed together at the same time. This only becomes possible with cooler assessment of the relative value of good and the relative non-value of evil. Then it can no longer be doubted, either, that a common life unites not only the Father and the "light" son, but the Father and his *dark* emanation. The unspeakable conflict posited by duality resolves itself in a fourth principle, which restores the unity of the first in its full development. The rhythm is built up in three steps, but the resultant symbol is a quaternity.

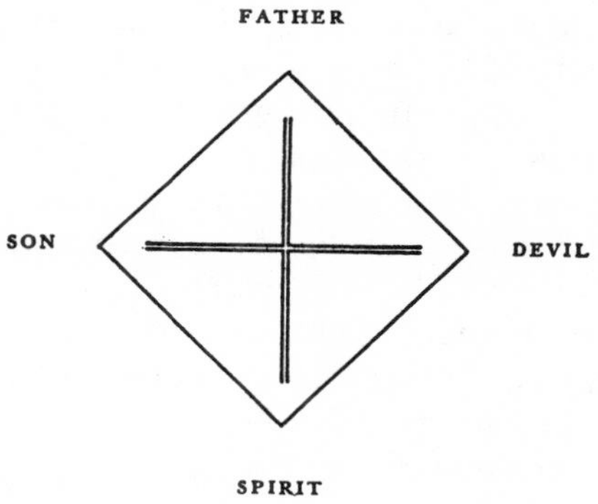

259 The dual aspect of the Father is by no means unknown to religious speculation.[23] This is proved by the allegory of the monoceros, or unicorn, who symbolizes Yahweh's angry moodiness. Like this irritable beast, he reduced the world to chaos and could only be moved to love in the lap of a pure virgin.[24] Luther was familiar with a *deus absconditus*. Murder, sudden death, war, sickness, crime, and every kind of abomination fall in with the unity of God. If God reveals his nature and takes on definite form as a man, then the opposites in him must fly apart: here good, there evil. So it was that the opposites latent in the Deity flew apart when the Son was begotten and manifested themselves in the struggle between Christ and the devil, with the Persian Ormuzd-Ahriman antithesis, perhaps, as the under-

23 God's antithetical nature is also expressed in his androgyny. Priscillian therefore calls him "masculofoemina," on the basis of Genesis 1:27: "So God created man in his own image . . . male and female created he them."

24 Cf. *Psychology and Alchemy*, pars. 520ff.

lying model. The world of the Son is the world of moral discord, without which human consciousness could hardly have progressed so far as it has towards mental and spiritual differentiation. That we are not unreservedly enthusiastic about this progress is shown by the fits of doubt to which our modern consciousness is subject.

260 Despite the fact that he is potentially redeemed, the Christian is given over to moral suffering, and in his suffering he needs the Comforter, the Paraclete. He cannot overcome the conflict on his own resources; after all, he didn't invent it. He has to rely on divine comfort and mediation, that is to say on the spontaneous revelation of the spirit, which does not obey man's will but comes and goes as *it* wills. This spirit is an autonomous psychic happening, a hush that follows the storm, a reconciling light in the darknesses of man's mind, secretly bringing order into the chaos of his soul. The Holy Ghost is a comforter like the Father, a mute, eternal, unfathomable One in whom God's love and God's terribleness come together in wordless union. And through this union the original meaning of the still-unconscious Father-world is restored and brought within the scope of human experience and reflection. Looked at from a quaternary standpoint, the Holy Ghost is a reconciliation of opposites and hence the answer to the suffering in the Godhead which Christ personifies.

261 The Pythagorean quaternity was a natural phenomenon, an archetypal image, but it was not yet a moral problem, let alone a divine drama. Therefore it "went underground." It was a purely naturalistic, intuitive idea born of the nature-bound mind. The gulf that Christianity opened out between nature and spirit enabled the human mind to think not only beyond nature but in opposition to it, thus demonstrating its divine freedom, so to speak. This flight from the darkness of nature's depths culminates in trinitarian thinking, which moves in a Platonic, "supracelestial" realm. But the question of the fourth, rightly or wrongly, remained. It stayed down "below," and from there threw up the heretical notion of the quaternity and the speculations of Hermetic philosophy.

262 In this connection I would like to call attention to Gerhard Dorn, a physician and alchemist, and a native of Frankfurt. He took great exception to the traditional quaternity of the basic

principles of his art, and also to the fourfold nature of its goal, the *lapis philosophorum*. It seemed to him that this was a heresy, since the principle that ruled the world was a Trinity. The quaternity must therefore be of the devil.[25] Four, he maintained, was a doubling of two, and two was made on the second day of Creation, but God was obviously not altogether pleased with the result of his handiwork that evening. The *binarius* is the devil of discord and, what is worse, of feminine nature. (In East and West alike even numbers are feminine.) The cause of dissatisfaction was that, on this ominous second day of Creation, just as with Ahura-Mazda, a split was revealed in God's nature. Out of it crept the "four-horned serpent," who promptly succeeded in seducing Eve, because she was related to him by reason of her binary nature. ("Man was created by God, woman by the ape of God.")

263 The devil is the aping shadow of God, the ἀντίμιμον πνεῦμα, in Gnosticism and also in Greek alchemy. He is "Lord of this world," in whose shadow man was born, fatally tainted with the original sin brought about by the devil. Christ, according to the Gnostic view, cast off the shadow he was born with and remained without sin. His sinlessness proves his essential lack of contamination with the dark world of nature-bound man, who tries in vain to shake off this darkness. ("Uns bleibt ein Erdenrest / zu tragen peinlich." [26]) Man's connection with physis, with the material world and its demands, is the cause of his anomalous position: on the one hand he has the capacity for enlightenment, on the other he is in thrall to the Lord of this world. ("Who will deliver me from the body of this death?") On account of his sinlessness, Christ on the contrary lives in the Platonic realm of pure ideas whither only man's thought can reach, but not he himself in his totality. Man is, in truth, the bridge spanning the gulf between "this world"—the realm of the dark Tricephalus—and the heavenly Trinity. That is why, even in the days of unqualified belief in the Trinity, there was always a quest for the lost fourth, from the time of the Neo-pythagoreans down to Goethe's *Faust*. Although these seekers thought of themselves as Christians, they were really Christians

25 Cf. above, pars. 104ff.

26 *Faust*, Part II, Act 5. ("Earth's residue to bear / Hath sorely pressed us." Trans. by Bayard Taylor.)

only on the side, devoting their lives to a work whose purpose it was to redeem the "four-horned serpent," the fallen Lucifer, and to free the *anima mundi* imprisoned in matter. What in their view lay hidden in matter was the *lumen luminum,* the *Sapientia Dei,* and their work was a "gift of the Holy Spirit." Our quaternity formula confirms the rightness of their claims; for the Holy Ghost, as the synthesis of the original One which then became split, issues from a source that is both light and dark. "For the powers of the right and the left unite in the harmony of wisdom," we are told in the Acts of John.[27]

264 It will have struck the reader that two corresponding elements cross one another in our quaternity schema. On the one hand we have the polaristic identity of Christ and his adversary, and on the other the unity of the Father unfolded in the multiplicity of the Holy Ghost. The resultant cross is the symbol of the suffering Godhead that redeems mankind. This suffering could not have occurred, nor could it have had any effect at all, had it not been for the existence of a power opposed to God, namely "this world" and its Lord. The quaternity schema recognizes the existence of this power as an undeniable fact by fettering trinitarian thinking to the reality of this world. The Platonic freedom of the spirit does not make a whole judgment possible: it wrenches the light half of the picture away from the dark half. This freedom is to a large extent a phenomenon of civilization, the lofty preoccupation of that fortunate Athenian whose lot it was not to be born a slave. We can only rise above nature if somebody else carries the weight of the earth for us. What sort of philosophy would Plato have produced had he been his own house-slave? What would the Rabbi Jesus have taught if he had had to support a wife and children? If he had had to till the soil in which the bread he broke had grown, and weed the vineyard in which the wine he dispensed had ripened? The dark weight of the earth must enter into the picture of the whole. In "this world" there is no good without its bad, no day without its night, no summer without its winter. But civilized man can live without the winter, for he can protect himself against the cold; without dirt, for he can wash; without sin, for he can prudently cut himself off from his fellows and thereby avoid many an occasion for evil. He can deem himself good and pure, because hard

27 Cf. James, *The Apocryphal New Testament,* p. 255.

necessity does not teach him anything better. The natural man, on the other hand, has a wholeness that astonishes one, though there is nothing particularly admirable about it. It is the same old unconsciousness, apathy, and filth.

265 If, however, God is born as a man and wants to unite mankind in the fellowship of the Holy Ghost, he must suffer the terrible torture of having to endure the world in all its reality. This is the cross he has to bear, and he himself is a cross. The whole world is God's suffering, and every individual man who wants to get anywhere near his own wholeness knows that this is the way of the cross.

266 These thoughts are expressed with touching simplicity and beauty in the Negro film *The Green Pastures*.[28] For many years God ruled the world with curses, thunder, lightning, and floods, but it never prospered. Finally he realized that he would have to become a man himself in order to get at the root of the trouble.

267 After he had experienced the world's suffering, this God who became man left behind him a Comforter, the Third Person of the Trinity, who would make his dwelling in many individuals still to come, none of whom would enjoy the privilege or even the possibility of being born without sin. In the Paraclete, therefore, God is closer to the real man and his darkness than he is in the Son. The light God bestrides the bridge—Man—from the day side; God's shadow, from the night side. What will be the outcome of this fearful dilemma, which threatens to shatter the frail human vessel with unknown storms and intoxications? It may well be the revelation of the Holy Ghost out of man himself. Just as man was once revealed out of God, so, when the circle closes, God may be revealed out of man. But since, in this world, an evil is joined to every good, the ἀντίμιμον πνεῦμα will twist the indwelling of the Paraclete into a self-deification of man, thereby causing an inflation of self-importance of which we had a foretaste in the case of Nietzsche. The more unconscious we are of the religious problem in the future, the greater the danger of our putting the divine germ within us to some ridiculous or demoniacal use, puffing ourselves up with it instead of remaining conscious that we are no more than the

28 [From a play by Marc Connelly, adapted from stories by Roark Bradford based on American Negro folk-themes.—EDITORS.]

stable in which the Lord is born. Even on the highest peak we shall never be "beyond good and evil," and the more we experience of their inextricable entanglement the more uncertain and confused will our moral judgment be. In this conflict, it will not help us in the least to throw the moral criterion on the rubbish heap and to set up new tablets after known patterns; for, as in the past, so in the future the wrong we have done, thought, or intended will wreak its vengeance on our souls, no matter whether we turn the world upside down or not. Our knowledge of good and evil has dwindled with our mounting knowledge and experience, and will dwindle still more in the future, without our being able to escape the demands of ethics. In this utmost uncertainty we need the illumination of a holy and whole-making spirit—a spirit that can be anything rather than our reason.

II. THE PSYCHOLOGY OF THE QUATERNITY

268 As I have shown in the previous chapter, one can think out the problem of the fourth without having to discard a religious terminology. The development of the Trinity into a quaternity can be represented in projection on metaphysical figures, and at the same time the exposition gains in plasticity. But any statements of this kind can—and for scientific reasons, must—be reduced to man and his psychology, since they are mental products which cannot be presumed to have any metaphysical validity. They are, in the first place, projections of psychic processes, and nobody really knows what they are "in themselves," i.e., if they exist in an unconscious sphere inaccessible to man. At any rate, science ought not to treat them as anything other than projections. If it acts otherwise, it loses its independence. And since it is not a question of individual fantasies but—at least so far as the Trinity is concerned—of a collective phenomenon, we must assume that the development of the idea of the Trinity is a collective process, representing a differentiation of consciousness that has been going on for several thousand years.

269 In order to interpret the Trinity-symbol psychologically, we have to start with the individual and regard the symbol as an expression of his psyche, rather as if it were a dream-image. It is

possible to do this because even collective ideas once sprang from single individuals and, moreover, can only be "had" by individuals. We can treat the Trinity the more easily as a dream in that its life is a drama, as is also the case with every dream that is moderately well developed.

270 Generally speaking, the father denotes the earlier state of consciousness when one was still a child, still dependent on a definite, ready-made pattern of existence which is habitual and has the character of law. It is a passive, unreflecting condition, a mere awareness of what is given, without intellectual or moral judgment.[1] This is true both individually and collectively.

271 The picture changes when the accent shifts to the son. On the individual level the change usually sets in when the son starts to put himself in his father's place. According to the archaic pattern, this takes the form of quasi-father-murder—in other words, violent identification with the father followed by his liquidation. This, however, is not an advance; it is simply a retention of the old habits and customs with no subsequent differentiation of consciousness. No detachment from the father has been effected. Legitimate detachment consists in conscious differentiation from the father and from the habitus represented by him. This requires a certain amount of knowledge of one's own individuality, which cannot be acquired without moral discrimination and cannot be held on to unless one has understood its meaning.[2] Habit can only be replaced by a mode of life consciously chosen and acquired. The Christianity symbolized by the "Son" therefore forces the individual to discriminate and to reflect, as was noticeably the case with those Church Fathers[3] who laid such emphasis on ἐπιστήμη (knowledge) as opposed to

1 Yahweh approaches the moral problem comparatively late—only in Job. Cf. "Answer to Job," in this volume.

2 Koepgen (p. 231) therefore calls Jesus, quite rightly, the first "autonomous" personality.

3 Justin Martyr, *Apologia* II: "that we may not remain children of necessity and ignorance, but of choice and knowledge." Clement of Alexandria, *Stromata,* I, 9: "And how necessary is it for him who desires to be partaker of the power of God, to treat of intellectual subjects by philosophizing!" II, 4: "Knowledge accordingly is characterized by faith; and faith, by a kind of divine mutual and reciprocal correspondence, becomes characterized by knowledge." VII, 10: "For by it (Gnosis) faith is perfected, inasmuch as it is solely by it that the believer becomes perfect." "And knowledge is the strong and sure demonstration of what is received by faith." (Trans. by Wilson, I, p. 380; II, pp. 10, 446–47.)

ἀνάγκη (necessity) and ἄγνοια (ignorance). The same tendency is apparent in the New Testament controversies over the Jews' righteousness in the eyes of the law, which stands exclusively for the old habitus.

272 The third step, finally, points beyond the "Son" into the future, to a continuing realization of the "spirit," i.e., a living activity proceeding from "Father" and "Son" which raises the subsequent stages of consciousness to the same level of independence as that of "Father" and "Son." This extension of the *filiatio,* whereby men are made children of God, is a metaphysical projection of the psychic change that has taken place. The "Son" represents a transition stage, an intermediate state, part child, part adult. He is a transitory phenomenon, and it is thanks to this fact that the "Son"-gods die an early death. "Son" means the transition from a permanent initial stage called "Father" and "auctor rerum" to the stage of being a father oneself. And this means that the son will transmit to his children the procreative spirit of life which he himself has received and from which he himself was begotten. Brought down to the level of the individual, this symbolism can be interpreted as follows: the state of unreflecting awareness known as "Father" changes into the reflective and rational state of consciousness known as "Son." This state is not only in opposition to the still-existing earlier state, but, by virtue of its conscious and rational nature, it also contains many latent possibilities of dissociation. Increased discrimination begets conflicts that were unconscious before but must now be faced, because, unless they are clearly recognized, no moral decisions can be taken. The stage of the "Son" is therefore a conflict situation *par excellence:* the choice of possible ways is menaced by just as many possibilities of error. "Freedom from the law" brings a sharpening of opposites, in particular of the moral opposites. Christ crucified between two thieves is an eloquent symbol of this fact. The exemplary life of Christ is in itself a "transitus" and amounts therefore to a bridge leading over to the third stage, where the initial stage of the Father is, as it were, recovered. If it were no more than a repetition of the first stage, everything that had been won in the second stage—reason and reflection—would be lost, only to make room for a renewed state of semiconsciousness, of an irrational and unreflecting nature. To avoid this, the values of the

second stage must be held fast; in other words, reason and reflection must be preserved intact. Though the new level of consciousness acquired through the emancipation of the son continues in the third stage, it must recognize that *it* is not the source of the ultimate decisions and flashes of insight which rightly go by the name of "gnosis," but that these are inspired by a higher authority which, in projected form, is known as the "Holy Ghost." Psychologically speaking, "inspiration" comes from an unconscious function. To the naïve-minded person the agent of inspiration appears as an "intelligence" correlated with, or even superior to, consciousness, for it often happens that an idea drops in on one like a saving *deus ex machina.*

273 Accordingly, the advance to the third stage means something like a recognition of the unconscious, if not actual subordination to it.[4] Adulthood is reached when the son reproduces his own childhood state by voluntarily submitting to a paternal authority, either in psychological form, or factually in projected form, as when he recognizes the authority of the Church's teachings. This authority can, of course, be replaced by all manner of substitutes, which only proves that the transition to the third stage is attended by unusual spiritual dangers, consisting chiefly in rationalistic deviations that run counter to the instincts.[5] Spiritual transformation does not mean that one should remain a child, but that the adult should summon up enough honest self-criticism admixed with humility to see where, and in relation to what, he must behave as a child—irrationally, and with unreflecting receptivity. Just as the transition from the first stage to the second demands the sacrifice of childish dependence, so, at the transition to the third stage, an exclusive independence has to be relinquished.

274 It is clear that these changes are not everyday occurrences, but are very fateful transformations indeed. Usually they have a numinous character, and can take the form of conversions, illuminations, emotional shocks, blows of fate, religious or

4 Submission to any metaphysical authority is, from the psychological standpoint, submission to the unconscious. There are no scientific criteria for distinguishing so-called metaphysical factors from psychic ones. But this does not mean that psychology denies the existence of metaphysical factors.

5 The Church knows that the "discernment of spirits" is no simple matter. It knows the dangers of subjective submission to God and therefore reserves the right to act as a director of conscience.

mystical experiences, or their equivalents. Modern man has such hopelessly muddled ideas about anything "mystical," or else such a rationalistic fear of it, that, if ever a mystical experience should befall him, he is sure to misunderstand its true character and will deny or repress its numinosity. It will then be evaluated as an inexplicable, irrational, and even pathological phenomenon. This sort of misinterpretation is always due to lack of insight and inadequate understanding of the complex relationships in the background, which as a rule can only be clarified when the conscious data are supplemented by material derived from the unconscious. Without this, too many gaps remain unfilled in a man's experience of life, and each gap is an opportunity for futile rationalizations. If there is even the slightest tendency to neurotic dissociation, or an indolence verging upon habitual unconsciousness, then false causalities will be preferred to truth every time.

275 The numinous character of these experiences is proved by the fact that they are *overwhelming*—an admission that goes against not only our pride, but against our deep-rooted fear that consciousness may perhaps lose its ascendency, for pride is often only a reaction covering up a secret fear. How thin these protective walls are can be seen from the positively terrifying suggestibility that lies behind all psychic mass movements, beginning with the simple folk who call themselves "Jehovah's Witnesses," the "Oxford Groups" (so named for reasons of prestige[6]) among the upper classes, and ending with the National Socialism of a whole nation—all in search of the unifying mystical experience!

276 Anyone who does not understand the events that befall him is always in danger of getting stuck in the transitional stage of the Son. The criterion of adulthood does not consist in being a member of certain sects, groups, or nations, but in submitting to the spirit of one's own independence. Just as the "Son" proceeds from the "Father," so the "Father" proceeds from the

6 The "Oxford Movement" was originally the name of the Catholicizing trend started by the Anglican clergy in Oxford, 1833. [Whereas the "Oxford Groups," or "Moral Rearmament Movement," were founded in 1921, also at Oxford, by Frank Buchman as "a Christian revolution . . . the aim of which is a new social order under the dictatorship of the Spirit of God, and which issues in personal, social racial, national, and supernational renaissance" (Buchman, cited in *Webster's International Dictionary,* 2nd edn., 1950).—EDITORS.]

stage of the "Son," yet this Father is not a mere repetition of the original Father or an identification with him, but one in whom the vitality of the "Father" continues its procreative work. This third stage, as we have seen, means articulating one's ego-consciousness with a supraordinate totality, of which one cannot say that it is "I," but which is best visualized as a more comprehensive being, though one should of course keep oneself conscious all the time of the anthropomorphism of such a conception. Hard as it is to define, this unknown quantity can be experienced by the psyche and is known in Christian parlance as the "Holy Ghost," the breath that heals and makes whole. Christianity claims that this breath also has personality, which in the circumstances could hardly be otherwise. For close on two thousand years history has been familiar with the figure of the Cosmic Man, the Anthropos, whose image has merged with that of Yahweh and also of Christ. Similarly, the saints who received the stigmata became Christ-figures in a visible and concrete sense, and thus carriers of the Anthropos-image. They symbolize the working of the Holy Ghost among men. The Anthropos is a symbol that argues in favour of the personal nature of the "totality," i.e., the self. If, however, you review the numerous symbols of the self, you will discover not a few among them that have no characteristics of human personality at all. I won't back up this statement with psychological case histories, which are *terra incognita* to the layman anyway, but will only refer to the historical material, which fully confirms the findings of modern scientific research. Alchemical symbolism has produced, aside from the personal figures, a whole series of non-human forms, geometrical configurations like the sphere, circle, square, and octagon, or chemical symbols like the Philosophers' Stone, the ruby, diamond, quicksilver, gold, water, fire, and spirit (in the sense of a volatile substance). This choice of symbols tallies more or less with the modern products of the unconscious.[7] I might mention in this connection that there are numerous theriomorphic spirit symbols, the most important Christian ones being the lamb, the dove, and the snake (Satan). The snake symbolizing the Gnostic Nous and the Agathodaimon has a pneumatic significance (the devil, too, is a spirit). These symbols express the non-human character of the totality or self, as was

7 Cf. *Psychology and Alchemy,* Part II.

reported long ago when, at Pentecost, the spirit descended on the disciples in tongues of fire. From this point of view we can share something of Origen's perplexity as to the nature of the Holy Ghost. It also explains why the Third Person of the Trinity, unlike Father and Son, has no personal quality.[8] "Spirit" is not a personal designation but the qualitative definition of a substance of aeriform nature.

277 Whenever, as in the present instance, the unconscious makes such sweepingly contradictory statements, experience tells us that the situation is far from simple. The unconscious is trying to express certain facts for which there are no conceptual categories in the conscious mind. The contents in question need not be "metaphysical," as in the case of the Holy Ghost. Any content that transcends consciousness, and for which the apperceptive apparatus does not exist, can call forth the same kind of paradoxical or antinomial symbolism. For a naïve consciousness that sees everything in terms of black and white, even the unavoidable dual aspect of "man and his shadow" can be transcendent in this sense and will consequently evoke paradoxical symbols. We shall hardly be wrong, therefore, if we conjecture that the striking contradictions we find in our spirit symbolism are proof that the Holy Ghost is a *complexio oppositorum* (union of opposites). Consciousness certainly possesses no conceptual category for anything of this kind, for such a union is simply inconceivable except as a violent collision in which the two sides cancel each other out. This would mean their mutual annihilation.

278 But the spontaneous symbolism of the *complexio oppositorum* points to the exact opposite of annihilation, since it ascribes to the product of their union either everlasting duration, that is to say incorruptibility and adamantine stability, or supreme and inexhaustible efficacy.[9]

279 Thus the spirit as a *complexio oppositorum* has the same formula as the "Father," the *auctor rerum,* who is also, accord-

8 Thomas Aquinas (*Summa theologica,* I, xxxvi, art. 1): "Non habet nomen proprium" (he has no proper name). I owe this reference to the kindness of Fr. Victor White, O.P.

9 Both these categories are, as we know, attributes of the *lapis philosophorum* and of the symbols of the self.

ing to Nicholas of Cusa, a union of opposites.[10] The "Father," in fact, contains the opposite qualities which appear in his son and his son's adversary. Riwkah Schärf [11] has shown just how far the monotheism of the Old Testament was obliged to make concessions to the idea of the "relativity" of God. The Book of Job comes within a hair's breadth of the dualism which flowered in Persia for some centuries before and after Christ, and which also gave rise to various heretical movements within Christianity itself. It was only to be expected, therefore, that, as we said above, the dual aspect of the "Father" should reappear in the Holy Ghost, who in this way effects an apocatastasis of the Father. To use an analogy from physics, the Holy Ghost could be likened to the stream of photons arising out of the destruction of matter, while the "Father" would be the primordial energy that promotes the formation of protons and electrons with their positive and negative charges. This, as the reader will understand, is not an explanation, but an analogy which is possible because the physicist's models ultimately rest on the same archetypal foundations that also underlie the speculations of the theologian. Both are psychology, and it too has no other foundation.

III. GENERAL REMARKS ON SYMBOLISM

280 Although it is extremely improbable that the Christian Trinity is derived directly from the triadic World-Soul in the *Timaeus,* it is nevertheless rooted in the same archetype. If we wish to describe the phenomenology of this archetype, we shall have to consider all the aspects which go to make up the total picture. For instance, in our analysis of the *Timaeus,* we found that the number three represents an intellectual schema only, and that the second mixture reveals the resistance of the "recalcitrant fourth" ingredient, which we meet again as the "adversary" of the Christian Trinity. Without the fourth the three have no reality as we understand it; they even lack meaning,

10 It should not be forgotten, however, that the opposites which Nicholas had in mind were very different from the psychological ones.

11 Cf. "Die Gestalt des Satans im Alten Testament," in *Symbolik des Geistes,* pp. 153ff.

for a "thought" has meaning only if it refers to a possible or actual reality. This relationship to reality is completely lacking in the idea of the Trinity, so much so that people nowadays tend to lose sight of it altogether, without even noticing the loss. But we can see what this loss means when we are faced with the problem of reconstruction—that is to say in all those cases where the conscious part of the psyche is cut off from the unconscious part by a dissociation. This split can only be mended if consciousness is able to formulate conceptions which give adequate expression to the contents of the unconscious. It seems as if the Trinity plus the incommensurable "fourth" were a conception of this kind. As part of the doctrine of salvation it must, indeed, have a saving, healing, wholesome effect. During the process of integrating the unconscious contents into consciousness, undoubted importance attaches to the business of seeing how the dream-symbols relate to trivial everyday realities. But, in a deeper sense and on a long-term view, this procedure is not sufficient, as it fails to bring out the significance of the archetypal contents. These reach down, or up, to quite other levels than so-called common sense would suspect. As *a priori* conditions of all psychic events, they are endued with a dignity which has found immemorial expression in godlike figures. No other formulation will satisfy the needs of the unconscious. The unconscious is the unwritten history of mankind from time unrecorded. Rational formulae may satisfy the present and the immediate past, but not the experience of mankind as a whole. This calls for the all-embracing vision of the myth, as expressed in symbols. If the symbol is lacking, man's wholeness is not represented in consciousness. He remains a more or less accidental fragment, a suggestible wisp of consciousness, at the mercy of all the utopian fantasies that rush in to fill the gap left by the totality symbols. A symbol cannot be made to order as the rationalist would like to believe. It is a legitimate symbol only if it gives expression to the immutable structure of the unconscious and can therefore command general acceptance. So long as it evokes belief spontaneously, it does not require to be understood in any other way. But if, from sheer lack of understanding, belief in it begins to wane, then, for better or worse, one must use understanding as a tool if the incalculable consequences of a loss are to be avoided. What should we then put in place of the symbol? Is there anybody who knows a better way of expressing something that has never yet been understood?

281 As I have shown in *Psychology and Alchemy* and elsewhere, trinity and quaternity symbols occur fairly frequently in dreams, and from this I have learnt that the idea of the Trinity is based on something that can be experienced and must, therefore, have a meaning. This insight was not won by a study of the traditional sources. If I have succeeded in forming an intelligible conception of the Trinity that is in any way based on empirical reality, I have been helped by dreams, folklore, and the myths in which these number motifs occur. As a rule they appear spontaneously in dreams, and such dreams look very banal from the outside. There is nothing at all of the myth or fairytale about them, much less anything religious. Mostly it is three men and a woman, either sitting at a table or driving in a car, or three men and a dog, a huntsman with three hounds, three chickens in a coop from which the fourth has escaped, and suchlike. These things are indeed so banal that one is apt to overlook them. Nor do they wish to say anything more specific, at first, than that they refer to functions and aspects of the dreamer's personality, as can easily be ascertained when they appear as three or four known persons with well-marked characteristics, or as the four principal colours, red, blue, green, and yellow. It happens with some regularity that these colours are correlated with the four orienting functions of consciousness. Only when the dreamer begins to reflect that the four are an allusion to his total personality does he realize that these banal dream-motifs are like shadow pictures of more important things. The fourth figure is, as a rule, particularly instructive: it soon becomes incompatible, disagreeable, frightening, or in some way odd, with a different sense of good and bad, rather like a Tom Thumb beside his three normal brothers. Naturally the situation can be reversed, with three odd figures and one normal one. Anybody with a little knowledge of fairytales will know that the seemingly enormous gulf that separates the Trinity from these trivial happenings is by no means unbridgeable. But this is not to say that the Trinity can be reduced to this level. On the contrary, the Trinity represents the most perfect form of the archetype in

question. The empirical material merely shows, in the smallest and most insignificant psychic detail, how the archetype works. This is what makes the archetype so important, firstly as an organizing schema and a criterion for judging the quality of an individual psychic structure, and secondly as a vehicle of the synthesis in which the individuation process culminates. This goal is symbolized by the putting together of the four; hence the quaternity is a symbol of the self, which is of central importance in Indian philosophy and takes the place of the Deity. In the West, any amount of quaternities were developed during the Middle Ages; here I would mention only the *Rex gloriae* with the four symbols of the evangelists (three theriomorphic, one anthropomorphic). In Gnosticism there is the figure of Barbelo ("God is four"). These examples and many others like them bring the quaternity into closest relationship with the Deity, so that, as I said earlier, it is impossible to distinguish the self from a God-image. At any rate, I personally have found it impossible to discover a criterion of distinction. Here faith or philosophy alone can decide, neither of which has anything to do with the empiricism of the scientist.

282 One can, then, explain the God-image aspect of the quaternity as a reflection of the self, or, conversely, explain the self as an *imago Dei* in man. Both propositions are psychologically true, since the self, which can only be perceived subjectively as a most intimate and unique thing, requires universality as a background, for without this it could not manifest itself in its absolute separateness. Strictly speaking, the self must be regarded as the extreme opposite of God. Nevertheless we must say with Angelus Silesius: "He cannot live without me, nor I without him." So although the empirical symbol requires two diametrically opposite interpretations, neither of them can be proved valid. The symbol means both and is therefore a paradox. This is not the place to say anything more about the role these number symbols play in practice; for this I must refer the reader to the dream material in *Psychology and Alchemy,* Part II.

*

283 In view of the special importance of quaternity symbolism one is driven to ask how it came about that a highly differentiated form of religion like Christianity reverted to the archaic

triad in order to construct its trinitarian God-image.[1] With equal justification one could also ask (as has, in fact, been done) with what right Christ is presumed to be a symbol of the self, since the self is by definition a *complexio oppositorum,* whereas the Christ figure wholly lacks a dark side? (In dogma, Christ is *sine macula peccati*—'unspotted by sin.')

284 Both questions touch on the same problem. I always seek the answer to such questions on empirical territory, for which reason I must now cite the concrete facts. It is a general rule that most geometrical or numerical symbols have a quaternary character. There are also ternary or trinitarian symbols, but in my experience they are rather rare. On investigating such cases carefully, I have found that they were distinguished by something that can only be called a "medieval psychology." This does not imply any backwardness and is not meant as a value judgment, but only as denoting a special problem. That is to say, in all these cases there is so much unconsciousness, and such a large degree of primitivity to match it, that a spiritualization appears necessary as a compensation. The saving symbol is then a triad in which the fourth is lacking because it has to be unconditionally rejected.

285 In my experience it is of considerable practical importance that the symbols aiming at wholeness should be correctly understood by the doctor. They are the remedy with whose help neurotic dissociations can be repaired, by restoring to the conscious mind a spirit and an attitude which from time immemorial have been felt as solving and healing in their effects. They are "représentations collectives" which facilitate the much-needed union of conscious and unconscious. This union cannot be accomplished either intellectually or in a purely practical sense, because in the former case the instincts rebel and in the latter case reason and morality. Every dissociation that falls within the category of the psychogenic neuroses is due to a conflict of this kind, and the conflict can only be resolved through the symbol. For this purpose the dreams produce symbols which in the last analysis coincide with those recorded throughout history. But the dream-images can be taken up into the dreamer's consciousness, and grasped by his reason and feeling, only if his conscious mind possesses the intellectual categories and moral

[1] In the Greek Church the Trinity is called τριάς.

feelings necessary for their assimilation. And this is where the psychotherapist often has to perform feats that tax his patience to the utmost. The synthesis of conscious and unconscious can only be implemented by a conscious confrontation with the latter, and this is not possible unless one understands what the unconscious is saying. During this process we come upon the symbols investigated in the present study, and in coming to terms with them we re-establish the lost connection with ideas and feelings which make a synthesis of the personality possible. The loss of gnosis, i.e., knowledge of the ultimate things, weighs much more heavily than is generally admitted. Faith alone would suffice too, did it not happen to be a charisma whose true possession is something of a rarity, except in spasmodic form. Were it otherwise, we doctors could spare ourselves much thankless work. Theology regards our efforts in this respect with mistrustful mien, while pointedly declining to tackle this very necessary task itself. It proclaims doctrines which nobody understands, and demands a faith which nobody can manufacture. This is how things stand in the Protestant camp. The situation in the Catholic camp is more subtle. Of especial importance here is the ritual with its sacral action, which dramatizes the living occurrence of archetypal meaning and thus makes a direct impact on the unconscious. Can any one, for instance, deny the impression made upon him by the sacrament of the Mass, if he has followed it with even a minimum of understanding? Then again, the Catholic Church has the institution of confession and the director of conscience, which are of the greatest practical value when these activities devolve upon suitable persons. The fact that this is not always so proves, unfortunately, to be an equally great disadvantage. Thirdly, the Catholic Church possesses a richly developed and undamaged world of dogmatic ideas, which provide a worthy receptacle for the plethora of figures in the unconscious and in this way give visible expression to certain vitally important truths with which the conscious mind should keep in touch. The faith of a Catholic is not better or stronger than the faith of a Protestant, but a person's unconscious is gripped by the Catholic form no matter how weak his faith may be. That is why, once he slips out of this form, he may easily fall into a fanatical atheism, of a kind that is particularly to be met with in Latin countries.

6. CONCLUSION

286 Because of its noetic character, the Trinity expresses the need for a spiritual development that demands independence of thought. Historically we can see this striving at work above all in scholastic philosophy, and it was these preliminary exercises that made the scientific thinking of modern man possible. Also, the Trinity is an archetype whose dominating power not only fosters spiritual development but may, on occasion, actually enforce it. But as soon as the spiritualization of the mind threatens to become so one-sided as to be deleterious to health, the compensatory significance of the Trinity necessarily recedes into the background. Good does not become better by being exaggerated, but worse, and a small evil becomes a big one through being disregarded and repressed. The shadow is very much a part of human nature, and it is only at night that no shadows exist.

287 As a psychological symbol the Trinity denotes, first, the homoousia or essential unity of a three-part process, to be thought of as a process of unconscious maturation taking place within the individual. To that extent the three Persons are personifications of the three phases of a regular, instinctive psychic occurrence that always tends to express itself in the form of mythologems and ritualistic customs (for instance, the initiations at puberty, and the various rites for birth, marriage,

sickness, war, and death). As the medical lore of the ancient Egyptians shows, myths as well as rites have a psychotherapeutic value, and they still have today.

288 Second, the Trinity denotes a process of conscious realization continuing over the centuries.

289 Third, the Trinity lays claim not only to *represent* a personification of psychic processes in three roles, but to *be* the one God in three Persons, who all share the same divine nature. In God there is no advance from the potential to the actual, from the possible to the real, because God is pure reality, the "actus purus" itself. The three Persons differ from one another by reason of the different manner of their origin, or their procession (the Son begotten by the Father and the Holy Ghost proceeding from both—*procedit a patre filioque*). The homoousia, whose general recognition was the cause of so many controversies, is absolutely necessary from a psychological standpoint, because, regarded as a psychological symbol, the Trinity represents the progressive transformation of one and the same substance, namely the psyche as a whole. The homoousia together with the *filioque* assert that Christ and the Holy Ghost are both of the same substance as the Father. But since, psychologically, Christ must be understood as a symbol of the self, and the descent of the Holy Ghost as the self's actualization in man, it follows that the self must represent something that is of the substance of the Father too. This formulation is in agreement with the psychological statement that the symbols of the self cannot be distinguished empirically from a God-image. Psychology, certainly, can do no more than establish the fact that they *are* indistinguishable. This makes it all the more remarkable that the "metaphysical" statement should go so much further than the psychological one. Indistinguishability is a negative constatation merely; it does not rule out the possibility that a distinction may exist. It may be that the distinction is simply not perceived. The dogmatic assertion, on the other hand, speaks of the Holy Ghost making us "children of God," and this filial relationship is indistinguishable in meaning from the *υἱότης* (sonship) or *filiatio* of Christ. We can see from this how important it was that the homoousia should triumph over the homoiousia (*similarity* of substance); for, through the descent of the Holy Ghost, the self of man enters into a relationship of

unity with the substance of God. As ecclesiastical history shows, this conclusion is of immense danger to the Church—it was, indeed, the main reason why the Church did not insist on any further elaboration of the doctrine of the Holy Ghost. Its continued development would lead, on a negative estimate, to explosive schisms, and on a positive estimate straight into psychology. Moreover, the gifts of the Holy Ghost are somewhat mixed: not all of them are unreservedly welcome, as St. Paul has already pointed out. Also, St. Thomas Aquinas observes that revelation is a gift of the spirit that does not stand in any clearly definable relationship to moral endowment.[1] The Church must reserve the right to decide what is a working of the Holy Ghost and what is not, thereby taking an exceedingly important and possibly disagreeable decision right out of the layman's hands. That the spirit, like the wind, "bloweth where it listeth" is something that alarmed even the Reformers. The third as well as the first Person of the Trinity can wear the aspect of a *deus absconditus,* and its action, like that of fire, may be no less destructive than beneficial when regarded from a purely human standpoint.

290 "Creation" in the sense of "matter" is not included in the Trinity formula, at any rate not explicitly. In these circumstances there are only two possibilities: either the material world is real, in which case it is an intrinsic part of the divine "actus purus," or it is unreal, a mere illusion, because outside the divine reality. The latter conclusion is contradicted firstly by God's incarnation and by his whole work of salvation, secondly by the autonomy and eternality of the "Prince of this world," the devil, who has merely been "overcome" but is by no means destroyed—and cannot be destroyed because he is eternal. But if the reality of the created world *is* included in the "actus purus," then the devil is there too—Q.E.D. This situation gives rise to a quaternity, albeit a very different quaternity from the one anathematized by the fourth Lateran Council. The question there debated was whether God's essence could claim a place

[1] "St. Thomas emphasizes that prophetic revelation is, as such, independent of good morals—not to speak of personal sanctity" (*De veritate,* xii, 5; *Summa theol.,* I–II, p. 172). I take this remark from the MS. of an essay on "St. Thomas's Conception of Revelation," by Fr. Victor White, O.P., with the kind permission of the author.

alongside the three Persons or not. But the question we are confronted with here is the independent position of a creature endowed with autonomy and eternality: the fallen angel. He is the fourth, "recalcitrant" figure in our symbolical series, the intervals between which correspond to the three phases of the trinitarian process. Just as, in the *Timaeus,* the adversary is the second half of the second pair of opposites, without whom the world-soul would not be whole and complete, so, too, the devil must be added to the *trias* as τὸ ἓν τέταρτον (the One as the Fourth),[2] in order to make it a totality. If the Trinity is understood as a *process,* as I have tried to do all along, then, by the addition of the Fourth, this process would culminate in a condition of absolute totality. Through the intervention of the Holy Ghost, however, man is included in the divine process, and this means that the principle of separateness and autonomy over against God—which is personified in Lucifer as the God-opposing will—is included in it too. But for this will there would have been no creation and no work of salvation either. The shadow and the opposing will are the necessary conditions for all actualization. An object that has no will of its own, capable, if need be, of opposing its creator, and with no qualities other than its creator's, such an object has no independent existence and is incapable of ethical decision. At best it is just a piece of clockwork which the Creator has to wind up to make it function. Therefore Lucifer was perhaps the one who best understood the divine will struggling to create a world and who carried out that will most faithfully. For, by rebelling against God, he became the active principle of a creation which opposed to God a counter-will of its own. Because God willed this, we are told in Genesis 3 that he gave man the power to will otherwise. Had he not done so, he would have created nothing but a machine, and then the incarnation and the redemption would never have come about. Nor would there have been any revelation of the Trinity, because everything would have remained One for ever.

291 The Lucifer legend is in no sense an absurd fairytale; like the story of the serpent in the Garden of Eden, it is a "therapeutic" myth. We naturally boggle at the thought that good and evil are both contained in God, and we think God could not possibly want such a thing. We should be careful, though, not to

2 The Axiom of Maria. Cf. *Psychology and Alchemy,* pars. 209f.

pare down God's omnipotence to the level of our human opinions; but that is just how we do think, despite everything. Even so, it would not do to impute all evil to God: thanks to his moral autonomy, man can put down a sizable portion of it to his own account. Evil is a relative thing, partly avoidable, partly fate—just as virtue is, and often one does not know which is worse. Think of the fate of a woman married to a recognized saint! What sins must not the children commit in order to feel their lives their own under the overwhelming influence of such a father! Life, being an energic process, needs the opposites, for without opposition there is, as we know, no energy. Good and evil are simply the moral aspects of this natural polarity. The fact that we have to feel this polarity so excruciatingly makes human existence all the more complicated. Yet the suffering that necessarily attaches to life cannot be evaded. The tension of opposites that makes energy possible is a universal law, fittingly expressed in the *yang* and *yin* of Chinese philosophy. Good and evil are feeling-values of human provenance, and we cannot extend them beyond the human realm. What happens beyond this is beyond our judgment: God is not to be caught with human attributes. Besides, where would the *fear* of God be if only good—i.e., what seems good to us—were to be expected from him? After all, eternal damnation doesn't bear much resemblance to goodness as we understand it! Although good and evil are unshakable as moral values, they still need to be subjected to a bit of psychological revision. Much, that is to say, that proves to be abysmally evil in its ultimate effects does not come from man's wickedness but from his stupidity and unconsciousness. One has only to think of the devastating effects of Prohibition in America or of the hundred thousand autos-da-fé in Spain, which were all caused by a praiseworthy zeal to save people's souls. One of the toughest roots of all evil is unconsciousness, and I could wish that the saying of Jesus, "Man, if thou knowest what thou doest, thou art blessed, but if thou knowest not, thou art accursed, and a transgressor of the law,"[3] were still in the gospels, even though it has only one authentic source. It might well be the motto for a new morality.

292 The individuation process is invariably started off by the patient's becoming conscious of the shadow, a personality

[3] Cf. James, *The Apocryphal New Testament,* p. 33.

component usually with a negative sign. This "inferior" personality is made up of everything that will not fit in with, and adapt to, the laws and regulations of conscious life. It is compounded of "disobedience" and is therefore rejected not on moral grounds only, but also for reasons of expediency. Closer investigation shows that there is at least one function in it which ought to collaborate in orienting consciousness. Or rather, this function does collaborate, not for the benefit of conscious, purposive intentions, but in the interests of unconscious tendencies pursuing a different goal. It is this fourth, "inferior" function which acts autonomously towards consciousness and cannot be harnessed to the latter's intentions. It lurks behind every neurotic dissociation and can only be annexed to consciousness if the corresponding unconscious contents are made conscious at the same time. But this integration cannot take place and be put to a useful purpose unless one can admit the tendencies bound up with the shadow and allow them some measure of realization—tempered, of course, with the necessary criticism. This leads to disobedience and self-disgust, but also to self-reliance, without which individuation is unthinkable. The ability to "will otherwise" must, unfortunately, be real if ethics are to make any sense at all. Anyone who submits to the law from the start, or to what is generally expected, acts like the man in the parable who buried his talent in the earth. Individuation is an exceedingly difficult task: it always involves a conflict of duties, whose solution requires us to understand that our "counter-will" is also an aspect of God's will. One cannot individuate with mere words and convenient self-deceptions, because there are too many destructive possibilities in the offing. One almost unavoidable danger is that of getting stuck in the conflict and hence in the neurotic dissociation. Here the therapeutic myth has a helpful and loosening effect, even when the patient shows not a trace of conscious understanding. The felt presence of the archetype is enough; it only fails to work when the possibility of conscious understanding is there, within the patient's reach. In those circumstances it is positively deleterious for him to remain unconscious, though this happens frequently enough in our Christian civilization today. So much of what Christian symbolism taught has gone by the board for large numbers of people, without their ever having understood what they have lost. Civilization does not consist in progress as such and in mindless destruction of the old values, but in developing and refining the good that has been won.

293 Religion is a "revealed" way of salvation. Its ideas are products of a pre-conscious knowledge which, always and everywhere, expresses itself in symbols. Even if our intellect does not grasp them, they still work, because our unconscious acknowledges them as exponents of universal psychic facts. For this reason faith is enough—if it is there. Every extension and intensification of rational consciousness, however, leads us further away from the sources of the symbols and, by its ascendency, prevents us from understanding them. That is the situation today. One cannot turn the clock back and force oneself to believe "what one knows is not true." But one could give a little thought to what the symbols really mean. In this way not only would the incomparable treasures of our civilization be conserved, but we should also gain new access to the old truths which have vanished from our "rational" purview because of the strangeness of their symbolism. How can a man be God's Son and be born of a virgin? That is a slap in the face of reason. But did not Justin Martyr point out to his contemporaries that exactly the same thing was said of their heroes, *and* get himself listened to? That was because man's consciousness in those days did not find the symbols as outlandish as they are for us. Today such dogmas fall on deaf ears, because nothing in our known world responds to such assertions. But if we understand these things for what they are, as symbols, then we can only marvel at the unfathomable wisdom that is in them and be grateful to the institution which has not only conserved them, but developed them dogmatically. The man of today lacks the very understanding that would help him to believe.

294 If I have ventured to submit old dogmas, now grown stale, to psychological scrutiny, I have certainly not done so in the priggish conceit that I knew better than others, but in the sincere conviction that a dogma which has been such a bone of contention for so many centuries cannot possibly be an empty fantasy. I felt it was too much in line with the *consensus omnium,* with the archetype, for that. It was only when I realized this that I was able to establish any relationship with the dogma at all. As a metaphysical "truth" it remained wholly inaccessible to me, and I suspect that I am by no means the only one to find himself

in that position. A knowledge of the universal archetypal background was, in itself, sufficient to give me the courage to treat "that which is believed always, everywhere, by everybody" as a *psychological fact* which extends far beyond the confines of Christianity, and to approach it as an object of scientific study, as a *phenomenon* pure and simple, regardless of the "metaphysical" significance that may have been attached to it. I know from my own experience that this latter aspect has never contributed in the slightest to my belief or to my understanding. It told me absolutely nothing. However, I was forced to admit that the "symbolum" possesses the highest degree of actuality inasmuch as it was regarded by countless millions of people, for close on two thousand years, as a valid statement concerning those things which one cannot see with the eyes or touch with the hands. It is this fact that needs to be understood, for of "metaphysical truth" we know only that part which man has made, unless the unbiddable gift of faith lifts us beyond all dubiety and all uneasy investigation. It is dangerous if these matters are only objects of belief;[4] for where there is belief there is doubt, and the fiercer and naïver the belief the more devastating the doubt once it begins to dawn. One is then infinitely cleverer than all the benighted heads of the Middle Ages.

295 These considerations have made me extremely cautious in my approach to the further metaphysical significance that may possibly underlie archetypal statements. There is nothing to stop their ultimate ramifications from penetrating to the very ground of the universe. We alone are the dumb ones if we fail to notice it. Such being the case, I cannot pretend to myself that the object of archetypal statements has been explained and disposed of merely by our investigation of its psychological aspects. What I have put forward can only be, at best, a more or less successful or unsuccessful attempt to give the inquiring mind some access to one side of the problem—the side that can be approached. It would be presumptuous to expect more than this. If I have merely succeeded in stimulating discussion, then my purpose is more than fulfilled. For it seems to me that the world, if it should lose sight of these archetypal statements, would be threatened with unspeakable impoverishment of mind and soul.

4 I am thinking here of the *sola fide* standpoint of the Protestants.

II

TRANSFORMATION SYMBOLISM IN THE MASS

[First published as a lecture in *Eranos Jahrbuch 1940/41;* later published in revised and expanded form in *Von den Wurzeln des Bewusstseins* (Zurich, 1954). The present translation is made from the 1954 version. It was published in slightly different form in *The Mysteries* (Papers from the Eranos Yearbooks, 2; New York, 1955; London, 1956).—EDITORS.]

1. INTRODUCTION [1]

296 The Mass is a still-living mystery, the origins of which go back to early Christian times. It is hardly necessary to point out that it owes its vitality partly to its undoubted psychological efficacy, and that it is therefore a fit subject for psychological study. But it should be equally obvious that psychology can only approach the subject from the phenomenological angle, for the realities of faith lie outside the realm of psychology.

297 My exposition falls into four parts: in this introduction I indicate some of the New Testament sources of the Mass, with notes on its structure and significance. In section 2, I recapitulate the sequence of events in the rite. In 3, I cite a parallel from pagan antiquity to the Christian symbolism of sacrifice and transformation: the visions of Zosimos. Finally, in 4, I attempt a psychological discussion of the sacrifice and transformation.

*

298 The oldest account of the sacrament of the Mass is to be found in I Corinthians 11:23ff.:

[1] The following account and examination of the principal symbol in the Mass is not concerned either with the Mass as a whole, or with its liturgy in particular, but solely with the ritual actions and texts which relate to the transformation process in the strict sense. In order to give the reader an adequate account of this, I had to seek professional help. I am especially indebted to the theologian Dr. Gallus Jud for reading through and correcting the first two sections.

For the tradition which I have received of the Lord and handed down to you is that the Lord Jesus, on the night he was betrayed, took bread, gave thanks, broke it, and said: *This is my body for you; do this in remembrance of me. And after he had supped, he took the chalice also, and said: This chalice is the new testament in my blood.* As often as you drink, do this in remembrance of me. For as often as you eat this bread and drink the chalice, you declare the death of the Lord, until he comes.[2]

299 Similar accounts are to be found in Matthew, Mark, and Luke. In John the corresponding passage speaks of a "supper,"[3] but there it is connected with the washing of the disciples' feet. At this supper Christ utters the words which characterize the meaning and substance of the Mass (John 15:1, 4, 5). "I am the true vine." "Abide in me, and I in you." "I am the vine, ye are the branches." The correspondence between the liturgical accounts points to a traditional source outside the Bible. There is no evidence of an actual feast of the Eucharist until after A.D. 150.

300 The Mass is a Eucharistic feast with an elaborately developed liturgy. It has the following structure:

CONSECRATION
↗ ↘
OBLATION → COMMUNION
↗ ↘
PRELIMINARIES → CONCLUSION

301 As this investigation is concerned essentially with the symbol of transformation, I must refrain from discussing the Mass as a whole.

302 In the sacrifice of the Mass two distinct ideas are blended together: the ideas of *deipnon* and *thysia*. *Thysia* comes from the verb *θύειν*, 'to sacrifice' or 'to slaughter'; but it also has the mean-

2 [This is a translation of the Karl von Weizsäcker version (1875) used here by the author. Elsewhere the Biblical quotations are taken from the AV and occasionally from the RSV and the DV. Following are the Greek and Latin (Vulgate) versions of the italicized portion of this passage.—TRANS.]

"*. . . τοῦτο μού ἐστιν τὸ σῶμα τὸ ὑπὲρ ὑμῶν. τοῦτο ποιεῖτε εἰς τὴν ἐμὴν ἀνάμνησιν. ὡσαύτως καὶ τὸ ποτήριον μετὰ τὸ δειπνῆσαι λέγων· τοῦτο τὸ ποτήριον ἡ καινὴ διαθήκη ἐστὶν ἐν τῷ ἐμῷ αἵματι.*"

". . . hoc est corpus meum, quod pro vobis tradetur: hoc facite in meam commemorationem. Similiter et calicem, postquam coenavit, dicens: Hic calix novum testamentum est in meo sanguine."

3 *δεῖπνον*, 'coena.'

ing of 'blazing' or 'flaring up.' This refers to the leaping sacrificial fire by which the gift offered to the gods was consumed. Originally the food-offering was intended for the nourishment of the gods; the smoke of the burnt sacrifice carried the food up to their heavenly abode. At a later stage the smoke was conceived as a spiritualized form of food-offering; indeed, all through the Christian era up to the Middle Ages, spirit (or *pneuma*) continued to be thought of as a fine, vaporous substance.[4]

303 *Deipnon* means 'meal.' In the first place it is a meal shared by those taking part in the sacrifice, at which the god was believed to be present. It is also a "sacred" meal at which "consecrated" food is eaten, and hence a *sacrifice* (from *sacrificare,* 'to make sacred,' 'to consecrate').

304 The dual meaning of *deipnon* and *thysia* is implicitly contained in the words of the sacrament: "the body which (was given) for you." [5] This may mean either "which was given to you to eat" or, indirectly, "which was given for you to God." The idea of a meal immediately invests the word 'body' with the meaning of σάρξ, 'flesh' (as an edible substance). In Paul, σῶμα and σάρξ are practically identical.[6]

305 Besides the authentic accounts of the institution of the sacrament, we must also consider Hebrews 13:10–15 as a possible source for the Mass:

> We have an altar, whereof they have no right to eat which serve the tabernacle. For the bodies of those beasts, whose blood is brought into the sanctuary by the high priest for sin, are burned without the camp. Wherefore Jesus also, that he might sanctify the people with his own blood, suffered without the gate. Let us go forth therefore unto him without the camp, bearing his reproach. For here have we no continuing city, but we seek one to come. By him therefore let us offer the sacrifice of praise to God continually. . . .

306 As a further source we might mention Hebrews 7:17: "Thou art a priest for ever after the order of Melchisedec." [7] The idea

[4] This of course has nothing to do with the official conception of spirit by the Church. [5] "τὸ σῶμα τὸ ὑπὲρ ὑμῶν."

[6] Käsemann, *Leib und Leib Christi,* p. 120.

[7] Dr. Jud kindly drew my attention to the equally relevant passage in Malachi 1:10–11: "Who is there even among you that would shut the doors for nought? neither do ye kindle fire on mine altar for nought. . . . And in every place incense shall be offered unto my name, and a pure offering . . ."

of perpetual sacrifice and of an eternal priesthood is an essential component of the Mass. Melchisedec, who according to Hebrews 7:3 was "without father, without mother, without descent, having neither beginning of days, nor end of life, but made like unto the Son of God," was believed to be a pre-Christian incarnation of the Logos.

307 The idea of an eternal priesthood and of a sacrifice offered to God "continually" brings us to the true *mysterium fidei,* the transformation of the substances, which is the third aspect of the Mass. The ideas of *deipnon* and *thysia* do not in themselves imply or contain a mystery, although, in the burnt offering which is reduced to smoke and ashes by the fire, there is a primitive allusion to a transformation of substance in the sense of its spiritualization. But this aspect is of no practical importance in the Mass, where it only appears in subsidiary form in the censing, as an incense-offering. The *mysterium,* on the other hand, manifests itself clearly enough in the eternal priest "after the order of Melchisedec" and in the sacrifice which he offers to God "continually." The manifestation of an order outside time involves the idea of a *miracle* which takes place "vere, realiter, substantialiter" at the moment of transubstantiation, for the substances offered are no different from natural objects, and must in fact be definite commodities whose nature is known to everybody, namely pure wheaten bread and wine. Furthermore, the officiating priest is an ordinary human being who, although he bears the indelible mark of the priesthood upon him and is thus empowered to offer sacrifice, is nevertheless not yet in a position to be the instrument of the divine self-sacrifice enacted in the Mass.[8] Nor is the congregation standing behind him yet purged from sin, consecrated, and itself transformed into a sacrificial gift. The ritual of the Mass takes this situation and transforms it step by step until the climax is reached—the Conse-

[8] That is to say, not before he has accomplished the preparatory part of the service. In offering these gifts the priest is not the "master" of the sacrifice. "Rather that which causes them to be sacrificed in the first place is sanctifying grace. For that is what their sacrifice means: their sanctification. The man who each time performs the sacred act is the servant of grace, and that is why the gifts and their sacrifice are always pleasing to God. The fact that the servant may be bad does not affect them in any way. The priest is only the servant, and even this he has from grace, not from himself." Joseph Kramp, S.J., *Die Opferanschauungen der römischen Messliturgie,* p. 148.

cration, when Christ himself, as sacrificer and sacrificed, speaks the decisive words through the mouth of the priest. At that moment Christ is present in time and space. Yet his presence is not a reappearance, and therefore the inner meaning of the consecration is not a repetition of an event which occurred once in history, but the revelation of something existing in eternity, a rending of the veil of temporal and spatial limitations which separates the human spirit from the sight of the eternal. This event is necessarily a mystery, because it is beyond the power of man to conceive or describe. In other words, the rite is necessarily and in every one of its parts a *symbol.* Now a symbol is not an arbitrary or intentional sign standing for a known and conceivable fact, but an admittedly anthropomorphic—hence limited and only partly valid—expression for something suprahuman and only partly conceivable. It may be the best expression possible, yet it ranks below the level of the mystery it seeks to describe. The Mass is a symbol in this sense. Here I would like to quote the words of Father Kramp: "It is generally admitted that the sacrifice is a *symbolic* act, by which I mean that the offering of a material gift to God has no purpose in itself, but merely serves as a means to express an idea. And the choice of this means of expression brings a wide range of anthropomorphism into play: man confronts God as he confronts his own kind, almost as if God were a human being. We offer a gift to God as we offer it to a good friend or to an earthly ruler." [9]

308 In so far, then, as the Mass is an anthropomorphic symbol standing for something otherworldly and beyond our power to conceive, its symbolism is a legitimate subject for comparative psychology and analytical research. My psychological explanations are, of course, exclusively concerned with the symbolical expression.

9 Ibid., p. 17.

2. THE SEQUENCE OF THE TRANSFORMATION RITE

309 The rite of transformation may be said to begin with the Offertory, an antiphon recited during the offering of the sacrificial gifts. Here we encounter the first ritual act relating to the transformation.[1]

I. OBLATION OF THE BREAD

310 The Host is lifted up towards the cross on the altar, and the priest makes the sign of the cross over it with the paten. The bread is thus brought into relation with Christ and his death on the cross; it is marked as a "sacrifice" and thereby becomes sacred. The elevation exalts it into the realm of the spiritual: it is a preliminary act of spiritualization. Justin makes the interesting remark that the presentation of the cleansed lepers in the temple was an image of the Eucharistic bread.[2] This links up with the later alchemical idea of the imperfect or "leprous" substance which is made perfect by the *opus*. (*Quod natura relinquit imperfectum, arte perficitur.*—"What nature leaves imperfect is perfected by the art.")

1 In the account that follows I have made extensive use of Brinktrine, *Die Heilige Messe in ihrem Werden und Wesen*.

2 "Τύπος τοῦ ἄρτου τῆς εὐχαριστίας."

II. PREPARATION OF THE CHALICE

311 This is still more solemn than that of the bread, corresponding to the "spiritual" nature of the wine, which is reserved for the priest.[3] Some water is mingled with the wine.

312 The mixing of water with the wine originally referred to the ancient custom of not drinking wine unless mixed with water. A drunkard was therefore called *akratopotes,* an 'unmixed drinker.' In modern Greek, wine is still called κρασί (mixture). From the custom of the Monophysite Armenians, who did not add any water to the Eucharistic wine (so as to preserve the exclusively divine nature of Christ), it may be inferred that water has a hylical, or physical, significance and represents man's material nature. The mixing of water and wine in the Roman rite would accordingly signify that divinity is mingled with humanity as indivisibly as the wine with the water.[4] St. Cyprian (bishop of Carthage, d. 258) says that the wine refers to Christ, and the water to the congregation as the body of Christ. The significance of the water is explained by an allusion to the Book of Revelation 17:15: "The waters which thou sawest, where the whore sitteth, are peoples, and multitudes, and nations, and tongues." (In alchemy, *meretrix* the whore is a synonym for the *prima materia,* the *corpus imperfectum* which is sunk in darkness, like the man who wanders in darkness, unconscious and unredeemed. This idea is foreshadowed in the Gnostic image of Physis, who with passionate arms draws the Nous down from heaven and wraps him in her dark embrace.) As the water is an imperfect or even leprous substance, it has to be blessed and consecrated before being mixed, so that only a purified body may be joined to the wine of the spirit, just as Christ is to be united only with a pure and sanctified congregation. Thus this part of the rite has the special significance of preparing a perfect body—the glorified body of resurrection.

313 At the time of St. Cyprian the communion was generally celebrated with water.[5] And, still later, St. Ambrose (bishop of

[3] That is, in the Roman rite. In the Greek Uniate rites, communion is received in bread *and* wine.

[4] This is the interpretation of Yves, bishop of Chartres (d. 1116).

[5] Cyprian attacks this heretical custom in his letter to Caecilius. Letter 63 to Caecilius, Migne, *P.L.,* vol. 4, cols. 372ff. (trans. by Carey, pp. 181ff.).

Milan, d. 397) says: "In the shadow there was water from the rock, as it were the blood of Christ." [6] The water communion is prefigured in John 7:37–39: "If any man thirst, let him come unto me, and drink. He that believeth on me, as the scripture hath said, out of his belly flow rivers of living water. (But this he spake of the Spirit, which they that believe on him should receive: for the Holy Ghost was not yet given, because that Jesus was not yet glorified.)" And also in John 4:14: "But whosoever drinketh of the water that I shall give him shall never thirst; but the water that I shall give him shall be in him a well of water springing up into everlasting life." The words "as the scripture hath said, out of his belly shall flow rivers of living water" do not occur anywhere in the Old Testament. They must therefore come from a writing which the author of the Johannine gospel obviously regarded as holy, but which is not known to us. It is just possible that they are based on Isaiah 58:11: "And the Lord shall guide thee continually, and satisfy thy soul in drought, and make fat thy bones: and thou shalt be like a watered garden, and like a spring of water, whose waters fail not." Another possibility is Ezekiel 47:1: "Afterward he brought me again unto the door of the house; and, behold, waters issued out from under the threshold of the house eastward . . . and the waters came down from under from the right side of the house, at the south side of the altar." In the Church Order of Hippolytus (d. *c.* 235) the water chalice is associated with the baptismal font, where the inner man is renewed as well as the body.[7] This interpretation comes very close to the baptismal *krater* of Poimandres [8] and to the Hermetic basin filled with *nous* which God gave to those seeking ἔννοια.[9] Here the water signifies the *pneuma,* i.e., the spirit of prophecy, and also the doctrine which a man receives

6 "In umbra erat aqua de petra quasi sanguis ex Christo." The *umbra,* 'shadow,' refers to the foreshadowing in the Old Testament, in accordance with the saying: "Umbra in lege, imago in evangelio, veritas in coelestibus" (The shadow in the Law, the image in the Gospel, the truth in Heaven). Note that this remark of Ambrose does not refer to the Eucharist but to the water symbolism of early Christianity in general; and the same is true of the passages from John. St. Augustine himself says: "There the rock was Christ; for to us that is Christ which is placed on the altar of God." *Tractatus in Joannem,* XLV, 9 (trans. by Innes).

7 Connolly, ed., *The So-called Egyptian Church Order and Derived Documents.*

8 Berthelot, *Collection des anciens alchimistes grecs,* III, li. 8.

9 *Corpus Hermeticum,* Lib. IV, 4, in *Hermetica,* I, p. 151.

and passes on to others.[10] The same image of the spiritual water occurs in the "Odes of Solomon": [11]

For there went forth a stream, and became a river great and broad; . . . and all the thirsty upon earth were given to drink of it; and thirst was relieved and quenched; for from the Most High the draught was given. Blessed then are the ministers of that draught who are entrusted with that water of His; they have assuaged the dry lips, and the will that had fainted they have raised up; and souls that were near departing they have caught back from death; and limbs that had fallen they straightened and set up; they gave strength for their feebleness and light to their eyes. For everyone knew them in the Lord, and they lived by the water of life for ever.[12]

314 The fact that the Eucharist was also celebrated with water shows that the early Christians were mainly interested in the symbolism of the mysteries and not in the literal observance of the sacrament. (There were several other variants—"galactophagy," for instance—which all bear out this view.)

315 Another, very graphic, interpretation of the wine and water is the reference to John 19:34: "And forthwith came there out blood and water." Deserving of special emphasis is the remark of St. John Chrysostom (patriarch of Constantinople, d. 407), that in drinking the wine Christ drank his own blood. (See Section 3, on Zosimos.)

316 In this section of the Mass we meet the important prayer:

O God, who in creating human nature, didst wonderfully dignify it, and hast still more wonderfully renewed it; grant that, by the mystery of this water and wine, we may be made partakers of his divinity who vouchsafed to become partaker of our humanity, Jesus Christ. . . .[13]

10 Strack and Billerbeck, *Kommentar zum Neuen Testament aus Talmud und Midrasch,* II, p. 492.

11 A collection of Gnostic hymns from the 2nd cent.

12 Ode VI in *The Odes of Solomon,* ed. Bernard, p. 55, after the J. Rendel Harris version. Cf. the ὕδωρ θεῖον, the *aqua permanens* of early alchemy, also the treatise of Komarius (Berthelot, IV, xx).

13 "Deus, qui humanae substantiae dignitatem mirabiliter condidisti, et mirabilius reformasti; da nobis per huius aquae et vini mysterium, eius divinitatis esse consortes, qui humanitatis nostrae fieri dignatus est particeps, Jesus Christus . . ." [Here and throughout this essay the English translation is taken from *The Small Missal,* London, 1924.—Trans.]

III. ELEVATION OF THE CHALICE

317 The lifting up of the chalice in the air prepares the spiritualization (i.e., volatilization) of the wine.[14] This is confirmed by the invocation to the Holy Ghost which immediately follows (*Veni sanctificator*), and it is even more evident in the Mozarabic liturgy, which has "Veni spiritus sanctificator." [15] The invocation serves to infuse the wine with holy spirit, for it is the Holy Ghost who begets, fulfils, and transforms (cf. the "Obumbratio Mariae," Pentecostal fire). After the elevation, the chalice was, in former times, set down to the right of the Host, to correspond with the blood that flowed from the right side of Christ.

IV. CENSING OF THE SUBSTANCES AND THE ALTAR

318 The priest makes the sign of the cross three times over the substances with the thurible, twice from right to left and once from left to right.[16] The counterclockwise movement (from right to left) corresponds psychologically to a circumambulation downwards, in the direction of the unconscious, while the clockwise (left-to-right) movement goes in the direction of consciousness. There is also a complicated censing of the altar.[17]

319 The censing has the significance of an incense offering and is therefore a relic of the original *thysia*. At the same time it signifies a transformation of the sacrificial gifts and of the altar, a spiritualization of all the physical substances subserving the rite. Finally, it is an apotropaic ceremony to drive away any demonic forces that may be present, for it fills the air with the fragrance of the *pneuma* and renders it uninhabitable by evil spirits. The vapour also suggests the sublimated body, the *corpus volatile sive spirituale,* or wraithlike "subtle body." Rising up as a "spiritual" substance, the incense implements and represents the ascent of

14 This is *my* interpretation and not that of the Church, which sees in this only an act of devotion.

15 "Mozarabic" from Arabic *musta'rib,* 'Arabianized,' with reference to the Visigothic-Spanish form of ritual. [The Latin phrases: "Come, O sanctifying one." "Come, O sanctifying spirit."—EDITORS.]

16 The circumambulation from left to right is strictly observed in Buddhism.

17 The censing is only performed at High Mass.

prayer—hence the *Dirigatur, Domine, oratio mea, sicut incensum, in conspectu tuo.*[18]

320 The censing brings the preparatory, spiritualizing rites to an end. The gifts have been sanctified and prepared for the actual transubstantiation. Priest and congregation are likewise purified by the prayers *Accendat in nobis Dominus ignem sui amoris* and *Lavabo inter innocentes,*[19] and are made ready to enter into the mystic union of the sacrificial act which now follows.

V. THE EPICLESIS

321 The *Suscipe, sancta Trinitas,* like the *Orate, fratres,* the *Sanctus,* and the *Te igitur,* is a propitiatory prayer which seeks to insure the acceptance of the sacrifice. Hence the Preface that comes after the Secret is called *Illatio* in the Mozarabic rite (the equivalent of the Greek ἀναφορά), and in the old Gallican liturgy is known as *Immolatio* (in the sense of *oblatio*), with reference to the presentation of the gifts. The words of the *Sanctus,* "Benedictus qui venit in nomine Domini,"[20] point to the expected appearance of the Lord which has already been prepared, on the ancient principle that a "naming" has the force of a "summons." After the Canon there follows the "Commemoration of the Living," together with the prayers *Hanc igitur* and *Quam oblationem.* In the Mozarabic Mass these are followed by the Epiclesis (invocation): "Adesto, adesto Jesu, bone Pontifex, in medio nostri: sicut fuisti in medio discipulorum tuorum."[21] This naming likewise has the original force of a summons. It is an intensification of the *Benedictus qui venit,* and it may be, and sometimes was, regarded as the actual manifestation of the Lord, and hence as the culminating point of the Mass.

18 ["Let my prayer, O Lord, ascend like incense in thy sight."]

19 ["May the Lord enkindle in us the fire of his love." / "I will wash my hands among the innocent."]

20 ["Blessed is he that cometh in the name of the Lord."]

21 ["Be present, be present in our midst, O Jesus, great High Priest: as thou wert in the midst of thy disciples."]

VI. THE CONSECRATION

322 This, in the Roman Mass, is the climax, the transubstantiation of the bread and wine into the body and blood of Christ. The formula for the consecration of the bread runs: [22]

Qui pridie quam pateretur, accepit panem in sanctas ac venerabiles manus suas, et elevatis oculis in caelum ad te Deum, Patrem suum omnipotentem, tibi gratias agens, benedixit, fregit, deditque discipulis suis, dicens: Accipite, et manducate ex hoc omnes. Hoc est enim Corpus meum.

And for the consecration of the chalice:

Simili modo postquam coenatum est, accipiens et hunc praeclarum Calicem in sanctas ac venerabiles manus suas, item tibi gratias agens, benedixit, deditque discipulis suis, dicens: Accipite, et bibite ex eo omnes. Hic est enim Calix Sanguinis mei, novi et aeterni testamenti: mysterium fidei: qui pro vobis et pro multis effundetur in remissionem peccatorum. Haec quotiescumque feceritis, in mei memoriam facietis.

323 The priest and congregation, as well as the substances and the altar, have now been progressively purified, consecrated, exalted, and spiritualized by means of the prayers and rites which began with the Preliminaries and ended with the Canon, and are thus prepared as a mystical unity for the divine epiphany. Hence the uttering of the words of the consecration signifies Christ himself speaking in the first person, his living presence in the *corpus mysticum* of priest, congregation, bread, wine, and incense, which together form the mystical unity offered for sacrifice. At this moment the eternal character of the one divine sacrifice is made evident: it is experienced at a particular time and a particular place, as if a window or a door had been opened upon that which lies beyond space and time. It is in this sense that we have to understand the words of St. Chrysostom: "And this word once uttered in any church, at any altar, makes perfect the sacrifice from that day to this, and till his Second Coming." It is clear that only by our Lord's presence in his words, and by their virtue, is the imperfect body of the sacrifice made perfect,

22 According to the edict of the Church these words ought not, on account of their sacredness, to be translated into any profane tongue. Although there are missals that sin against this wise edict, I would prefer the Latin text to stand untranslated.

and not by the preparatory action of the priest. Were this the efficient cause, the rite would be no different from common magic. The priest is only the *causa ministerialis* of the transubstantiation. The real cause is the living presence of Christ which operates spontaneously, as an act of divine grace.

324 Accordingly, John of Damascus (d. 754) says that the words have a consecrating effect no matter by what priest they be spoken, as if Christ were present and uttering them himself. And Duns Scotus (d. 1308) remarks that, in the sacrament of the Last Supper, Christ, by an act of will, offers himself as a sacrifice in every Mass, through the agency of the priest.[23] This tells us plainly enough that the sacrificial act is not performed by the priest, but by Christ himself. The agent of transformation is nothing less than the divine will working through Christ. The Council of Trent declared that in the sacrifice of the Mass "the selfsame Christ is contained and bloodlessly sacrificed,"[24] although this is not a repetition of the historical sacrifice but a bloodless renewal of it. As the sacramental words have the power to accomplish the sacrifice, being an expression of God's will, they can be described metaphorically as the sacrificial knife or sword which, guided by his will, consummates the *thysia*. This comparison was first drawn by the Jesuit father Lessius (d. 1623), and has since gained acceptance as an ecclesiastical figure of speech. It is based on Hebrews 4:12: "For the word of God is quick, and powerful, and sharper than any two-edged sword," and perhaps even more on the Book of Revelation 1:16: "And out of his mouth went a sharp two-edged sword." The "mactation theory" first appeared in the sixteenth century. Its originator, Cuesta, bishop of Leon (d. 1560), declared that Christ was slaughtered by the priest. So the sword metaphor followed quite naturally.[25] Nicholas Cabasilas, archbishop of Thessalonica (d.

23 Klug, in *Theologie und Glaube,* XVIII (1926), 335f. Cited by Brinktrine, p. 192.

24 "idem ille Christus continetur et incruente immolatur." Sessio XXII. Denzinger and Bannwart, *Enchiridion Symbolorum,* p. 312.

25 "Missa est sacrificium hac ratione quia Christus aliquo modo moritur et a sacerdote mactatur" (The Mass is a sacrifice for the reason that in it Christ dies after a certain manner, and is slain by the priest). Hauck, *Realenzyklopädie,* XII, p. 693. The question of the *mactatio* had already been raised by Nicholas Cabasilas of Thessalonica: "De divino altaris sacrificio," in Migne, *P.G.,* vol. 150, cols. 363ff. The sword as a sacrificial instrument also occurs in the Zosimos visions (see section 3).

c. 1363), gives a vivid description of the corresponding rite in the Greek Orthodox Church:

The priest cuts a piece of bread from the loaf, reciting the text: "As a lamb he was led to the slaughter." Laying it on the table he says: "The lamb of God is slain." Then a sign of the cross is imprinted on the bread and a small lance is stabbed into its side, to the text: "And one of the soldiers with a spear pierced his side, and forthwith came there out blood and water." With these words water and wine are mixed in the chalice, which is placed beside the bread.

The δῶρον (gift) also represents the giver; that is to say, Christ is both the sacrificer and the sacrificed.

325 Kramp writes: "Sometimes the *fractio* and sometimes the *elevatio* which precedes the Pater noster was taken as symbolizing the death of Christ, sometimes the sign of the cross at the end of the *Supplices,* and sometimes the *consecratio;* but no one ever thought of taking a symbol like the 'mystical slaughter' as a sacrifice which constitutes the essence of the Mass. So it is not surprising that there is no mention of any 'slaughter' in the liturgy." [26]

VII. THE GREATER ELEVATION

326 The consecrated substances are lifted up and shown to the congregation. The Host in particular represents a beatific vision of heaven, in fulfilment of Psalm 27:8: "Thy face, Lord, will I seek," for in it the Divine Man is present.

VIII. THE POST-CONSECRATION

327 There now follows the significant prayer *Unde et memores,* which I give in full together with the *Supra quae* and *Supplices:*

Wherefore, O Lord, we thy servants, as also thy holy people, calling to mind the blessed passion of the same Christ thy Son our Lord, his resurrection from hell, and glorious ascension into heaven, offer unto thy most excellent majesty, of thy gifts and grants, a pure Host, a holy Host, an immaculate Host, the holy bread of eternal life, and the chalice of everlasting salvation.

26 Kramp, p. 56.

Upon which vouchsafe to look down with a propitious and serene countenance, and to accept them, as thou wert graciously pleased to accept the gifts of thy just servant Abel, and the sacrifice of our patriarch Abraham, and that which thy high priest Melchisedec offered to thee, a holy sacrifice, an immaculate Host.

We most humbly beseech thee, almighty God, command these things to be carried by the hands of thy holy angel to thy altar on high, in the sight of thy divine majesty, that as many of us as, by participation at this altar, shall receive the most sacred body and blood of thy Son, may be filled with all heavenly benediction and grace. Through the same Christ, our Lord. Amen.[27]

328 The first prayer shows that in the transformed substances there is an allusion to the resurrection and glorification of our Lord, and the second prayer recalls the sacrifices prefigured in the Old Testament. Abel sacrificed a lamb; Abraham was to sacrifice his son, but a ram was substituted at the last moment. Melchisedec offers no sacrifice, but comes to meet Abraham with bread and wine. This sequence is probably not accidental—it forms a sort of crescendo. Abel is essentially the son, and sacrifices an animal; Abraham is essentially the father—indeed, the "tribal father"—and therefore on a higher level. He does not offer a choice possession merely, but is ready to sacrifice the best and dearest thing he has—his only son. Melchisedec ("teacher of righteousness"), is, according to Hebrews 7 : 1, king of Salem and "priest of the most high God," El 'Elyon. Philo Byblius mentions a Ἐλιοῦν ὁ ὕψιστος as a Canaanite deity,[28] but he cannot be identical with Yahweh. Abraham nevertheless acknowledges the

27 "Unde et memores, Domine, nos servi tui, sed et plebs tua sancta, eiusdem Christi Filii tui, Domini nostri, tam beatae passionis, nec non et ab inferis resurrectionis, sed et in caelos gloriosae ascensionis: offerimus praeclarae majestati tuae de tuis donis ac datis, hostiam puram, hostiam sanctam, hostiam immaculatam, Panem sanctum vitae aeternae, et Calicem salutis perpetuae.

"Supra quae propitio ac sereno vultu respicere digneris: et accepta habere, sicuti accepta habere dignatus es munera pueri tui justi Abel, et sacrificium Patriarchae nostri Abrahae: et quod tibi obtulit summus sacerdos tuus Melchisedech, sanctum sacrificium, immaculatam hostiam.

"Supplices te rogamus, omnipotens Deus: jube haec perferri per manus sancti Angeli tui in sublime altare tuum, in conspectu divinae majestatis tuae: ut, quotquot ex hac altaris participatione sacrosanctum Filii tui corpus, et sanguinem sumpserimus, omni benedictione caelesti et gratia repleamur. Per eundem Christum, Dominum nostrum. Amen."

28 Eusebius, *Evangelica praeparatio,* I, 10, 11 (Migne, *P.G.*, vol. 21, col. 30).

priesthood of Melchisedec[29] by paying him "a tenth part of all." By virtue of his priesthood, Melchisedec stands above the patriarch, and his feasting of Abraham has the significance of a priestly act. We must therefore attach a symbolical meaning to it, as is in fact suggested by the bread and wine. Consequently the symbolical offering ranks even higher than the sacrifice of a son, which is still the sacrifice of somebody else. Melchisedec's offering is thus a prefiguration of Christ's sacrifice of himself.

329 In the prayer *Supplices te rogamus* we beseech God to bring the gifts "by the hands of thy holy angel to thy altar on high." This singular request derives from the apocryphal *Epistolae Apostolorum,* where there is a legend that Christ, before he became incarnate, bade the archangels take his place at God's altar during his absence.[30] This brings out the idea of the eternal priesthood which links Christ with Melchisedec.

IX. END OF THE CANON

330 Taking up the Host, the priest makes the sign of the cross three times over the chalice, and says: "Through Him, and with Him, and in Him." Then he makes the sign of the cross twice between himself and the chalice. This establishes the identity of Host, chalice, and priest, thus affirming once more the unity of all parts of the sacrifice. The union of Host and chalice signifies the union of the body and blood, i.e., the quickening of the body with a soul, for blood is equivalent to soul. Then follows the *Pater noster.*

X. BREAKING OF THE HOST ("FRACTIO")

331 The prayer "Deliver us, O Lord, we beseech thee, from all evils, past, present, and to come" lays renewed emphasis on the petition made in the preceding *Pater noster:* "but deliver us from evil." The connection between this and the sacrificial death of Christ lies in the descent into hell and the breaking of the

29 "Sidik" is a Phoenician name for God. Sir Leonard Woolley gives a very interesting explanation of this in his report on the excavations at Ur: *Abraham: Recent Discoveries and Hebrew Origins.*

30 Kramp, p. 98.

infernal power. The breaking of the bread that now follows is symbolic of Christ's death. The Host is broken in two over the chalice. A small piece, the *particula,* is broken off from the left half and used for the rite of *consignatio* and *commixtio.* In the Byzantine rite the bread is divided into four, the four pieces being marked with letters as follows:

IΣ

NI KA

XΣ

This means "'Ἰησοῦς Χριστὸς νικᾷ"—'Jesus Christ is victorious.' The peculiar arrangement of the letters obviously represents a quaternity, which as we know always has the character of wholeness. This quaternity, as the letters show, refers to Christ glorified, king of glory and Pantokrator.

332 Still more complicated is the Mozarabic *fractio:* the Host is first broken into two, then the left half into five parts, and the right into four. The five are named *corporatio* (*incarnatio*), *nativitas, circumcisio, apparitio,* and *passio;* and the four *mors, resurrectio, gloria, regnum.* The first group refers exclusively to the human life of our Lord, the second to his existence beyond this world. According to the old view, five is the number of the natural ("hylical") man, whose outstretched arms and legs form, with the head, a pentagram. Four, on the other hand, signifies eternity and totality (as shown for instance by the Gnostic name "Barbelo," which is translated as "fourness is God"). This symbol, I would add in passing, seems to indicate that extension in space signifies God's suffering (on the cross) and, on the other hand, his dominion over the universe.

XI. CONSIGNATIO

333 The sign of the cross is made over the chalice with the *particula,* and then the priest drops it into the wine.

XII. COMMIXTIO

334 This is the mingling of bread and wine, as explained by Theodore of Mopsuestia (d. 428?): ". . . he combines them into one, whereby it is made manifest to everybody that although

they are two they are virtually one." [31] The text at this point says: "May this mixture and consecration [*commixtio et consecratio*] of the body and blood of our Lord help us," etc. The word 'consecration' may be an allusion to an original consecration by contact, though that would not clear up the contradiction since a consecration of both substances has already taken place. Attention has therefore been drawn to the old custom of holding over the sacrament from one Mass to another, the Host being dipped in wine and then preserved in softened, or mixed, form. There are numerous rites that end with minglings of this kind. Here I would only mention the consecration by water, or the mixed drink of honey and milk which the neophytes were given after communion in the Church Order of Hippolytus.

335 The *Leonine Sacramentary* (seventh century) interprets the *commixtio* as a mingling of the heavenly and earthly nature of Christ. The later view was that it symbolizes the resurrection, since in it the blood (or soul) of our Lord is reunited with the body lying in the sepulchre. There is a significant reversal here of the original rite of baptism. In baptism, the body is immersed in water for the purpose of transformation; in the *commixtio,* on the other hand, the body, or *particula,* is steeped in wine, symbolizing spirit, and this amounts to a glorification of the body. Hence the justification for regarding the *commixtio* as a symbol of the resurrection.

XIII. CONCLUSION

336 On careful examination we find that the sequence of ritual actions in the Mass contains, sometimes clearly and sometimes by subtle allusions, a representation in condensed form of the life and sufferings of Christ. Certain phases overlap or are so close together that there can be no question of conscious and deliberate condensation. It is more likely that the historical evolution of the Mass gradually led to its becoming a concrete picture of the most important aspects of Christ's life. First of all (in the *Benedictus qui venit* and *Supra quae*) we have an anticipation and prefiguration of his coming. The uttering of the words

31 Rücker, ed., *Ritus baptismi et missae quam descripsit Theodorus ep. Mopsuestanus.*

of consecration corresponds to the incarnation of the Logos, and also to Christ's passion and sacrificial death, which appears again in the *fractio*. In the *Libera nos* there is an allusion to the descent into hell, while the *consignatio* and *commixtio* hint at resurrection.

337 In so far as the offered gift is the sacrificer himself, in so far as the priest and congregation offer themselves in the sacrificial gift, and in so far as Christ is both sacrificer and sacrificed, there is a mystical unity of all parts of the sacrificial act.[32] The combination of offering and offerer in the single figure of Christ is implicit in the doctrine that just as bread is composed of many grains of wheat, and wine of many grapes, so the mystical body of the Church is made up of a multitude of believers. The mystical body, moreover, includes both sexes, represented by the bread and wine.[33] Thus the two substances—the masculine wine and the feminine bread—also signify the androgynous nature of the mystical Christ.

338 The Mass thus contains, as its essential core, the mystery and miracle of God's transformation taking place in the human sphere, his becoming Man, and his return to his absolute existence in and for himself. Man, too, by his devotion and self-sacrifice as a ministering instrument, is included in the mysterious process. God's offering of himself is a voluntary act of love, but the actual sacrifice was an agonizing and bloody death brought about by men *instrumentaliter et ministerialiter*. (The words *incruente immolatur*—'bloodlessly sacrificed'—refer only to the rite, not to the thing symbolized.) The terrors of death on the cross are an indispensable condition for the transformation. This is in the first place a bringing to life of substances which are in themselves lifeless, and, in the second, a substantial alteration of them, a spiritualization, in accordance with the ancient conception of *pneuma* as a subtle material entity (the *corpus glorificationis*). This idea is expressed in the concrete participation in the body and blood of Christ in the Communion.

32 This unity is a good example of *participation mystique*, which Lévy-Bruhl stressed as being one of the main characteristics of primitive psychology—a view that has recently been contested by ethnologists in a very short-sighted manner. The idea of unity should not, however, be regarded as "primitive" but rather as showing that *participation mystique* is a characteristic of symbols in general. The symbol always includes the unconscious, hence man too is contained in it. The *numinosity* of the symbol is an expression of this fact.

33 Kramp, p. 55.

3. PARALLELS TO THE TRANSFORMATION MYSTERY

I. THE AZTEC "TEOQUALO"

339 Although the Mass itself is a unique phenomenon in the history of comparative religion, its symbolic content would be profoundly alien to man were it not rooted in the human psyche. But if it is so rooted, then we may expect to find similar patterns of symbolism both in the earlier history of mankind and in the world of pagan thought contemporary with it. As the prayer *Supra quae* shows, the liturgy of the Mass contains allusions to the "prefigurations" in the Old Testament, and thus indirectly to ancient sacrificial symbolism in general. It is clear, then, that in Christ's sacrifice and the Communion one of the deepest chords in the human psyche is struck: human sacrifice and ritual anthropophagy. Unfortunately I cannot enter into the wealth of ethnological material in question here, so must content myself with mentioning the ritual slaying of the king to promote the fertility of the land and the prosperity of his people, the renewal and revivification of the gods through human sacrifice, and the totem meal, the purpose of which was to reunite the participants with the life of their ancestors. These hints will suffice to show how the symbols of the Mass penetrate into the deepest layers of the psyche and its history. They are evidently

among the most ancient and most central of religious conceptions. Now with regard to these conceptions there is still a widespread prejudice, not only among laymen, but in scientific circles too, that beliefs and customs of this kind must have been "invented" at some time or other, and were then handed down and imitated, so that they would not exist at all in most places unless they had got there in the manner suggested. It is, however, always precarious to draw conclusions from our modern, "civilized" mentality about the primitive state of mind. Primitive consciousness differs from that of the present-day white man in several very important respects. Thus, in primitive societies, "inventing" is very different from what it is with us, where one novelty follows another. With primitives, life goes on in the same way for generations; nothing alters, except perhaps the language. But that does not mean that a new one is "invented." Their language is "alive" and can therefore change, a fact that has been an unpleasant discovery for many lexicographers of primitive languages. Similarly, no one "invents" the picturesque slang spoken in America; it just springs up in inexhaustible abundance from the fertile soil of colloquial speech. Religious rites and their stock of symbols must have developed in much the same way from beginnings now lost to us, and not just in one place only, but in many places at once, and also at different periods. They have grown spontaneously out of the basic conditions of human nature, which are never invented but are everywhere the same.

340 So it is not surprising that we find religious rites which come very close to Christian practices in a field untouched by classical culture. I mean the rites of the Aztecs, and in particular that of the *teoqualo,* 'god-eating,' as recorded by Fray Bernardino de Sahagún, who began his missionary work among the Aztecs in 1529, eight years after the conquest of Mexico. In this rite, a doughlike paste was made out of the crushed and pounded seeds of the prickly poppy (*Argemone mexicana*) and moulded into the figure of the god Huitzilopochtli:

> And upon the next day the body of Huitzilopochtli died.
>
> And he who slew him was the priest known as Quetzalcoatl. And that with which he slew him was a dart, pointed with flint, which he shot into his heart.
>
> He died in the presence of Moctezuma and of the keeper of the

god, who verily spoke to Huitzilopochtli—who verily appeared before him, who indeed could make him offerings; and of four masters of the youths, front rank leaders. Before all of them died Huitzilopochtli.

And when he had died, thereupon they broke up his body of . . . dough. His heart was apportioned to Moctezuma.

And as for the rest of his members, which were made, as it were, to be his bones, they were distributed and divided up among all. . . . Each year . . . they ate it. . . . And when they divided up among themselves his body made of . . . dough, it was broken up exceeding small, very fine, as small as seeds. The youths ate it.

And of this which they ate, it was said: "The god is eaten." And of those who ate it, it was said: "They guard the god." [1]

341 The idea of a divine body, its sacrifice in the presence of the high priest to whom the god appears and with whom he speaks, the piercing with the spear, the god's death followed by ritual dismemberment, and the eating (*communio*) of a small piece of his body, are all parallels which cannot be overlooked and which caused much consternation among the worthy Spanish Fathers at the time.

342 In Mithraism, a religion that sprang up not long before Christianity, we find a special set of sacrificial symbols and, it would seem, a corresponding ritual which unfortunately is known to us only from dumb monuments. There is a *transitus,* with Mithras carrying the bull; a bull-sacrifice for seasonal fertility; a stereotyped representation of the sacrificial act, flanked on either side by dadophors carrying raised and lowered torches; and a meal at which pieces of bread marked with crosses were laid on the table. Even small bells have been found, and these probably have some connection with the bell which is sounded at Mass. The Mithraic sacrifice is essentially a self-sacrifice, since the bull is a world bull and was originally identical with Mithras himself. This may account for the singularly agonized expression on the face of the *tauroktonos,*[2] which bears comparison with Guido Reni's *Crucifixion.* The Mithraic *transitus* is a motif that corresponds to Christ carrying the cross, just as the

1 Bernardino de Sahagún, *General History of the Things of New Spain,* Book 3: *The Origin of the Gods,* trans. by Anderson and Dibble, pp. 5f. (slightly modified).

2 Cumont, *Textes et monuments,* I, p. 182. [And cf. Jung, *Symbols of Transformation,* p. 428 and frontispiece.—EDITORS.]

transformation of the beast of sacrifice corresponds to the resurrection of the Christian God in the form of food and drink. The representations of the sacrificial act, the tauroctony (bull-slaying), recall the crucifixion between two thieves, one of whom is raised up to paradise while the other goes down to hell.

343 These few references to the Mithras cult are but one example of the wealth of parallels offered by the legends and rites of the various Near Eastern gods who die young, are mourned, and rise again. For anyone who knows these religions at all, there can be no doubt as to the basic affinity of the symbolic types and ideas.[3] At the time of primitive Christianity and in the early days of the Church, the pagan world was saturated with conceptions of this kind and with philosophical speculations based upon them, and it was against this background that the thought and visionary ideas of the Gnostic philosophers were unfolded.

II. THE VISION OF ZOSIMOS

344 A characteristic representative of this school of thought was Zosimos of Panopolis, a natural philosopher and alchemist of the third century A.D., whose works have been preserved, though in corrupt state, in the famous alchemical Codex Marcianus, and were published in 1887 by Berthelot in his *Collection des anciens alchimistes grecs*. In various portions of his treatises[4] Zosimos relates a number of dream-visions, all of which appear to go back to one and the same dream.[5] He was clearly a non-Christian Gnostic, and in particular—so one gathers from the famous passage about the *krater*[6]—an adherent of the Poimandres sect, and therefore a follower of Hermes. Although alchemical literature abounds in parables, I would hesitate to class these dream-visions among them. Anyone acquainted with the language of the alchemists will recognize that their parables are mere allegories of ideas that were common knowledge. In the allegorical figures and actions, one can usually see at once

3 Cf. Frazer's *The Golden Bough,* Part III: "The Dying God." For the Eucharistic meal of fish, see *Aion,* pars. 174ff., 181ff.

4 *Alchimistes,* III, i, 2, 3; III, v; III, vi.

5 Cf. my paper "The Visions of Zosimos," par. 86, which quotes the relevant passages.

6 *Alchimistes,* III, li, 8. Cf. supra, par. 313.

what substances and what procedures are being referred to under a deliberately theatrical disguise. There is nothing of this kind in the Zosimos visions. Indeed, it comes almost as a surprise to find the alchemical interpretation, namely that the dream and its impressive machinery are simply an illustration of the means for producing the "divine water." Moreover, a parable is a self-contained whole, whereas our vision varies and amplifies a single theme as a dream does. So far as one can assess the nature of these visions at all, I should say that even in the original text the contents of an imaginative meditation have grouped themselves round the kernel of an actual dream and been woven into it. That there really was such a meditation is evident from the fragments of it that accompany the visions in the form of a commentary. As we know, meditations of this kind are often vividly pictorial, as if the dream were being continued on a level nearer to consciousness. In his *Lexicon alchemiae,* Martin Ruland, writing in Frankfort in 1612, defines the meditation that plays such an important part in alchemy as an "internal colloquy with someone else, who is nevertheless not seen, it may be with God, with oneself, or with one's good angel." The latter is a milder and less obnoxious form of the *paredros,* the familiar spirit of ancient alchemy, who was generally a planetary demon conjured up by magic. It can hardly be doubted that real visionary experiences originally lay at the root of these practices, and a vision is in the last resort nothing less than a dream which has broken through into the waking state. We know from numerous witnesses all through the ages that the alchemist, in the course of his imaginative work, was beset by visions of all kinds,[7] and was sometimes even threatened with madness.[8] So the visions of Zosimos are not something unusual or unknown in alchemical experience, though they are perhaps the most important self-revelations ever bequeathed to us by an alchemist.

345 I cannot reproduce here the text of the visions in full, but will give as an example the first vision, in Zosimos' own words:

And while I said this I fell asleep, and I saw a sacrificial priest standing before me, high up on an altar, which was in the shape of a

7 Cf. the examples given in *Psychology and Alchemy,* pars. 347f.

8 Olympiodorus says this is particularly the effect of lead. Cf. Berthelot, II, iv, 43.

shallow bowl. There were fifteen steps leading up to the altar. And the priest stood there, and I heard a voice from above say to me: "Behold, I have completed the descent down the fifteen steps of darkness and I have completed the ascent up the steps of light. And he who renews me is the priest, casting away the grossness of the body, and by compelling necessity I am sanctified and now stand in perfection as a spirit [*pneuma*]." And I perceived the voice of him who stood upon the altar, and I inquired of him who he was. And he answered me in a fine voice, saying: "I am Ion, priest of the innermost hidden sanctuary, and I submit myself to an unendurable torment. For there came one in haste at early morning, who overpowered me and pierced me through with the sword and cut me in pieces, yet in such a way that the order of my limbs was preserved. And he drew off the scalp of my head with the sword, which he wielded with strength, and he put the bones and the pieces of flesh together and with his own hand burned them in the fire, until I perceived that I was transformed and had become spirit. And that is my unendurable torment." And even as he spoke this, and I held him by force to converse with me, his eyes became as blood. And he spewed out all his own flesh. And I saw how he changed into a manikin [ἀνθρωπάριον, i.e., an homunculus] who had lost a part of himself. And he tore his flesh with his own teeth, and sank into himself.

346 In the course of the visions the Hiereus (priest) appears in various forms. At first he is split into the figures of the Hiereus and the Hierourgon (sacrificer), who is charged with the performance of the sacrifice. But these figures blend into one in so far as both suffer the same fate. The sacrificial priest submits voluntarily to the torture by which he is transformed. But he is also the sacrificer who is sacrificed, since he is pierced through with the sword and ritually dismembered.[9] The *deipnon* consists in his tearing himself to pieces with his own teeth and eating himself; the *thysia,* in his flesh being sacrificially burned on the altar.

347 He is the Hiereus in so far as he rules over the sacrificial rite as a whole, and over the human beings who are transformed during the *thysia.* He calls himself a guardian of spirits. He is also known as the "Brazen Man" and as Xyrourgos, the barber.

[9] The dismemberment motif belongs in the wider context of rebirth symbolism. Consequently it plays an important part in the initiation experiences of shamans and medicine men, who are dismembered and then put together again. For details, see Eliade, *Shamanism,* ch. II.

The brazen or leaden man is an allusion to the spirits of the metals, or planetary demons, as protagonists of the sacrificial drama. In all probability they are *paredroi* who were conjured up by magic, as may be deduced from Zosimos' remark that he "held him by force" to converse with him. The planetary demons are none other than the old gods of Olympus who finally expired only in the eighteenth century, as the "souls of the metals"—or rather, assumed a new shape, since it was in this same century that paganism openly arose for the first time (in the French Revolution).

348 Somewhat more curious is the term 'barber,' which we find in other parts of the visions,[10] for there is no mention of cutting the hair or shaving. There is, however, a scalping, which in our context is closely connected with the ancient rites of flaying and their magical significance.[11] I need hardly mention the flaying of Marsyas, who is an unmistakable parallel to the son-lover of Cybele, namely Attis, the dying god who rises again. In one of the old Attic fertility rites an ox was flayed, stuffed, and set up on its feet. Herodotus (IV, 60) reports a number of flaying ceremonies among the Scythians, and especially scalpings. In general, flaying signifies transformation from a worse state to a better, and hence renewal and rebirth. The best examples are to be found in the religion of ancient Mexico.[12] Thus, in order to renew the moon-goddess a young woman was decapitated and skinned, and a youth then put the skin round him to represent the risen goddess. The prototype of this renewal is the snake casting its skin every year, a phenomenon round which primitive fantasy has always played. In our vision the skinning is restricted to the head, and this can probably be explained by the underlying idea of spiritual transformation. Since olden times shaving the head has been associated with consecration,

10 [Cf. Berthelot, III, i, 3 and v, 1–2; and "The Visions of Zosimos," par. 86.—EDITORS.]

11 Cf. Frazer's *The Golden Bough,* Part IV: *Adonis, Attis, Osiris,* pp. 242ff. and p. 405, and my *Symbols of Transformation,* pars. 594f. Cf. also Colin Campbell, *The Miraculous Birth of King Amon-Hotep III,* p. 142, concerning the presentation of the dead man, Sen-nezem, before Osiris, Lord of Amentet: "In this scene the god is usually represented enthroned. Before and behind him, hanging from a pole, is the dripping skin of a slain bull that was slaughtered to yield up the soul of Osiris at his reconstruction, with the vase underneath to catch the blood."

12 Cf. Eduard Seler's account in Hastings, *Encyclopedia,* VIII, pp. 615f.

that is, with spiritual transformation or initiation. The priests of Isis had their heads shaved quite bald, and the tonsure, as we know, is still in use at the present day. This "symptom" of transformation goes back to the old idea that the transformed one becomes like a new-born babe (neophyte, *quasimodogenitus*) with a hairless head. In the myth of the night sea journey, the hero loses all his hair during his incubation in the belly of the monster, because of the terrific heat.[13] The custom of tonsure, which is derived from these primitive ideas, naturally presupposes the presence of a ritual barber.[14] Curiously enough, we come across the barber in that old alchemical "mystery," the *Chymical Wedding* of 1616.[15] There the hero, on entering the mysterious castle, is pounced on by invisible barbers, who give him something very like a tonsure.[16] Here again the initiation and transformation process is accompanied by a shaving.[17]

349 In one variant of these visions there is a dragon who is killed and sacrificed in the same manner as the priest and therefore seems to be identical with him. This makes one think of those far from uncommon medieval pictures, not necessarily alchemical, in which a serpent is shown hanging on the Cross in place of Christ. (*Psychology and Alchemy,* fig. 217. Note the comparison of Christ with the serpent of Moses in John 3: 14.)

350 A notable aspect of the priest is the leaden homunculus, and this is none other than the leaden spirit or planetary demon Saturn. In Zosimos' day Saturn was regarded as a Hebrew god,

13 [*Symbols of Transformation,* pars. 309f.; *Psychology and Alchemy,* par. 490.]

14 Barbers were comparatively well-to-do people in ancient Egypt, and evidently did a flourishing trade. Cf. Erman, *Life in Ancient Egypt,* p. 304: "Barbers, all of whom must . . . have lived in easy circumstances."

15 The real author of the *Chymische Hochzeit* was Johann Valentin Andreae. [It appeared under the pseudonym "Christian Rosencreutz," dated 1459, but actually published at Strasbourg, 1616. Concerning Andreae, cf. "The Psychology of the Transference," par. 407 and n. 18.—EDITORS.]

16 As Andreae must have been a learned alchemist, he might very well have got hold of a copy of the Codex Marcianus and seen the writings of Zosimos. Manuscript copies exist in Gotha, Leipzig, Munich, and Weimar. I know of only one printed edition, published in Italy in the 16th cent., which is very rare.

17 Hence the "shaving of a man" and the "plucking of a fowl," mentioned further on among the magical sacrificial recipes. A similar motif is suggested by the "changing of wigs" at the Egyptian judgment of the dead. Cf. the picture in the tomb of Sennezem (Campbell, p. 143). When the dead man is led before Osiris his wig is black; afterwards (at the sacrifice in the Papyrus of Ani) it is white.

presumably on account of the keeping holy of the Sabbath—Saturday means 'Saturn's Day' [18]—and also on account of the Gnostic parallel with the supreme archon Ialdabaoth ('child of chaos') who, as λεοντοειδής, may be grouped together with Baal, Kronos, and Saturn.[19] The later Arabic designation of Zosimos as al-'Ibrî (the Hebrew) does not of course prove that he himself was a Jew, but it is clear from his writings that he was acquainted with Jewish traditions.[20] The parallel between the Hebrew god and Saturn is of considerable importance as regards the alchemical idea of the transformation of the God of the Old Testament into the God of the New. The alchemists naturally attached great significance to Saturn,[21] for, besides being the outermost planet, the supreme archon (the Harranites named him "Primas"), and the demiurge Ialdabaoth, he was also the *spiritus niger* who lies captive in the darkness of matter, the deity or that part of the deity which has been swallowed up in his own creation. He is the dark god who reverts to his original luminous state in the mystery of alchemical transmutation. As the *Aurora Consurgens* says: "Blessed is he that shall find this science and into whom this prudence of Saturn floweth." [22]

351 The later alchemists were familiar not only with the ritual slaying of a dragon but also with the slaying of a lion, which took the form of his having all four paws cut off. Like the dragon, the lion devours himself, and so is probably only a variant.[23]

18 Plutarch, *Quaestiones convivales,* IV, 5, and Diogenes Laertius, II, §112; Reitzenstein, *Poimandres,* pp. 75f. and 112. In a text named "Ghāya al-hakīm," ascribed to Maslama al-Madjrītī, the following instructions are given when invoking Saturn: "Arrive vêtu à la manière des Juifs, car il est leur patron." Dozy and de Goeje, "Nouveaux documents pour l'étude de la religion des Harraniens," p. 350.

19 Origen, *Contra Celsum,* VI, 31. Mead, *Pistis Sophia,* ch. 45. Bousset, *Hauptprobleme der Gnosis,* pp. 351ff. Roscher, *Lexikon,* s.v. Kronos, II, col. 1496. The dragon (*κρόνος*) and Kronos are often confused.

20 Lippmann, *Entstehung und Ausbreitung der Alchemie,* II, p. 229.

21 Cf. *Aion,* pars. 128f.

22 "Beatus homo qui invenerit hanc scientiam et cui affluit providentia Saturni." [Ed. von Franz, pp. 37f.]

23 See the illustration in Reusner, *Pandora* (1588), and in *Le Songe de Poliphile,* trans. Béroalde de Verville (1600). [*Psych. and Alch.,* fig. 4.] Mostly the pictures show two lions eating one another. The uroboros, too, is often pictured in the form of two dragons engaged in the same process (*Viridarium chymicum,* 1624).

352 The vision itself indicates that the main purpose of the transformation process is the spiritualization of the sacrificing priest: he is to be changed into *pneuma*. We are also told that he would "change the bodies into blood, make the eyes to see and the dead to rise again." Later in the visions he appears in glorified form, shining white like the midday sun.

353 Throughout the visions it is clear that sacrificer and sacrificed are one and the same. This idea of the unity of the *prima* and *ultima materia*, of that which redeems and that which is to be redeemed, pervades the whole of alchemy from beginning to end. "Unus est lapis, una medicina, unum vas, unum regimen, unaque dispositio" is the key formula to its enigmatic language.[24] Greek alchemy expresses the same idea in the formula ἓν τὸ πᾶν. Its symbol is the uroboros, the tail-eating serpent. In our vision it is the priest as sacrificer who devours himself as the sacrifice. This recalls the saying of St. John Chrysostom that in the Eucharist Christ drinks his own blood. By the same token, one might add, he eats his own flesh. The grisly repast in the dream of Zosimos reminds us of the orgiastic meals in the Dionysus cult, when sacrificial animals were torn to pieces and eaten. They represent Dionysus Zagreus being torn to pieces by the Titans, from whose mangled remains the νέος Διόνυσος arises.[25]

354 Zosimos tells us that the vision represents or explains the "production of the waters." [26] The visions themselves only show the transformation into *pneuma*. In the language of the alchemists, however, spirit and water are synonymous,[27] as they are

24 Cf. the *Rosarium philosophorum*, in the *Artis auriferae* (1593), II, p. 206.

25 Cf. the Cretan fragment of Euripides (Dieterich, *Eine Mithrasliturgie*, p. 105):

> ἁγνὸν δὲ βίον τείνων ἐξ οὗ
> Διὸς Ἰδαίου μύστης γενόμην
> καὶ νυκτιπόλου Ζαγρέως βούτας
> τοὺς ὠμοφάγους δαῖτας τελέσας

(living a holy life, since I have been initiated into the mysteries of the Idaean Zeus, and eaten raw the flesh of Zagreus, the night-wandering shepherd).

26 [Cf. "The Visions of Zosimos," par. 86, III, i, 3, and—for the reference lower down to "blood"—III, v bis.]

27 "Est et coelestis aqua sive potius divina Chymistarum . . . pneuma, ex aetheris natura et essentia rerum quinta" (There is also the celestial, or rather the divine, water of the alchemists . . . the pneuma, having the nature of the pneuma and the quintessence of things).—Hermolaus Barbarus, *Coroll. in Dioscoridem*, cited in M. Maier, *Symbola aureae mensae* (1617), p. 174.

"Spiritus autem in hac arte nihil aliud quam aquam indicari . . ." (In this art, in the language of the early Christians, for whom water meant the *spiritus veritatis*. In the "Book of Krates" we read: "You make the bodies to liquefy, so that they mingle and become an homogeneous liquid; this is then named the 'divine water.' "[28] The passage corresponds to the Zosimos text, which says that the priest would "change the bodies into blood." For the alchemists, water and blood are identical. This transformation is the same as the *solutio* or *liquefactio,* which is a synonym for the *sublimatio,* for "water" is also "fire": "Item ignis . . . est aqua et ignis noster est ignis et non ignis" (For fire . . . is water and our fire is the fire that is no fire). "Aqua nostra" is said to be "ignea" (fiery).[29]

355 The "secret fire of our philosophy" is said to be "our mystical water," and the "permanent water" is the "fiery form of the true water." [30] The permanent water (the ὕδωρ θεῖον of the Greeks) also signifies "spiritualis sanguis," [31] and is identified with the blood and water that flowed from Christ's side. Heinrich Khunrath says of this water: "So there will open for thee an healing flood which issues from the heart of the son of the great world." It is a water "which the son of the great world pours forth from his body and heart, to be for us a true and natural Aqua vitae." [32] Just as a spiritual water of grace and truth flows from Christ's sacrifice, so the "divine water" is produced by a sacrificial act in the Zosimos vision. It is mentioned in the ancient

spirit means nothing else but water).—Theobaldus de Hoghelande, in the *Theatrum chemicum,* I (1602), p. 196. Water is a "spiritus extractus," or a "spiritus qui in ventre (corporis) occultus est et fiet aqua et corpus absque spiritu: qui est spiritualis naturae" (spirit which is hidden in the belly [of the substance], and water will be produced and a substance without spirit, which is of a spiritual nature).—J. D. Mylius, *Philosophia reformata* (1622), p. 150. This quotation shows how closely spirit and water were associated in the mind of the alchemist.

"Sed aqua coelestis gloriosa *scil.* aes nostrum ac argentum nostrum, sericum nostrum, totaque oratio nostra, quod est unum et idem *scil.* sapientia, quam Deus obtulit, quibus voluit" (But the glorious celestial water, namely our copper and our silver, our silk, and everything we talk about, is one and the same thing, namely the Wisdom, which God has given to whomsoever he wished).—"Consilium coniugii," in the *Ars chemica* (1566), p. 120.

28 Berthelot, *La Chimie au moyen âge,* III, p. 53.

29 Mylius, pp. 121 and 123. For the blood–water–fire equation see George Ripley, *Opera omnia chemica* (1649), pp. 162, 197, 295, 427.

30 Ripley, *Opera,* p. 62; *Rosarium,* p. 264.

31 Mylius, p. 42.

32 Khunrath, *Von hylealischen . . . Chaos* (1597), pp. 274f.

treatise entitled "Isis to Horus," [33] where the angel Amnael brings it to the prophetess in a drinking vessel. As Zosimos was probably an adherent of the Poimandres sect, another thing to be considered here is the *krater* which God filled with *nous* for all those seeking ἔννοια.[34] But *nous* is identical with the alchemical Mercurius. This is quite clear from the Ostanes quotation in Zosimos, which says: "Go to the streams of the Nile and there thou wilt find a stone which hath a spirit. Take and divide it, thrust in thy hand and draw out its heart, for its soul is in its heart." Commenting on this, Zosimos remarks that "having a spirit" is a metaphorical expression for the *exhydrargyrosis,* the expulsion of the quicksilver.[35]

356 During the first centuries after Christ the words *nous* and *pneuma* were used indiscriminately, and the one could easily stand for the other. Moreover the relation of Mercurius to "spirit" is an extremely ancient astrological fact. Like Hermes, Mercurius (or the planetary spirit Mercury) was a god of revelation, who discloses the secret of the art to the adepts. The *Liber quartorum,* which being of Harranite origin cannot be dated later than the tenth century, says of Mercurius: "Ipse enim aperit clausiones operum cum ingenio et intellectu suo" (For he opens with his genius and understanding the locked [insoluble] problems of the work).[36] He is also the "soul of the bodies," the "anima vitalis," [37] and Ruland defines him as "spirit which has become earth." [38] He is a spirit that penetrates into the depths of the material world and transforms it. Like the *nous,* he is symbolized by the serpent. In Michael Maier he points the way to the earthly paradise.[39] Besides being identified with Hermes Trismegistus,[40] he is also called the "mediator" [41] and,

33 Berthelot, *Alchimistes,* I, xiii. [Cf. "The Visions of Zosimos," pars. 97ff.]

34 Ibid., III, li, 8, and *Hermetica,* ed. Scott, I, p. 151.

35 Berthelot, *Alchimistes,* III, vi, 5.

36 Of the later authors I will mention only Johannes Christophorus Steeb, *Coelum sephiroticum* (1679, p. 138): "Omnis intellectus acuminis auctor . . . a coelesti mercurio omnem ingeniorum vim provenire" (The author of all deeper understanding . . . all the power of genius comes from the celestial Mercurius). For the astrological connection see Bouché-Leclercq, *L'Astrologie grecque,* pp. 312, 321–23.

37 "Aurora consurgens." In Mylius (p. 533) he is a giver of life.

38 *Lexicon.*

39 *Symbola,* p. 592.

40 Ibid., p. 600.

41 Ripley, *Opera,* Foreword, and in Khunrath's *Chaos.* In Plutarch, Mercurius acts as a kind of world soul.

as the Original Man, the "Hermaphroditic Adam."[42] From numerous passages it is clear that Mercurius is as much a fire as a water, both of which aptly characterize the nature of spirit.[43]

357 Killing with the sword is a recurrent theme in alchemical literature. The "philosophical egg" is divided with the sword, and with it the "King" is transfixed and the dragon or "corpus" dismembered, the latter being represented as the body of a man whose head and limbs are cut off.[44] The lion's paws are likewise cut off with the sword. For the alchemical sword brings about the *solutio* or *separatio* of the elements, thereby restoring the original condition of chaos, so that a new and more perfect body can be produced by a new *impressio formae,* or by a "new imagination." The sword is therefore that which "kills and vivifies," and the same is said of the permanent water or mercurial water. Mercurius is the giver of life as well as the destroyer of the old form. In ecclesiastical symbolism the sword which comes out of the mouth of the Son of Man in the Book of Revelation is, according to Hebrews 4:12, the Logos, the Word of God, and hence Christ himself. This analogy did not escape the notice of the alchemists, who were always struggling to give expression to their fantasies. Mercurius was their mediator and saviour, their *filius macrocosmi* (contrasted with Christ the *filius microcosmi*),[45] the solver and separator. So he too is a sword, for he is a "penetrating spirit" ("more piercing than a two-edged sword"!). Gerhard Dorn, an alchemist of the sixteenth century, says that in our world the sword was changed into Christ our Saviour. He comments as follows:

> After a long interval of time the Deus Optimus Maximus immersed himself in the innermost of his secrets, and he decided, out of the compassion of his love as well as for the demands of justice, to take the sword of wrath from the hand of the angel. And having hung the sword on the tree, he substituted for it a golden trident, and thus was the wrath of God changed into love. . . . When peace and

42 Gerhard Dorn, "Congeries Paracelsicae chemicae," in the *Theatrum chemicum,* I, p. 589.

43 Cf. "The Spirit Mercurius," pars. 255, 256ff.

44 Illustration in "Splendor solis," *Aureum vellus* (1598).

45 Cf. Khunrath, *Chaos,* and *Amphitheatrum sapientiae aeternae* (1604).

justice were united, the water of Grace flowed more abundantly from above, and now it bathes the whole world.[46]

[46] Dorn, "Speculativae philosophiae," in the *Theatrum chemicum,* I, pp. 284ff. The whole passage runs as follows:

"Post primam hominis inobedientiam, Dominus viam hanc amplissimam in callem strictissimam difficilimamque (ut videtis) restrinxit, in cuius ostio collocavit Cherubim angelum, ancipitem gladium manu tenentem, quo quidem arceret omnes ab introitu felicis patriae: hinc deflectentes Adae filii propter peccatum primi sui parentis, in sinistram latam sibimet viam construxerunt, quam evitastis. Longo postea temporis intervallo D. O. M. secreta secretorum suorum introivit, in quibus amore miserente, accusanteque iustitia, conclusit angelo gladium irae suae de manibus eripere, cuius loco tridentem hamum substituit aureum, gladio ad arborem suspenso: & sic mutata est ira Dei in amorem, servata iustitia: quod antequam fieret, fluvius iste non erat, ut iam, in se collectus, sed ante lapsum per totum orbem terrarum roris instar expansus aequaliter: post vero rediit unde processerat tandem, ut pax & iustitia sunt osculatae se, descendit affluentius ab alto manans aqua gratiae, totum nunc mundum alluens. In sinistram partem qui deflectunt, partim suspensum in arbore gladium videntes, eiusque noscentes historiam, quia mundo nimium sunt insiti, praetereunt: nonnulli videntes eius efficaciam perquirere negligunt, alii nec vident, nec vidisse voluissent: hi recta peregrinationem suam ad vallem dirigunt omnes, nisi per hamos resipiscentiae, vel poenitentiae nonnulli retrahantur ad montem Sion. Nostro iam saeculo (quod gratiae est) mutatus est gladius in Christum salvatorem nostrum qui crucis arborem pro peccatis nostris ascendit."

(After man's first disobedience the Lord straitened this wide road into a very narrow and difficult path, as you see. At its entrance he placed an angel of the Cherubim, holding in his hand a double-edged sword with which he was to keep all from entering into Paradise. Turning from thence on account of the sin of their first parents, the sons of Adam built for themselves a broad left-hand path: this you have shunned. After a long interval of time the Deus Optimus Maximus immersed himself in the innermost of his secrets, and he decided, out of the compassion of his love as well as for the demands of justice, to take the sword of wrath from the hand of the angel. And having hung the sword on the tree, he substituted for it a golden trident, and thus was the wrath of God changed into love, and justice remained unimpaired. Previous to this, however, the river was not collected into one as it is now, but before the Fall it was spread equally over the whole world, like dew. But later it returned to the place of its origin. When peace and justice were united, the water of Grace flowed more abundantly from above, and now it bathes the whole world. Some of those who take the left-hand path, on seeing the sword suspended from the tree, and knowing its history, pass it by, because they are too entangled in the affairs of this world; some, on seeing it, do not choose to inquire into its efficacy; others never see it and would not wish to see it. All these continue their pilgrimage into the valley, except for those who are drawn back to Mount Zion by the hook of repentance. Now in our age, which is an age of grace, the sword has become Christ our Saviour, who ascended the tree of the Cross for our sins.) Cf. "The Philosophical Tree," pars. 447ff.

358 This passage, which might well have occurred in an author like Rabanus Maurus or Honorius of Autun without doing them discredit, actually occurs in a context which throws light on certain esoteric alchemical doctrines, namely in a colloquy between Animus, Anima, and Corpus. There we are told that it is Sophia, the Sapientia, Scientia, or Philosophia of the alchemists, "de cuius fonte scaturiunt aquae" (from whose fount the waters gush forth). This Wisdom is the *nous* that lies hidden and bound in matter, the "serpens mercurialis" or "humidum radicale" that manifests itself in the "viventis aquae fluvius de montis apice" (stream of living water from the summit of the mountain).[47] That is the water of grace, the "permanent" and "divine" water which "now bathes the whole world." The apparent transformation of the God of the Old Testament into the God of the New is in reality the transformation of the *deus absconditus* (i.e., the *natura abscondita*) into the *medicina catholica* of alchemical wisdom.[48]

359 The divisive and separative function of the sword, which is of such importance in alchemy, is prefigured in the flaming sword of the angel that separated our first parents from paradise. Separation by a sword is a theme that can also be found in the Gnosis of the Ophites: the earthly cosmos is surrounded by a ring of fire which at the same time encloses paradise. But paradise and the ring of fire are separated by the "flaming sword." [49] An important interpretation of this flaming sword is given in Simon Magus: [50] there is an incorruptible essence potentially present in every human being, the divine *pneuma* "which is stationed above and below in the stream of water." Simon says of this *pneuma:* "I and thou, thou before me. I, who am after thee." It is a force "that generates itself, that causes itself to grow; it is its own mother, sister, bride, daughter; its own son, mother, father; a unity, a root of the whole." It is the very

47 Another remark of Dorn's points in the same direction: "The sword was suspended from a tree over the bank of the river" (p. 288).

48 A few pages later Dorn himself remarks: "Scitote, fratres, omnia quae superius dicta sunt et dicentur in posterum, intelligi posse de praeparationibus alchemicis" (Know, brothers, that everything which has been said above and everything which will be said in what follows can also be understood of the alchemical preparations).

49 Leisegang, *Die Gnosis,* pp. 171f.

50 The passage which follows occurs in Hippolytus, *Elenchos,* vi, pp. 4f.

ground of existence, the procreative urge, which is of fiery origin. Fire is related to blood, which "is fashioned warm and ruddy like fire." Blood turns into semen in men, and in women into milk. This "turning" is interpreted as "the flaming sword which turned every way, to keep the way of the tree of life." [51] The operative principle in semen and milk turns into mother and father. The tree of life is guarded by the turning (i.e., transforming) sword, and this is the "seventh power" which begets itself. "For if the flaming sword turned not, then would that fair Tree be destroyed, and perish utterly; but if it turneth into semen and milk, and there be added the Logos and the place of the Lord where the Logos is begotten, he who dwelleth potentially in the semen and milk shall grow to full stature from the littlest spark, and shall increase and become a power boundless and immutable, like to an unchanging Aeon, which suffereth no more change until measureless eternity." [52] It is clear from these remarkable statements of Hippolytus concerning the teachings of Simon Magus that the sword is very much more than an instrument which divides; it is itself the force which "turns" from something infinitesimally small into the infinitely great: from water, fire, and blood it becomes the limitless aeon. What it means is the transformation of the vital spirit in man into the Divine. The natural being becomes the divine *pneuma*, as in the vision of Zosimos. Simon's description of the creative *pneuma*, the true arcane substance, corresponds in every detail to the uroboros or *serpens mercurialis* of the Latinists. It too is its own father, mother, son, daughter, brother, and sister from the earliest beginnings of alchemy right down to the end.[53] It begets and sacrifices itself and is its own instrument of sacrifice, for it is a symbol of the deadly and life-giving water.[54]

360 Simon's ideas also throw a significant light on the above-quoted passage from Dorn, where the sword of wrath is transformed into Christ. Were it not that the philosophoumena of Hippolytus were first discovered in the nineteenth century, on Mount Athos, one might almost suppose that Dorn had made use of them. There are numerous other symbols in alchemy whose origin is so doubtful that one does not know whether to

51 Genesis 3 : 24. 52 Leisegang, p. 80.

53 That is why it is called "Hermaphroditus."

54 One of its symbols is the scorpion, which stings itself to death.

attribute them to tradition, or to a study of the heresiologists, or to spontaneous revival.[55]

361 The sword as the "proper" instrument of sacrifice occurs again in the old treatise entitled "Consilium coniugii de massa solis et lunae." This says: "Both must be killed with their own sword" ("both" referring to Sol and Luna).[56] In the still older "Tractatus Micreris," [57] dating perhaps from the twelfth century, we find the "fiery sword" in a quotation from Ostanes: "The great Astanus [Ostanes] said: Take an egg, pierce it with the fiery sword, and separate its soul from its body." [58] Here the sword is something that divides body and soul, corresponding to the division between heaven and earth, the ring of fire and paradise, or paradise and the first parents. In an equally old treatise, the "Allegoriae sapientum . . . supra librum Turbae," there is even mention of a sacrificial rite: "Take a fowl [*volatile*], cut off its head with the fiery sword, then pluck out its feathers, separate the limbs, and cook over a charcoal fire till it becomes of one colour." [59] Here we have a decapitation with the fiery sword, then a "clipping," or more accurately a "plucking," and finally a "cooking." The cock, which is probably what is meant here, is simply called "volatile," a fowl or winged creature, and this is a common term for spirit, but a spirit still nature-bound and imperfect, and in need of improvement. In another old treatise, with the very similar title "Allegoriae super librum Turbae," [60] we find the following supplementary variants: "Kill the mother [the *prima materia*], tearing off her hands and feet." "Take a viper . . . cut off its head and tail." "Take a cock . . . and pluck it alive." "Take a man, shave him, and drag him over the stone [i.e., dry him on the hot stone] till his body dies." "Take the glass vessel containing bridegroom and bride, throw

55 So far I have come across only one alchemical author who admits to having read the *Panarium* of Epiphanius, while declaring at the same time his sincere abhorrence of heresies. The silence of the alchemists in this matter is nothing to wonder at, since the mere proximity to heresy would have put them in danger of their lives. Thus even 90 years after the death of Trithemius of Spanheim, who was supposed to have been the teacher of Paracelsus, the abbot Sigismund of Seon had to compose a moving defence in which he endeavoured to acquit Trithemius of the charge of heresy. Cf. *Trithemius sui-ipsius vindex* (1616).

56 *Ars chemica,* p. 259. Printed in Manget (1702), II.

57 "Micreris" is probably a corruption of "Mercurius."

58 *Theatr. chem.,* V (1622), p. 103.

59 Ibid., p. 68.

60 *Artis auriferae,* I, pp. 139f.

them into the furnace, and roast them for three days, and they will be two in one flesh." "Take the white man from the vessel." [61]

362 One is probably right in assuming that these recipes are instructions for magical sacrifices, not unlike the Greek magic papyri.[62] As an example of the latter I will give the recipe from the Mimaut Papyrus (li. 2ff.): "Take a tomcat and make an Osiris of him [63] [by immersing] his body in water. And when you proceed to suffocate him, talk into his back." Another example from the same papyrus (li. 425): "Take a hoopoe, tear out its heart, pierce it with a reed, then cut it up and throw it into Attic honey."

363 Such sacrifices really were made for the purpose of summoning up the *paredros,* the familiar spirit. That this sort of thing was practised, or at any rate recommended, by the alchemists is clear from the "Liber Platonis quartorum," where it speaks of the "oblationes et sacrificia" offered to the planetary demon. A deeper and more sombre note is struck in the following passage, which I give in the original (and generally very corrupt) text: [64]

> Vas . . . oportet esse rotundae figurae: Ut sit artifex huius mutator firmamenti et testae capitis, ut cum sit res, qua indigemus, res simplex, habens partes similes, necesse est ipsius generationem, et in corpore habente similes partibus . . . proiicies ex testa capitis, videlicet capitis elementi hominis et massetur totum cum urina . . .
>
> (The vessel . . . must be round in shape. Thus the artifex must be the transformer of this firmament and of the brain-pan, just as the thing for which we seek is a simple thing having uniform parts. It is therefore necessary that you should generate it in a body [i.e., a vessel] of uniform parts . . . from the brain-pan, that is, from the head of the element Man, and that the whole should be macerated with urine . . .)

364 One asks oneself how literally this recipe is to be taken.[65] The following story from the "Ghāya al-hakīm" is exceedingly enlightening in this connection:

365 The Jacobite patriarch Dionysius I set it on record that in

61 Ibid., pp. 151, 140, 140, 139, 151, 151, resp.

62 *Papyri Graecae Magicae,* trans. and ed. by Karl Preisendanz.

63 ἀποθέωσις = 'sacrifice.'

64 *Theatr. chem.,* V, p. 153.

65 See also pp. 127, 128, 130, and 149 of the same work.

the year 765, a man who was destined for the sacrifice, on beholding the bloody head of his predecessor, was so terrified that he took flight and lodged a complaint with Abbas, the prefect of Mesopotamia, against the priests of Harran, who were afterwards severely punished. The story goes on to say that in 830 the Caliph Mamun told the Harranite envoys: "You are without doubt the people of the head, who were dealt with by my father Rashid." We learn from the "Ghāya" that a fair-haired man with dark-blue eyes was lured into a chamber of the temple, where he was immersed in a great jar filled with sesame oil. Only his head was left sticking out. There he remained for forty days, and during this time was fed on nothing but figs soaked in sesame oil. He was not given a drop of water to drink. As a result of this treatment his body became as soft as wax. The prisoner was repeatedly fumigated with incense, and magical formulae were pronounced over him. Eventually his head was torn off at the neck, the body remaining in the oil. The head was then placed in a niche on the ashes of burnt olives, and was packed round with cotton wool. More incense was burned before it, and the head would thereupon predict famines or good harvests, changes of dynasty, and other future events. Its eyes could see, though the lids did not move. It also revealed to people their inmost thoughts, and scientific and technical questions were likewise addressed to it.[66]

366 Even though it is possible that the real head was, in later times, replaced by a dummy, the whole idea of this ceremony, particularly when taken in conjunction with the above passage from the "Liber quartorum," seems to point to an original human sacrifice. The idea of a mysterious head is, however, considerably older than the school of Harran. As far back as Zosimos we find the philosophers described as "children of the golden head," and we also encounter the "round element," which Zosimos says is the letter omega (Ω). This symbol may well be interpreted as the head, since the "Liber quartorum" also associates the round vessel with the head. Zosimos, moreover, refers on several occasions to the "whitest stone, which is in the head."[67] Probably all these ideas go back to the severed head

66 Dozy and de Goeje, p. 365.

67 "Τὸν πάνυ λευκότατον λίθον τὸν ἐγκέφαλον." Berthelot, *Alchimistes,* III, xxix, 4. Cf. also I, iii, 1 and III, ii. 1.

of Osiris, which crossed the sea and was therefore associated with the idea of resurrection. The "head of Osiris" also plays an important part in medieval alchemy.

367 In this connection we might mention the legend that was current about Gerbert of Rheims, afterwards Pope Sylvester II (d. 1003). He was believed to have possessed a golden head which spoke to him in oracles. Gerbert was one of the greatest savants of his time, and well known as a transmitter of Arabic science.[68] Can it be that the translation of the "Liber quartorum," which is of Harranite origin, goes back to this author? Unfortunately there is little prospect of our being able to prove this.

368 It has been conjectured that the Harranite oracle head may be connected with the ancient Hebrew teraphim. Rabbinic tradition considers the teraphim to have been originally either the decapitated head or skull of a human being, or else a dummy head.[69] The Jews had teraphim about the house as a sort of lares and penates (who were plural spirits, like the Cabiri). The idea that they were heads goes back to I Samuel 19:13f., which describes how Michal, David's wife, put the teraphim in David's bed in order to deceive the messengers of Saul, who wanted to kill him. "Then Michal took an image and laid it on the bed and put a pillow of goats' hair at its head, and covered it with the clothes (RSV)." The "pillow of goats' hair" is linguistically obscure and has even been interpreted as meaning that the teraphim were goats. But it may also mean something woven or plaited out of goats' hair, like a wig, and this would fit in better with the picture of a man lying in bed. Further evidence for this comes from a legend in a collection of midrashim from the twelfth century, printed in Bin Gorion's *Die Sagen der Juden.* There it is said:

The teraphim were idols, and they were made in the following way. The head of a man, who had to be a first-born, was cut off and the hair plucked out. The head was then sprinkled with salt and anointed with oil. Afterwards a little plaque, of copper or gold, was inscribed with the name of an idol and placed under the tongue of the decapitated head. The head was set up in a room, candles were lit before it, and the people made obeisance. And if any man fell

68 Thorndike, *A History of Magic and Experimental Science,* I, p. 705.

69 *Jewish Encyclopaedia,* XII, s.v. "Teraphim," pp. 108f.

down before it, the head began to speak, and answered all questions that were addressed to it.[70]

369 This is an obvious parallel to the Harranite ritual with the head. The tearing out of the hair seems significant, since it is an equivalent of scalping or shearing, and is thus a rebirth mystery. It is conceivable that in later times the bald skull was covered with a wig for a rite of renewal, as is also reported from Egypt.

370 It seems probable that this magical procedure is of primitive origin. I am indebted to the South African writer, Laurens van der Post, for the following report from a lecture which he gave in Zurich in 1951:

> The tribe in question was an offshoot of the great Swazi nation—a Bantu people. When, some years ago, the old chief died, he was succeeded by his son, a young man of weak character. He soon proved to be so unsatisfactory a chief that his uncles called a meeting of the tribal elders. They decided that something must be done to strengthen their chief, so they consulted the witch doctors. The witch doctors treated him with a medicine which proved ineffective. Another meeting was held and the witch doctors were asked to use the strongest medicine of all on the chief because the situation was becoming desperate. A half brother of the chief, a boy of twelve, was chosen to provide the material for the medicine.
>
> One afternoon a sorcerer went up to the boy, who was tending cattle, and engaged him in conversation. Then, emptying some powder from a horn into his hand, he took a reed and blew the powder into the ears and nostrils of the boy. A witness told me that the lad thereupon began to sway like a drunken person and sank to the ground shivering. He was then taken to the river bed and tied to the roots of a tree. More powder was sprinkled round about, the sorcerer saying: "This person will no longer eat food but only earth and roots."
>
> The boy was kept in the river bed for nine months. Some people say a cage was made and put into the stream, with the boy inside it, for hours on end, so that the water should flow over him and make his skin white. Others reported seeing him crawling about in the river bed on his hands and knees. But all were so frightened that, although there was a mission school only one hundred yards away,

70 Josef bin Gorion, *Die Sagen der Juden,* p. 325. I am indebted to Dr. Riwkah Schärf for drawing my attention to this passage.

no one except those directly concerned in the ritual would go near him. All are agreed that at the end of nine months this fat, normal, healthy boy was like an animal and quite white-skinned. One woman said, "His eyes were white and the whole of his body was white as white paper."

On the evening that the boy was to be killed a veteran witch doctor was summoned to the chief's kraal and asked to consult the tribal spirits. This he did in the cattle kraal, and after selecting an animal for slaughter he retired to the chief's hut. There the witch doctor was handed parts of the dead boy's body: first the head in a sack, then a thumb and a toe. He cut off the nose and ears and lips, mixed them with medicine, and cooked them over a fire in a broken clay pot. He stuck two spears on either side of the pot. Then those present—twelve in all including the weak chief—leaned over the pot and deeply inhaled the steam. All save the boy's mother dipped their fingers in the pot and licked them. She inhaled but refused to dip her fingers in the pot. The rest of the body the witch doctor mixed into a kind of bread for doctoring the tribe's crops.

371 Although this magical rite is not actually a "head mystery," it has several things in common with the practices previously mentioned. The body is macerated and transformed by long immersion in water. The victim is killed, and the salient portions of the head form the main ingredient of the "strengthening" medicine which was concocted for the chief and his immediate circle. The body is kneaded into a sort of bread, and this is obviously thought of as a strengthening medicine for the tribe's crops as well. The rite is a transformation process, a sort of rebirth after nine months of incubation in the water. Laurens van der Post thinks that the purpose of the "whitening" [71] was to assimilate the mana of the white man, who has the political power. I agree with this view, and would add that painting with white clay often signifies transformation into ancestral spirits, in the same way as the neophytes are made invisible in the Nandi territory, in Kenya, where they walk about in portable, cone-shaped grass huts and demonstrate their invisibility to everyone.

372 Skull worship is widespread among primitives. In Melanesia and Polynesia it is chiefly the skulls of the ancestors that are worshipped, because they establish connections with the spirits

71 Cf. the alchemical *albedo* and *homo albus*.

or serve as tutelary deities, like the head of Osiris in Egypt. Skulls also play a considerable role as sacred relics. It would lead us too far to go into this primitive skull worship, so I must refer the reader to the literature.[72] I would only like to point out that the cut-off ears, nose, and mouth can represent the head as parts that stand for the whole. There are numerous examples of this. Equally, the head or its parts (brain, etc.) can act as magical food or as a means for increasing the fertility of the land.

373 It is of special significance for the alchemical tradition that the oracle head was also known in Greece. Aelian [73] reports that Cleomenes of Sparta had the head of his friend Archonides preserved in a jar of honey, and that he consulted it as an oracle. The same was said of the head of Orpheus. Onians [74] rightly emphasizes the fact that the *ψυχή*, whose seat was in the head, corresponds to the modern "unconscious," and that at that stage of development consciousness was identified with *θυμός* (breath) and *φρένες* (lungs), and was localized in the chest or heart region. Hence Pindar's expression for the soul—*αἴωνος εἴδωλον* (image of Aion)—is extraordinarily apt, for the collective unconscious not only imparts "oracles" but forever represents the microcosm (i.e., the form of a physical man mirroring the Cosmos).

374 There is no evidence to show that any of the parallels we have drawn are historically connected with the Zosimos visions. It seems rather to be a case partly of parallel traditions (transmitted, perhaps, chiefly through the Harran school), and partly of spontaneous fantasies arising from the same archetypal background from which the traditions were derived in the first place. As my examples have shown, the imagery of the Zosimos visions, however strange it may be, is by no means isolated, but is interwoven with older ideas some of which were certainly, and others quite possibly, known to Zosimos, as well as with parallels of uncertain date which continued to mould the speculations of the alchemists for many centuries to come. Religious thought in the early Christian era was not completely cut off from all contact with these conceptions; it was in fact influenced by them, and in turn it fertilized the minds of the natural philosophers during later centuries. Towards the end of the sixteenth century

72 Hastings, VI, pp. 535f. 73 *Varia historia,* XII, 8.

74 Onians, *The Origins of European Thought,* pp. 101ff.

the alchemical *opus* was even represented in the form of a Mass. The author of this tour de force was the Hungarian alchemist, Melchior Cibinensis. I have elaborated this parallel in my book *Psychology and Alchemy*.[75]

375 In the visions of Zosimos, the Hiereus who is transformed into *pneuma* represents the transformative principle at work in nature and the harmony of opposing forces. Chinese philosophy formulated this process as the enantiodromian interplay of Yin and Yang.[76] But the curious personifications and symbols characteristic not only of these visions but of alchemical literature in general show in the plainest possible terms that we are dealing with a psychic process that takes place mainly in the unconscious and therefore can come into consciousness only in the form of a dream or vision. At that time and until very much later no one had any idea of the unconscious; consequently all unconscious contents were projected into the object, or rather were found in nature as apparent objects or properties of matter and were not recognized as purely internal psychic events. There is some evidence that Zosimos was well aware of the spiritual or mystical side of his art, but he believed that what he was concerned with was a spirit that dwelt in natural objects, and not something that came from the human psyche. It remained for modern science to despiritualize nature through its so-called objective knowledge of matter. All anthropomorphic projections were withdrawn from the object one after another, with a twofold result: firstly man's mystical identity with nature[77] was curtailed as never before, and secondly the projections falling back into the human soul caused such a terrific activation of the unconscious that in modern times man was compelled to postulate the existence of an unconscious psyche. The first beginnings of this can be seen in Leibniz and Kant, and then, with mounting intensity, in Schelling, Carus, and von Hartmann, until finally modern psychology discarded the last metaphysical claims of the philosopher-psychologists and restricted the idea of the psyche's existence to the psychological statement, in other

75 Pars. 480–89.

76 The classical example being *The I Ching or Book of Changes.*

77 Mystical or *unconscious* identity occurs in every case of projection, because the content projected upon the extraneous object creates an apparent relationship between it and the subject.

words, to its phenomenology. So far as the dramatic course of the Mass represents the death, sacrifice and resurrection of a god and the inclusion and active participation of the priest and congregation, its phenomenology may legitimately be brought into line with other fundamentally similar, though more primitive, religious customs. This always involves the risk that sensitive people will find it unpleasant when "small things are compared with great." In fairness to the primitive psyche, however, I would like to emphasize that the "holy dread" of civilized man differs but little from the awe of the primitive, and that the God who is present and active in the mystery is a mystery for both. No matter how crass the outward differences, the similarity or equivalence of meaning should not be overlooked.

4. THE PSYCHOLOGY OF THE MASS

I. GENERAL REMARKS ON THE SACRIFICE

376 Whereas I kept to the Church's interpretation when discussing the transformation rite in section 2, in the present section I shall treat this interpretation as a symbol. Such a procedure does not imply any evaluation of the content of religious belief. Scientific criticism must, of course, adhere to the view that when something is held as an opinion, thought to be true, or believed, it does not posit the existence of any real fact other than a psychological one. But that does not mean that a *mere nothing* has been produced. Rather, expression has been given to the psychic reality underlying the statement of the belief or rite as its empirical basis. When psychology "explains" a statement of this kind, it does not, in the first place, deprive the *object* of this statement of any reality—on the contrary, it is granted a psychic reality—and in the second place the intended metaphysical *statement* is not, on that account, turned into an hypostasis, since it was never anything more than a psychic phenomenon. Its specifically "metaphysical" coloration indicates that its object is beyond the reach of human perception and understanding except in its psychic mode of manifestation, and therefore cannot be judged. But every science reaches its end in the unknowable. Yet it would not be a science at all if it

regarded its temporary limitations as definitive and denied the existence of anything outside them. No science can consider its hypotheses to be the final truth.

377 The psychological explanation and the metaphysical statement do not contradict one another any more than, shall we say, the physicist's explanation of matter contradicts the as yet unknown or unknowable nature of matter. The very existence of a belief has in itself the reality of a psychic fact. Just what we posit by the concept "psyche" is simply unknowable, for psychology is in the unfortunate position where the observer and the observed are ultimately identical. Psychology has no Archimedean point outside, since all perception is of a psychic nature and we have only indirect knowledge of what is non-psychic.

378 The ritual event that takes place in the Mass has a dual aspect, human and divine. From the human point of view, gifts are offered to God at the altar, signifying at the same time the self-oblation of the priest and the congregation. The ritual act consecrates both the gifts and the givers. It commemorates and represents the Last Supper which our Lord took with his disciples, the whole Incarnation, Passion, death, and resurrection of Christ. But from the divine point of view this anthropomorphic action is only the outer shell or husk in which what is really happening is not a human action at all but a divine event. For an instant the life of Christ, eternally existent outside time, becomes visible and is unfolded in temporal succession, but in condensed form, in the sacred action: Christ incarnates as a man under the aspect of the offered substances, he suffers, is killed, is laid in the sepulchre, breaks the power of the underworld, and rises again in glory. In the utterance of the words of consecration the Godhead intervenes, Itself acting and truly present, and thus proclaims that the central event in the Mass is Its act of grace, in which the priest has only the significance of a minister. The same applies to the congregation and the offered substances: they are all ministering causes of the sacred event. The presence of the Godhead binds all parts of the sacrificial act into a mystical unity, so that it is God himself who offers himself as a sacrifice in the substances, in the priest, and in the congregation, and who, in the human form of the Son, offers himself as an atonement to the Father.

379 Although this act is an eternal happening taking place within the divinity, man is nevertheless included in it as an essential component, firstly because God clothes himself in our human nature, and secondly because he needs the ministering co-operation of the priest and congregation, and even the material substances of bread and wine which have a special significance for man. Although God the Father is of one nature with God the Son, he appears in time on the one hand as the eternal Father and on the other hand as a man with limited earthly existence. Mankind as a whole is included in God's human nature, which is why man is also included in the sacrificial act. Just as, in the sacrificial act, God is both *agens* and *patiens,* so too is man according to his limited capacity. The *causa efficiens* of the transubstantiation is a spontaneous act of God's grace. Ecclesiastical doctrine insists on this view and even tends to attribute the preparatory action of the priest, indeed the very existence of the rite, to divine prompting,[1] rather than to slothful human nature with its load of original sin. This view is of the utmost importance for a psychological understanding of the Mass. Wherever the magical aspect of a rite tends to prevail, it brings the rite nearer to satisfying the individual ego's blind greed for power, and thus breaks up the mystical body of the Church into separate units. Where, on the other hand, the rite is conceived as the action of God himself, the human participants have only an instrumental or "ministering" significance. The Church's view therefore presupposes the following psychological situation: human consciousness (represented by the priest and congregation) is confronted with an autonomous event which, taking place on a "divine" and "timeless" plane transcending consciousness, is in no way dependent on human action, but which impels man to act by seizing upon him as an instrument and making him the exponent of a "divine" happening. In the ritual action man places himself at the disposal of an autonomous and "eternal" agency operating outside the categories of human consciousness—*si parva licet componere magnis*—in much the same way that a good actor does not merely represent the drama, but allows himself to be overpowered by the genius of the dramatist. The beauty of the ritual action is one of its

[1] John 6:44: "No man can come to me, except the Father which hath sent me draw him."

essential properties, for man has not served God rightly unless he has also served him in beauty. Therefore the rite has no practical utility, for that would be making it serve a purpose—a purely human category. But everything divine is an end-in-itself, perhaps the only legitimate end-in-itself we know. How something eternal can "act" at all is a question we had better not touch, for it is simply unanswerable. Since man, in the action of the Mass, is a tool (though a tool of his own free will), he is not in a position to know anything about the hand which guides him. The hammer cannot discover within itself the power which makes it strike. It is something outside, something autonomous, which seizes and moves him. What happens in the consecration is essentially a miracle, and is meant to be so, for otherwise we should have to consider whether we were not conjuring up God by magic, or else lose ourselves in philosophical wonder how anything eternal can act at all, since action is a process in time with a beginning, a middle, and an end. It is necessary that the transubstantiation should be a cause of wonder and a miracle which man can in no wise comprehend. It is a *mysterium* in the sense of a δρώμενον and δεικνύμενον, a secret that is acted and displayed. The ordinary man is not conscious of anything in himself that would cause him to perform a "mystery." He can only do so if and when *it* seizes upon *him*. This seizure, or rather the sensed or presumed existence of a power outside consciousness which seizes him, is the miracle par excellence, really and truly a miracle when one considers *what* is being represented. What in the world could induce us to represent an absolute impossibility? What is it that for thousands of years has wrung from man the greatest spiritual effort, the loveliest works of art, the profoundest devotion, the most heroic self-sacrifice, and the most exacting service? What else but a miracle? It is a miracle which is not man's to command; for as soon as he tries to work it himself, or as soon as he philosophizes about it and tries to comprehend it intellectually, the bird is flown. A miracle is something that arouses man's wonder precisely because it seems inexplicable. And indeed, from what we know of human nature we could never explain why men are constrained to such statements and to such beliefs. (I am thinking here of the impossible statements made by all religions.) There must be some compelling reason for this, even though it is not to be found in ordinary experience. The very absurdity and impossibility of the statements vouches for the existence of this reason. That is the real ground for belief, as was formulated most brilliantly in Tertullian's "prorsus credibile, quia ineptum."[2] An improbable opinion has to submit sooner or later to correction. But the statements of religion are the most improbable of all and yet they persist for thousands of years.[3] Their wholly unexpected vitality proves the existence of a sufficient cause which has so far eluded scientific investigation. I can, as a psychologist, only draw attention to this fact and emphasize my belief that there are no facile "nothing but" explanations for psychic phenomena of this kind.

380 The dual aspect of the Mass finds expression not only in the contrast between human and divine action, but also in the dual aspect of God and the God-man, who, although they are by nature a unity, nevertheless represent a duality in the ritual drama. Without this "dichotomy of God," if I may use such a term, the whole act of sacrifice would be inconceivable and would lack actuality. According to the Christian view God has never ceased to be God, not even when he appeared in human form in the temporal order. The Christ of the Johannine gospel declares: "I and my Father are one. He that hath seen me hath seen the Father" (John 10:30, 14:9). And yet on the Cross Christ cries out: "My God, my God, why hast thou forsaken me?" This contradiction must exist if the formula "very God and very man" is psychologically true. And if it is true, then the different sayings of Christ are in no sense a contradiction. Being "very man" means being at an extreme remove and utterly different from God. "De profundis clamavi ad te, Domine"—this cry demonstrates both, the remoteness and the nearness, the outermost darkness and the dazzling spark of the Divine. God in his humanity is presumably so far from himself that he has to seek himself through absolute self-surrender. And where would God's wholeness be if he could not be the "wholly

2 "Et mortuus est Dei filius, prorsus credibile est, quia ineptum est. Et sepultus resurrexit; certum est, quia impossibile est" (And the Son of God is dead, which is to be believed because it is absurd. And buried He rose again, which is certain because it is impossible). Migne, *P.L.*, vol. 2, col. 751.

3 The audacity of Tertullian's argument is undeniable, and so is its danger, but that does not detract from its psychological truth.

other"? Accordingly it is with some psychological justification, so it seems to me, that when the Gnostic Nous fell into the power of Physis he assumed the dark chthonic form of the serpent, and the Manichaean "Original Man" in the same situation actually took on the qualities of the Evil One. In Tibetan Buddhism all gods without exception have a peaceful and a wrathful aspect, for they reign over all the realms of being. The dichotomy of God into divinity and humanity and his return to himself in the sacrificial act hold out the comforting doctrine that in man's own darkness there is hidden a light that shall once again return to its source, and that this light actually *wanted* to descend into the darkness in order to deliver the Enchained One who languishes there, and lead him to light everlasting. All this belongs to the stock of pre-Christian ideas, being none other than the doctrine of the "Man of Light," the Anthropos or Original Man, which the sayings of Christ in the gospels assume to be common knowledge.

II. THE PSYCHOLOGICAL MEANING OF SACRIFICE

(a) *The Sacrificial Gifts*

381 Kramp, in his book on the Roman liturgy, makes the following observations about the substances symbolizing the sacrifice:

> Now bread and wine are not only the ordinary means of subsistence for a large portion of humanity, they are also to be had all over the earth (which is of the greatest significance as regards the world-wide spread of Christianity). Further, the two together constitute the perfect food of man, who needs both solid and liquid sustenance. Because they can be so regarded as the typical food of man, they are best fitted to serve as a symbol of human life and human personality, a fact which throws significant light on the gift-symbol.[4]

382 It is not immediately apparent why precisely bread and wine should be a "symbol of human life and human personality." This interpretation looks very like a conclusion *a posteriori* from the special meaning which attaches to these substances in the Mass. In that case the meaning would be due to the liturgy and not to the substances themselves, for no one could imagine that

[4] *Die Opferanschauungen,* p. 55.

bread and wine, in themselves, signify human life or human personality. But, in so far as bread and wine are important products of culture, they do express a vital human striving. They represent a definite cultural achievement which is the fruit of attention, patience, industry, devotion, and laborious toil. The words "our daily bread" express man's anxious care for his existence. By producing bread he makes his life secure. But in so far as he "does not live by bread alone," bread is fittingly accompanied by wine, whose cultivation has always demanded a special degree of attention and much painstaking work. Wine, therefore, is equally an expression of cultural achievement. Where wheat and the vine are cultivated, civilized life prevails. But where agriculture and vine-growing do not exist, there is only the uncivilized life of nomads and hunters.

383 So in offering bread and wine man is in the first instance offering up the products of his culture, the best, as it were, that human industry produces. But the "best" can be produced only by the best in man, by his conscientiousness and devotion. Cultural products can therefore easily stand for the psychological conditions of their production, that is, for those human virtues which alone make man capable of civilization.[5]

384 As to the special nature of these substances, bread is undoubtedly a food. There is a popular saying that wine "fortifies," though not in the same sense as food "sustains." It stimulates and "makes glad the heart of man" by virtue of a certain volatile substance which has always been called "spirit." It is thus, unlike innocuous water, an "inspiriting" drink, for a spirit or god dwells within it and produces the ecstasy of intoxication. The wine miracle at Cana was the same as the miracle in the temple of Dionysus, and it is profoundly significant that, on the Damascus Chalice, Christ is enthroned among vine tendrils like Dionysus himself.[6] Bread therefore represents the physical means of subsistence, and wine the spiritual. The offering up of bread and wine is the offering of both the physical and the spiritual fruits of civilization.

[5] My reason for saying this is that every symbol has an objective and a subjective—or psychic—origin, so that it can be interpreted on the "objective level" as well as on the "subjective level." This is a consideration of some importance in dream-analysis. Cf. *Psychological Types,* Defs. 38 and 50.

[6] Further material in Eisler, *Orpheus—the Fisher,* pp. 280f.

385 But, however sensible he was of the care and labour lavished upon them, man could hardly fail to observe that these cultivated plants grew and flourished according to an inner law of their own, and that there was a power at work in them which he compared to his own life breath or vital spirit. Frazer has called this principle, not unjustly, the "corn spirit." Human initiative and toil are certainly necessary, but even more necessary, in the eyes of primitive man, is the correct and careful performance of the ceremonies which sustain, strengthen, and propitiate the vegetation numen.[7] Grain and wine therefore have something in the nature of a soul, a specific life principle which makes them appropriate symbols not only of man's cultural achievements, but also of the seasonally dying and resurgent god who is their life spirit. Symbols are never simple—only signs and allegories are simple. The symbol always covers a complicated situation which is so far beyond the grasp of language that it cannot be expressed at all in any unambiguous manner.[8] Thus the grain and wine symbols have a fourfold layer of meaning:

1. as agricultural products;
2. as products requiring special processing (bread from grain, wine from grapes);
3. as expressions of psychological achievement (work, industry, patience, devotion, etc.) and of human vitality in general;
4. as manifestations of mana or of the vegetation daemon.

386 From this list it can easily be seen that a symbol is needed to sum up such a complicated physical and psychic situation. The simplest symbolical formula for this is "bread and wine," giving these words the original complex significance which they have always had for tillers of the soil.

(*b*) *The Sacrifice*

387 It is clear from the foregoing that the sacrificial gift is symbolic, and that it embraces everything which is expressed by the symbol, namely the physical product, the processed substance, the psychological achievement, and the autonomous, daemonic life principle of cultivated plants. The value of the gift is en-

7 Similarly, in hunting, the *rites d'entrée* are more important than the hunt itself, for on these rites the success of the hunt depends.

8 Cf. *Psychological Types,* Def. 51.

hanced when it is the best or the first fruits. Since bread and wine are the best that agriculture can offer, they are by the same token man's best endeavour. In addition, bread symbolizes the visible manifestation of the divine numen which dies and rises again, and wine the presence of a pneuma which promises intoxication and ecstasy.[9] The classical world thought of this pneuma as Dionysus, particularly the suffering Dionysus Zagreus, whose divine substance is distributed throughout the whole of nature. In short, what is sacrificed under the forms of bread and wine is nature, man, and God, all combined in the unity of the symbolic gift.

388 The offering of so significant a gift at once raises the question: Does it lie within man's power to offer such a gift at all? Is he psychologically competent to do so? The Church says no, since she maintains that the sacrificing priest is Christ himself. But, since man is included in the gift—included, as we have seen, twice over—the Church also says yes, though with qualifications. On the side of the sacrificer there is an equally complicated, symbolic state of affairs, for the symbol is Christ himself, who is both the sacrificer and the sacrificed. This symbol likewise has several layers of meaning which I shall proceed to sort out in what follows.

389 The act of making a sacrifice consists in the first place in giving something which belongs to me. Everything which belongs to me bears the stamp of "mineness," that is, it has a subtle identity with my ego. This is vividly expressed in certain primitive languages, where the suffix of animation is added to an object—a canoe, for instance—when it belongs to me, but not when it belongs to somebody else. The affinity which all the things bearing the stamp of "mineness" have with my personality is aptly characterized by Lévy-Bruhl[10] as *participation mystique*. It is an irrational, unconscious identity, arising from the fact that anything which comes into contact with me is not only itself, but also a symbol. This symbolization comes about firstly because every human being has unconscious contents, and secondly because every object has an unknown side. Your watch, for instance. Unless you are a watchmaker, you would hardly presume to say that you know how it works. Even if you do, you wouldn't know anything about the molecular structure of the

9 Leisegang, *Der Heilige Geist,* pp. 248ff.

10 *How Natives Think.*

steel unless you happened to be a mineralogist or a physicist. And have you ever heard of a scientist who knew how to repair his pocket watch? But where two unknowns come together, it is impossible to distinguish between them. The unknown in man and the unknown in the thing fall together in one. Thus there arises an unconscious identity which sometimes borders on the grotesque. No one is permitted to touch what is "mine," much less use it. One is affronted if "my" things are not treated with sufficient respect. I remember once seeing two Chinese rickshaw boys engaged in furious argument. Just as they were about to come to blows, one of them gave the other's rickshaw a violent kick, thus putting an end to the quarrel. So long as they are unconscious our unconscious contents are always projected, and the projection fixes upon everything "ours," inanimate objects as well as animals and people. And to the extent that "our" possessions are projection carriers, they are *more* than what they are in themselves, and function as such. They have acquired several layers of meaning and are therefore symbolical, though this fact seldom or never reaches consciousness. In reality, our psyche spreads far beyond the confines of the conscious mind, as was apparently known long ago to the old alchemist who said that the soul was for the greater part outside the body.[11]

390 When, therefore, I give away something that is "mine," what I am giving is essentially a symbol, a thing of many meanings; but, owing to my unconsciousness of its symbolic character, it adheres to my ego, because it is part of my personality. Hence there is, explicitly or implicitly, a personal claim bound up with every gift. There is always an unspoken "give that thou mayest receive." Consequently the gift always carries with it a personal intention, for the mere giving of it is not a sacrifice. It only becomes a sacrifice if I give up the implied intention of receiving something in return. If it is to be a true sacrifice, the gift must be given as if it were being destroyed.[12] Only then is it possible

11 Michael Sendivogius, "Tractatus de sulphure" (16th cent.), in the *Musaeum hermeticum* (1678), p. 617: "[Anima] quae extra corpus multa profundissima imaginatur" ([The soul] which imagines many things of the utmost profundity outside the body).

12 The parallel to this is total destruction of the sacrificial gift by burning, or by throwing it into water or into a pit.

for the egoistic claim to be given up. Were the bread and wine simply given without any consciousness of an egoistic claim, the fact that it was unconscious would be no excuse, but would on the contrary be sure proof of the existence of a *secret* claim. Because of its egoistic nature, the offering would then inevitably have the character of a magical act of propitiation, with the unavowed purpose and tacit expectation of purchasing the good will of the Deity. That is an ethically worthless simulacrum of sacrifice, and in order to avoid it the giver must at least make himself sufficiently conscious of his identity with the gift to recognize how far he is *giving himself up* in giving the gift. In other words, out of the natural state of identity with what is "mine" there grows the ethical task of sacrificing oneself, or at any rate that part of oneself which is identical with the gift. One ought to realize that when one gives or surrenders oneself there are corresponding claims attached, the more so the less one knows of them. The conscious realization of this alone guarantees that the giving is a real sacrifice. For if I know and admit that I am giving myself, forgoing myself, and do not want to be repaid for it, then I have sacrificed my claim, and thus a part of myself. Consequently, all absolute giving, a giving which is a total loss from the start, is a self-sacrifice. Ordinary giving for which no return is received is felt as a loss; but a sacrifice is meant to be like a loss, so that one may be sure that the egoistic claim no longer exists. Therefore the gift should be given as if it were being destroyed. But since the gift represents myself, I have in that case destroyed myself, given myself away without expectation of return. Yet, looked at in another way, this intentional loss is also a gain, for if you can give yourself it proves that you possess yourself. Nobody can give what he has not got. So anyone who can sacrifice himself and forgo his claim must have had it; in other words, he must have been conscious of the claim. This presupposes an act of considerable self-knowledge, lacking which one remains permanently unconscious of such claims. It is therefore quite logical that the confession of sin should come before the rite of transformation in the Mass. The self-examination is intended to make one conscious of the selfish claim bound up with every gift, so that it may be consciously given up; otherwise the gift is no sacrifice. The sacrifice proves that you possess yourself, for it does not mean just letting yourself be passively taken: it is a conscious and deliberate self-surrender, which proves that you have full control of yourself, that is, of your ego. The ego thus becomes the object of a moral act, for "I" am making a decision on behalf of an authority which is supraordinate to my ego nature. I am, as it were, deciding against my ego and renouncing my claim. The possibility of self-renunciation is an established psychological fact whose philosophical implications I do not propose to discuss. Psychologically, it means that the ego is a relative quantity which can be subsumed under various supraordinate authorities. What are these authorities? They are not to be equated outright with collective moral consciousness, as Freud wanted to do with his superego, but rather with certain psychic conditions which existed in man from the beginning and are not acquired by experience. Behind a man's actions there stands neither public opinion nor the moral code,[13] but the personality of which he is still unconscious. Just as a man still is what he always was, so he already is what he will become. The conscious mind does not embrace the totality of a man, for this totality consists only partly of his conscious contents, and for the other and far greater part, of his unconscious, which is of indefinite extent with no assignable limits. In this totality the conscious mind is contained like a smaller circle within a larger one. Hence it is quite possible for the ego to be made into an object, that is to say, for a more compendious personality to emerge in the course of development and take the ego into its service. Since this growth of personality comes out of the unconscious, which is by definition unlimited, the extent of the personality now gradually realizing itself cannot in practice be limited either. But, unlike the Freudian superego, it is still individual. It is in fact individuality in the highest sense, and therefore theoretically limited, since no individual can possibly display *every* quality. (I have called this process of realization the "individuation process.") So far as the personality is still potential, it can be called transcendent, and

13 If there were really nothing behind him but collective standards of value on the one hand and natural instincts on the other, every breach of morality would be simply a rebellion of instinct. In that case valuable and meaningful innovations would be impossible, for the instincts are the oldest and most conservative element in man and beast alike. Such a view forgets the creative instinct which, although it can behave like an instinct, is seldom found in nature and is confined almost exclusively to *Homo sapiens*.

so far as it is unconscious, it is indistinguishable from all those things that carry its projections—in other words, the unconscious personality merges with our environment in accordance with the above-named *participation mystique*. This fact is of the greatest practical importance because it renders intelligible the peculiar symbols through which this projected entity expresses itself in dreams. By this I mean the symbols of the outside world and the cosmic symbols. These form the psychological basis for the conception of man as a microcosm, whose fate, as we know, is bound up with the macrocosm through the astrological components of his character.

391 The term "self" seemed to me a suitable one for this unconscious substrate, whose actual exponent in consciousness is the ego. The ego stands to the self as the moved to the mover, or as object to subject, because the determining factors which radiate out from the self surround the ego on all sides and are therefore supraordinate to it. The self, like the unconscious, is an *a priori* existent out of which the ego evolves. It is, so to speak, an unconscious prefiguration of the ego. It is not I who create myself, rather I happen to myself. This realization is of fundamental importance for the psychology of religious phenomena, which is why Ignatius Loyola started off his *Spiritual Exercises* with "Homo creatus est" as their "fundamentum." But, fundamental as it is, it can be only half the psychological truth. If it were the whole truth it would be tantamount to determinism, for if man were merely a creature that came into being as a result of something already existing unconsciously, he would have no freedom and there would be no point in consciousness. Psychology must reckon with the fact that despite the causal nexus man does enjoy a feeling of freedom, which is identical with autonomy of consciousness. However much the ego can be proved to be dependent and preconditioned, it cannot be convinced that it has no freedom. An absolutely preformed consciousness and a totally dependent ego would be a pointless farce, since everything would proceed just as well or even better unconsciously. The existence of ego consciousness has meaning only if it is free and autonomous. By stating these facts we have, it is true, established an antinomy, but we have at the same time given a picture of things as they are. There are temporal, local, and individual differences in the degree of dependence and freedom. In reality

both are always present: the supremacy of the self and the hybris of consciousness.

392 This conflict between conscious and unconscious is at least brought nearer to a solution through our becoming aware of it. Such an act of realization is presupposed in the act of self-sacrifice. The ego must make itself conscious of its claim, and the self must cause the ego to renounce it. This can happen in two ways:

393 1. I renounce my claim in consideration of a general moral principle, namely that one must not expect repayment for a gift. In this case the "self" coincides with public opinion and the moral code. It is then identical with Freud's superego and for this reason it is projected into the environment and therefore remains unconscious as an autonomous factor.

394 2. I renounce my claim because I feel impelled to do so for painful inner reasons which are not altogether clear to me. These reasons give me no particular moral satisfaction; on the contrary, I even feel some resistance to them. But I must yield to the power which suppresses my egoistic claim. Here the self is integrated; it is withdrawn from projection and has become perceptible as a determining psychic factor. The objection that in this case the moral code is simply unconscious must be ruled out, because I am perfectly well aware of the moral criticism against which I would have to assert my egoism. Where the ego wish clashes with the moral standard, it is not easy to show that the tendency which suppresses it is individual and not collective. But where it is a case of conflicting loyalties, or we find ourselves in a situation of which the classic example is Hosea's marriage with the harlot, then the ego wish coincides with the collective moral standard, and Hosea would have been bound to accuse Jehovah of immorality. Similarly, the unjust steward would have had to admit his guilt. Jesus took a different view.[14] Experiences of this kind make it clear that the self cannot be equated either with collective morality or with natural instinct, but must be conceived as a determining factor whose nature is individual and unique. The superego is a necessary and unavoidable substitute for the experience of the self.

14 To the defiler of the Sabbath he said: "Man, if indeed thou knowest what thou doest, thou art blessed; but if thou knowest not, thou art cursed, and a transgressor of the law." James, *The Apocryphal New Testament*, p. 33.

95 These two ways of renouncing one's egoistic claim reveal not only a difference of attitude, but also a difference of situation. In the first case the situation need not affect me personally and directly; in the second, the gift must necessarily be a very personal one which seriously affects the giver and forces him to overcome himself. In the one case it is merely a question, say, of going to Mass; in the other it is more like Abraham's sacrifice of his son or Christ's decision in Gethsemane. The one may be felt very earnestly and experienced with all piety, but the other is the real thing.[15]

96 So long as the self is unconscious, it corresponds to Freud's superego and is a source of perpetual moral conflict. If, however, it is withdrawn from projection and is no longer identical with public opinion, then one is truly one's own yea and nay. The self then functions as a union of opposites and thus constitutes the most immediate experience of the Divine which it is psychologically possible to imagine.[16]

(*c*) *The Sacrificer*

97 What I sacrifice is my own selfish claim, and by doing this I give up myself. Every sacrifice is therefore, to a greater or lesser degree, a self-sacrifice. The degree to which it is so depends on the significance of the gift. If it is of great value to me and touches my most personal feelings, I can be sure that in giving up my egoistic claim I shall challenge my ego personality to revolt. I can also be sure that the power which suppresses this claim, and thus suppresses me, must be the self. Hence it is the self that causes me to make the sacrifice; nay more, it compels me to make it.[17] The self is the sacrificer, and I am the sacrificed gift, the human sacrifice. Let us try for a moment to look into Abraham's soul when he was commanded to sacrifice his only son.

15 In order to avoid misunderstandings, I must emphasize that I am speaking only from personal experience, and not of the mysterious reality which the Mass has for the believer.

16 Cf. the "uniting symbol" in *Psychological Types,* Def. 51.

17 In Indian philosophy we find a parallel in Prajapati and Purusha Narayana. Purusha sacrifices himself at the command of Prajapati, but at bottom the two are identical. Cf. the Shatapatha-Brahmana (Sacred Books of the East, XLIV, pp. 172ff.); also the Rig-Veda, X, 90 (trans. by Macnicol, pp. 28–29).

Quite apart from the compassion he felt for his child, would not a father in such a position feel himself as the victim, and feel that he was plunging the knife into his own breast? He would be at the same time the sacrificer and the sacrificed.

398 Now, since the relation of the ego to the self is like that of the son to the father, we can say that when the self calls on us to sacrifice ourselves, it is really carrying out the sacrificial act on itself. We know more or less what this act means to us, but what it means to the self is not so clear. As the self can only be comprehended by us in particular acts, but remains concealed from us as a whole because it is more comprehensive than we are, all we can do is to draw conclusions from the little of the self that we can experience. We have seen that a sacrifice only takes place when we feel the self actually carrying it out on ourselves. We may also venture to surmise that in so far as the self stands to us in the relation of father to son, the self in some sort feels our sacrifice as a sacrifice of itself. From that sacrifice we gain ourselves—our "self"—for we have only what we give. But what does the self gain? We see it entering into manifestation, freeing itself from unconscious projection, and, as it grips us, entering into our lives and so passing from unconsciousness into consciousness, from potentiality into actuality. What it is in the diffuse unconscious state we do not know; we only know that in becoming ourself it has become man.

399 This process of becoming human is represented in dreams and inner images as the putting together of many scattered units, and sometimes as the gradual emergence and clarification of something that was always there.[18] The speculations of alchemy, and also of some Gnostics, revolve round this process. It is

[18] This contradiction is unavoidable because the concept of the self allows only of antinomial statements. The self is by definition an entity more comprehensive than the conscious personality. Consequently the latter cannot pass any comprehensive judgment on the self; any judgment and any statement about it is incomplete and has to be supplemented (but not nullified) by a conditioned negative. If I assert, "The self exists," I must supplement this by saying, "But it seems not to exist." For the sake of completeness I must also invert the proposition and say, "The self does not exist, but yet seems to exist." Actually, this inversion is superfluous in view of the fact that the self is not a philosophical concept like Kant's "thing-in-itself," but an empirical concept of psychology, and can therefore be hypostatized if the above precautions are taken.

likewise expressed in Christian dogma, and more particularly in the transformation mystery of the Mass. The psychology of this process makes it easier to understand why, in the Mass, man appears as both the sacrificer and the sacrificed gift, and why it is not man who is these things, but God who is both; why God becomes the suffering and dying man, and why man, through partaking of the Glorified Body, gains the assurance of resurrection and becomes aware of his participation in Godhead.

400 As I have already suggested, the integration or humanization of the self is initiated from the conscious side by our making ourselves aware of our selfish aims; we examine our motives and try to form as complete and objective a picture as possible of our own nature. It is an act of self-recollection, a gathering together of what is scattered, of all the things in us that have never been properly related, and a coming to terms with oneself with a view to achieving full consciousness. (Unconscious self-sacrifice is merely an accident, not a moral act.) Self-recollection, however, is about the hardest and most repellent thing there is for man, who is predominantly unconscious. Human nature has an invincible dread of becoming more conscious of itself. What nevertheless drives us to it is the self, which demands sacrifice by sacrificing itself to us. Conscious realization or the bringing together of the scattered parts is in one sense an act of the ego's will, but in another sense it is a spontaneous manifestation of the self,[19] which was always there. Individuation appears, on the one hand, as the synthesis of a new unity which previously consisted of scattered particles, and on the other hand, as the revelation of something which existed before the ego and is in fact its father or creator and also its totality. Up to a point we create the self by making ourselves conscious of our unconscious contents, and to that extent it is our son. This is why the alchemists called their incorruptible substance—which means precisely the self—the *filius philosophorum*. But we are forced to make this effort by the unconscious presence of the self, which is all the time urging us to overcome our unconsciousness. From that point of view the self is the father. This accounts for certain alchemical terms, such as Mercurius Senex (Hermes Trismegistus) and Saturnus, who in Gnosticism was regarded as both

[19] In so far as it is the self that actuates the ego's self-recollection.

greybeard and youth, just as Mercurius was in alchemy. These psychological connections are seen most clearly in the ancient conceptions of the Original Man, the Protanthropos, and the Son of Man. Christ as the Logos is from all eternity, but in his human form he is the "Son of Man." [20] As the Logos, he is the world-creating principle. This corresponds with the relation of the self to consciousness, without which no world could be perceived at all. The Logos is the real *principium individuationis,* because everything proceeds from it, and because everything which is, from crystal to man, exists only in individual form. In the infinite variety and differentiation of the phenomenal world is expressed the essence of the *auctor rerum.* As a correspondence we have, on the one hand, the indefiniteness and unlimited extent of the unconscious self (despite its individuality and uniqueness), its creative relation to individual consciousness, and, on the other hand, the individual human being as a mode of its manifestation. Ancient philosophy paralleled this idea with the legend of the dismembered Dionysus, who, as creator, is the ἀμέριστος (undivided) νοῦς, and, as the creature, the μεμερισμένος (divided) νοῦς.[21] Dionysus is distributed throughout the whole of nature, and just as Zeus once devoured the throbbing heart of the god, so his worshippers tore wild animals to pieces in order to reintegrate his dismembered spirit. The gathering together of the light-substance in Barbelo-Gnosis and in Manichaeism points in the same direction. The psychological equivalent of this is the integration of the self through conscious assimilation of the split-off contents. Self-recollection is a gathering together of the self. It is in this sense that we have to understand the instructions which Monoimos gives to Theophrastus:

Seek him [God] from out thyself, and learn who it is that taketh possession of everything in thee, saying: *my* god, *my* spirit [νοῦς], *my* understanding, *my* soul, *my* body; and learn whence is sorrow and joy, and love and hate, and waking though one would not, and sleeping though one would not, and getting angry though one

20 If I use the unhistorical term "self" for the corresponding processes in the psyche, I do so out of a conscious desire not to trespass on other preserves, but to confine myself exclusively to the field of empirical psychology.

21 Firmicus Maternus, *De errore profanarum religionum,* 7, 8.

would not, and falling in love though one would not. And if thou shouldst closely investigate these things, thou wilt find Him in thyself, the One and the Many, like to that little point, for it is from thee that he hath his origin.[22]

401 Self-reflection or—what comes to the same thing—the urge to individuation gathers together what is scattered and multifarious, and exalts it to the original form of the One, the Primordial Man. In this way our existence as separate beings, our former ego nature, is abolished, the circle of consciousness is widened, and because the paradoxes have been made conscious the sources of conflict are dried up. This approximation to the self is a kind of repristination or apocatastasis, in so far as the self has an "incorruptible" or "eternal" character on account of its being pre-existent to consciousness.[23] This feeling is expressed in the words from the *benedictio fontis:* "Et quos aut sexus in corpore aut aetas discernit in tempore, omnes in unam pariat gratia mater infantiam" (And may Mother Grace bring forth into one infancy all those whom sex has separated in the body, or age in time).

402 The figure of the divine sacrificer corresponds feature for feature to the empirical modes of manifestation of the archetype that lies at the root of almost all known conceptions of God. This archetype is not merely a static image, but dynamic, full of movement. It is always a drama, whether in heaven, on earth, or in hell.[24]

(d) *The Archetype of Sacrifice*

403 Comparing the basic ideas of the Mass with the imagery of the Zosimos visions, we find that, despite considerable differences, there is a remarkable degree of similarity. For the sake of clearness I give the similarities and differences in tabular form.

22 Hippolytus, *Elenchos,* VIII, 15.

23 And also on account of the fact that the unconscious is only conditionally bound by space and time. The comparative frequency of telepathic phenomena proves that space and time have only a relative validity for the psyche. Evidence for this is furnished by Rhine's experiments. Cf. my "Synchronicity."

24 The word "hell" may strike the reader as odd in this connection. I would, however, recommend him to study the brothel scene in James Joyce's *Ulysses,* or James Hogg's *The Private Memoirs and Confessions of a Justified Sinner.*

Zosimos	*Mass*
SIMILARITIES	
1. The chief actors are two priests.	1. There is the priest, and Christ the eternal priest.
2. One priest slays the other.	2. The *Mactatio Christi* takes place as the priest pronounces the words of consecration.
3. Other human beings are sacrificed as well.	3. The congregation itself is a sacrificial gift.
4. The sacrifice is a voluntary self-sacrifice.	4. Christ offers himself freely as a sacrifice.
5. It is a painful death.	5. He suffers in the sacrificial act.
6. The victim is dismembered.	6. Breaking of the Bread.
7. There is a *thysia*.	7. Offering up of incense.
8. The priest eats his own flesh.	8. Christ drinks his own blood (St. Chrysostom).
9. He is transformed into spirit.	9. The substances are transformed into the body and blood of Christ.
10. A shining white figure appears, like the midday sun.	10. The Host is shown as the Beatific Vision ("Quaesivi vultum tuum, Domine") in the greater elevation.
11. Production of the "divine water."	11. The Grace conferred by the Mass; similarity of water chalice and font; water a symbol of grace.
DIFFERENCES	
1. The whole sacrificial process is an individual dream vision, a fragment of the unconscious depicting itself in dream consciousness.	1. The Mass is a conscious artifact, the product of many centuries and many minds.
2. The dreamer is only a spectator of the symbolic action.	2. Priest and congregation both participate in the mystery.
3. The action is a bloody and gruesome human sacrifice.	3. Nothing obnoxious; the *mactatio* itself is not mentioned. There is only the bloodless sacrifice of bread and wine (*incruente immolatur!*).

4. The sacrifice is accompanied by a scalping.	4. Nothing comparable.
5. It is also performed on a dragon, and is therefore an animal sacrifice.	5. Symbolic sacrifice of the Lamb.
6. The flesh is roasted.	6. The substances are spiritually transformed.
7. The meaning of the sacrifice is the production of the divine water, used for the transmutation of metals and, mystically, for the birth of the self.	7. The meaning of the Mass is the communion of the living Christ with his flock.
8. What is transformed in the vision is presumably the planetary demon Saturn, the supreme Archon (who is related to the God of the Hebrews). It is the dark, heavy, material principle in man—*hyle*—which is transformed into pneuma.	8. What is transformed in the Mass is God, who as Father begat the Son in human form, suffered and died in that form, and rose up again to his origin.

404 The gross concretism of the vision is so striking that one might easily feel tempted, for aesthetic and other reasons, to drop the comparison with the Mass altogether. If I nevertheless venture to bring out certain analogies, I do so not with the rationalistic intention of devaluing the sacred ceremony by putting it on a level with a piece of pagan nature worship. If I have any aim at all apart from scientific truth, it is to show that the most important mystery of the Catholic Church rests, among other things, on psychic conditions which are deeply rooted in the human soul.

405 The vision, which in all probability has the character of a dream, must be regarded as a spontaneous psychic product that was never consciously intended. Like all dreams, it is a product of nature. The Mass, on the other hand, is a product of man's mind or spirit, and is a definitely conscious proceeding. To use an old but not outmoded nomenclature, we can call the vision *psychic,* and the Mass *pneumatic.* The vision is undifferentiated raw material, while the Mass is a highly differentiated artifact. That is why the one is gruesome and the other beautiful. If the Mass is antique, it is antique in the best sense of the word,

and its liturgy is therefore satisfying to the highest requirements of the present day. In contrast to this, the vision is archaic and primitive, but its symbolism points directly to the fundamental alchemical idea of the incorruptible substance, namely to the self, which is beyond change. The vision is a piece of unalloyed naturalism, banal, grotesque, squalid, horrifying and profound as nature herself. Its meaning is not clear, but it allows itself to be divined with the abysmal uncertainty and ambiguity that pertain to all things nonhuman, suprahuman, and subhuman. The Mass, on the other hand, represents and clearly expresses the Deity itself, and clothes it in the garment of the most beautiful humanity.

406 From all this it is evident that the vision and the Mass are two different things, so different as to be almost incommensurable. But if we could succeed in reconstructing the natural process in the unconscious on which the Mass is psychically based, we should probably obtain a picture which would be rather more commensurable with the vision of Zosimos. According to the view of the Church, the Mass is based on the historical events in the life of Jesus. From this "real" life we can single out certain details that add a few concretistic touches to our picture and thus bring it closer to the vision. For instance, I would mention the scourging, the crowning with thorns, and the clothing in a purple robe, which show Jesus as the archaic sacrificed king. This is further emphasized by the Barabbas episode (the name means "son of the father") which leads to the sacrifice of the king. Then there is the agony of death by crucifixion, a shameful and horrifying spectacle, far indeed from any "incruente immolatur"! The right pleural cavity and probably the right ventricle of the heart were cut open by the spear, so that blood clots and serum flowed out. If we add these details to the process which underlies the Mass, we shall see that they form a striking equivalent to certain archaic and barbarous features of the vision. There are also the fundamental dogmatic ideas to be considered. As is shown by the reference to the sacrifice of Isaac in the prayer *Unde et memores,* the sacrifice has the character not only of a human sacrifice, but the sacrifice of a son—and an *only* son. That is the cruellest and most horrible kind of sacrifice we can imagine, so horrible that, as we know, Abraham

was not required to carry it out.[25] And even if he had carried it out, a stab in the heart with a knife would have been a quick and relatively painless death for the victim. Even the bloody Aztec ceremony of cutting out the heart was a swift death. But the sacrifice of the son which forms the essential feature of the Mass began with scourging and mockery, and culminated in six hours of suspension on a cross to which the victim was nailed hand and foot—not exactly a quick death, but a slow and exquisite form of torture. As if that were not enough, crucifixion was regarded as a disgraceful death for slaves, so that the physical cruelty is balanced by the moral cruelty.

407 Leaving aside for the moment the unity of nature of Father and Son—which it is possible to do because they are two distinct Persons who are not to be confused with one another—let us try to imagine the feelings of a father who saw his son suffering such a death, knowing that it was he himself who had sent him into the enemy's country and deliberately exposed him to this danger. Executions of this kind were generally carried out as an act of revenge or as punishment for a crime, with the idea that both father and son should suffer. The idea of punishment can be seen particularly clearly in the crucifixion between two thieves. The punishment is carried out on God himself, and the model for this execution is the ritual slaying of the king. The king is killed when he shows signs of impotence, or when failure of the crops arouses doubts as to his efficacy. Therefore he is killed in order to improve the condition of his people, just as God is sacrificed for the salvation of mankind.

408 What is the reason for this "punishment" of God? Despite the almost blasphemous nature of this question, we must nevertheless ask it in view of the obviously punitive character of the

25 How Jewish piety reacted to this sacrifice can be seen from the following Talmudic legend: " 'And I,' cried Abraham, 'swear that I will not go down from the altar until you have heard me. When you commanded me to sacrifice my son Isaac you offended against your word, "in Isaac shall your descendants be named." So if ever my descendants offend against you, and you wish to punish them, then remember that you too are not without fault, and forgive them.' 'Very well, then,' replied the Lord, 'there behind you is a ram caught in the thicket with his horns. Offer up that instead of your son Isaac. And if ever your descendants sin against me, and I sit in judgment over them on New Year's Day, let them blow the horn of a ram, that I may remember my words, and temper justice with mercy.' " Fromer and Schnitzer, *Legenden aus dem Talmud*, pp. 34f.

sacrifice. The usual explanation is that Christ was punished for our sins.[26] The dogmatic validity of this answer is not in question here. As I am in no way concerned with the Church's explanation, but only wish to reconstruct the underlying psychic process, we must logically assume the existence of a guilt proportionate to the punishment. If mankind is the guilty party, logic surely demands that mankind should be punished. But if God takes the punishment on himself, he exculpates mankind, and we must then conjecture that it is not mankind that is guilty, but God (which would logically explain why he took the guilt on himself). For reasons that can readily be understood, a satisfactory answer is not to be expected from orthodox Christianity. But such an answer may be found in the Old Testament, in Gnosticism, and in late Catholic speculation. From the Old Testament we know that though Yahweh was a guardian of the law he was not just, and that he suffered from fits of rage which he had every occasion to regret.[27] And from certain Gnostic systems it is clear that the *auctor rerum* was a lower archon who falsely imagined that he had created a perfect world, whereas in fact it was woefully imperfect. On account of his Saturnine disposition this demiurgic archon has affinities with the Jewish Yahweh, who was likewise a world creator. His work was imperfect and did not prosper, but the blame cannot be placed on the creature any more than one can curse the pots for being badly turned out by the potter! This argument led to the Marcionite Reformation and to purging the New Testament of elements derived from the Old. Even as late as the seventeenth century the learned Jesuit, Nicolas Caussin, declared that the unicorn was a fitting symbol for the God of the Old Testament, because in his wrath he reduced the world to confusion like an angry rhinoceros (unicorn), until, overcome by the love of a pure virgin, he was changed in her lap into a God of Love.[28]

26 Isaiah 53:5: "But he was wounded for our transgressions, he was bruised for our iniquities: the chastisement of our peace was upon him; and with his stripes we are healed."

27 See "Answer to Job," in this volume.

28 Caussin, *De symbolica Aegyptiorum sapientia. Polyhistor symbolicus, Electorum symbolorum, et Parabolarum historicarum stromata* (1618), p. 401. Cf. also Philippus Picinelli, *Mondo Simbolico*, p. 299: "Of a truth God, terrible beyond measure, appeared before the world peaceful and wholly tamed after dwelling in the womb of the most blessed Virgin. St. Bonaventura said that Christ was tamed and pacified by the most kindly Mary, so that he should not punish the sinner with eternal death."

409 In these explanations we find the natural logic we missed in the answer of the Church. God's guilt consisted in the fact that, as creator of the world and king of his creatures, he was inadequate and therefore had to submit to the ritual slaying. For primitive man the concrete king was perfectly suited to this purpose, but not for a higher level of civilization with a more spiritual conception of God. Earlier ages could still dethrone their gods by destroying their images or putting them in chains. At a higher level, however, one god could be dethroned only by another god, and when monotheism developed, God could only transform himself.

410 The fact that the transformative process takes the form of a "punishment"—Zosimos uses this very word (κόλασις)—may be due to a kind of rationalization or a need to offer some explanation of its cruelty. Such a need only arises at a higher level of consciousness with developed feeling, which then seeks an adequate reason for the revolting and incomprehensible cruelty of the procedure. (A modern parallel would be the experience of dismemberment in shamanistic initiations.) The readiest conjecture at this level is that some guilt or sin is being punished. In this way the transformation process acquires a moral function that can scarcely be conceived as underlying the original event. It seems more likely that a higher and later level of consciousness found itself confronted with an experience for which no sensible reasons or explanations had ever been given, but which it tried to make intelligible by weaving into it a moral aetiology. It is not difficult to see that dismemberment originally served the purpose of reconstituting the neophyte as a new and more effective human being. Initiation even has the aspect of a healing.[29] In the light of these facts, moral interpretation in terms of punishment seems beside the mark and arouses the suspicion that dismemberment has still not been properly understood. A moral interpretation is inadequate because it fails to understand the contradiction at the heart of its explanation, namely that guilt should be avoided if one doesn't want to be punished. But, for the neophyte, it would be a real sin if he shrank from the torture of initiation. The torture inflicted on him is *not* a punishment but the indispensable means of leading him towards his destiny. Also, these ceremonies often take place at so young an age that a guilt of corresponding proportions is quite out of

29 Eliade, *Shamanism,* esp. chs. II and VII.

the question. For this reason, the moralistic view of suffering as punishment seems to me not only inadequate but misleading. It is obviously a primitive attempt to give a psychological explanation of an age-old archetypal idea that had never before been the object of reflection. Such ideas and rituals, far from ever having been invented, simply happened and were acted long before they were thought. I have seen primitives practising rites of which none of them had the remotest idea what they meant, and in Europe we still find customs whose meaning has always been unconscious. First attempts at explanation usually turn out to be somewhat clumsy.

411 The aspect of torture, then, is correlated with a detached and observing consciousness that has not yet understood the real meaning of dismemberment. What is performed concretely on the sacrificial animal, and what the shaman believes to be actually happening to himself, appears on a higher level, in the vision of Zosimos, as a psychic process in which a product of the unconscious, an homunculus, is cut up and transformed. By all the rules of dream-interpretation, this is an aspect of the observing subject himself; that is to say, Zosimos sees himself as an homunculus, or rather the unconscious represents him as such, as an incomplete, stunted, dwarfish creature who is made of some heavy material (lead or bronze) and thus signifies the "hylical man." Such a one is dark, and sunk in materiality. He is essentially unconscious and therefore in need of transformation and enlightenment. For this purpose his body must be taken apart and dissolved into its constituents, a process known in alchemy as the *divisio, separatio* and *solutio,* and in later treatises as *discrimination* and *self-knowledge.*[30] This psychological process is admittedly painful and for many people a positive torture. But, as always, every step forward along the path of individuation is achieved only at the cost of suffering.

412 In the case of Zosimos there is of course no real consciousness of the transformative process, as is abundantly clear from his own interpretation of the vision: he thought the dream imagery was showing him the "production of the waters." We can see from this that he was still exteriorizing the transformation and did not feel it in any way as an alteration of his own psyche.

30 Particularly in Gerhard Dorn, "Speculativae philosophiae," *Theatrum chemicum,* I (1602), pp. 276f.

413 A similar state of affairs prevails in Christian psychology whenever the rites and dogmas are taken as merely external factors and are not experienced as inner events. But, just as the *imitatio Christi* in general, and the Mass in particular, endeavour to include the believer in the process of transformation, the Mass actually representing him as a sacrificial gift parallel with Christ, so a better understanding of Christianity raises it as high above the sphere of "mind" as the rite of the Mass is above the archaic level of the Zosimos vision. The Mass tries to effect a *participation mystique*—or identity—of priest and congregation with Christ, so that on the one hand the soul is assimilated to Christ and on the other hand the Christ-figure is recollected in the soul. It is a transformation of God and man alike, since the Mass is, at least by implication, a repetition of the whole drama of Incarnation.

III. THE MASS AND THE INDIVIDUATION PROCESS

414 Looked at from the psychological standpoint, Christ, as the Original Man (Son of Man, second Adam, τέλειος ἄνθρωπος), represents a totality which surpasses and includes the ordinary man, and which corresponds to the total personality that transcends consciousness.[31] We have called this personality the "self." Just as, on the more archaic level of the Zosimos vision, the homunculus is transformed into pneuma and exalted, so the mystery of the Eucharist transforms the soul of the empirical man, who is only a part of himself, into his totality, symbolically expressed by Christ. In this sense, therefore, we can speak of the Mass as the *rite of the individuation process.*

415 Reflections of this kind can be found very early on in the old Christian writings, as for instance in the Acts of John, one of the most important of the apocryphal texts that have come down to us.[32] That part of the text with which we are concerned here begins with a description of a mystical "round dance" which Christ instituted before his crucifixion. He told his disciples to hold hands and form a ring, while he himself stood

[31] Cf. my *Aion,* Ch. V.

[32] *The Apocryphal New Testament.* The Acts of John were probably written during the first half of the 2nd cent.

in the centre. As they moved round in a circle, Christ sang a song of praise, from which I would single out the following characteristic verses: [33]

> I will be saved and I will save, Amen.
> I will be loosed and I will loose,[34] Amen.
> I will be wounded and I will wound, Amen.
> I will be begotten and I will beget, Amen.
> I will eat and I will be eaten, Amen.
> . . .
> I will be thought, being wholly spirit, Amen.
> I will be washed and I will wash, Amen.
> Grace paces the round. I will blow the pipe. Dance
> the round all, Amen.
> . . .
> The Eight [ogdoad] sings praises with us, Amen.
> The Twelve paces the round aloft, Amen.
> To each and all it is given to dance, Amen.
> Who joins not the dance mistakes the event, Amen.
> . . .
> I will be united and I will unite, Amen.
> . . .
> A lamp am I to you that perceive me, Amen.
> A mirror am I to you that know me, Amen.
> A door am I to you that knock on me, Amen.
> A way am I to you the wayfarer.

Now as you respond to my dancing, behold yourself in me who speaks . . .

As you dance, ponder what I do, for yours is this human suffering which I will to suffer. For you would be powerless to understand your suffering had I not been sent to you as the Logos by the Father. . . . If you had understood suffering, you would have non-suffering. Learn to suffer, and you shall understand how not to suffer. . . . Understand the Word of Wisdom in me.[35]

416 I would like to interrupt the text here, as we have come to a natural break, and introduce a few psychological remarks. They will help us to understand some further passages that still have

[33] Ibid., pp. 253f., modified.

[34] [Or: I will be freed and I will free.—TRANS.]

[35] Trans. based on James, pp. 253f., and that of Ralph Manheim from the German of Max Pulver, "Jesus' Round Dance and Crucifixion according to the Acts of St. John," in *The Mysteries*, pp. 179f.

to be discussed. Although our text is obviously based on New Testament models, what strikes us most of all is its antithetical and paradoxical style, which has very little in common with the spirit of the Gospels. This feature only appears in a veiled way in the canonical writings, for instance in the parable of the unjust steward (Luke 16), in the Lord's Prayer ("Lead us not into temptation"), in Matthew 10:16 ("Be wise as serpents"), John 10:34 ("Ye are gods"), in the logion of the Codex Bezae to Luke 6:4,[36] in the apocryphal saying "Whoso is near unto me is near unto the fire," and so on. Echoes of the antithetical style can also be found in Matthew 10:26: ". . . . for nothing is covered that will not be revealed, or hidden that will not be known."

417 Paradox is a characteristic of the Gnostic writings. It does more justice to the *unknowable* than clarity can do, for uniformity of meaning robs the mystery of its darkness and sets it up as something that is *known*. That is a usurpation, and it leads the human intellect into hybris by pretending that it, the intellect, has got hold of the transcendent mystery by a cognitive act and has "grasped" it. The paradox therefore reflects a higher level of intellect and, by not forcibly representing the unknowable as known, gives a more faithful picture of the real state of affairs.

418 These antithetical predications show the amount of *reflection* that has gone into the hymn: it formulates the figure of our Lord in a series of paradoxes, as God and man, sacrificer and sacrificed. The latter formulation is important because the hymn was sung just before Jesus was arrested, that is, at about the moment when the synoptic gospels speak of the Last Supper and John—among other things—of the parable of the vine. John, significantly enough, does not mention the Last Supper, and in the Acts of John its place is taken by the "round dance." But the round table, like the round dance, stands for synthesis and union. In the Last Supper this takes the form of participation in the body and blood of Christ, i.e., there is an ingestion and assimilation of the Lord, and in the round dance there is a circular circumambulation round the Lord as the central point. Despite the outward difference of the symbols, they have a common meaning: Christ is taken into the midst of the disciples. But, although the two rites have this common basic meaning,

36 See James, p. 33.

the outward difference between them should not be overlooked. The classical Eucharistic feast follows the synoptic gospels, whereas the one in the Acts of John follows the Johannine pattern. One could almost say that it expresses, in a form borrowed from some pagan mystery feast, a more immediate relationship of the congregation to Christ, after the manner of the Johannine parable: "I am the vine, ye are the branches. He that abideth in me, and I in him, the same bringeth forth much fruit" (John 15:5). This close relationship is represented by the circle and central point: the two parts are indispensable to each other and equivalent. Since olden times the circle with a centre has been a symbol for the Deity, illustrating the wholeness of God incarnate: the single point in the centre and the series of points constituting the circumference. Ritual circumambulation often bases itself quite consciously on the cosmic picture of the starry heavens revolving, on the "dance of the stars," an idea that is still preserved in the comparison of the twelve disciples with the zodiacal constellations, as also in the depictions of the zodiac that are sometimes found in churches, in front of the altar or on the roof of the nave. Some such picture may well have been at the back of the medieval ball-game of pelota that was played in church by the bishop and his clergy.

419 At all events, the aim and effect of the solemn round dance is to impress upon the mind the image of the circle and the centre and the relation of each point along the periphery to that centre.[37] Psychologically this arrangement is equivalent to a mandala and is thus a symbol of the self,[38] the point of reference not only of the individual ego but of all those who are of like mind or who are bound together by fate. The self is not an ego but a supraordinate totality embracing the conscious and the unconscious. But since the latter has no assignable limits and

[37] Another idea of the kind is that every human being is a ray of sunlight. This image occurs in the Spanish poet Jorge Guillén, *Cantico: Fe de Vida,* pp. 24–25 ("Más allá," VI):

> Where could I stray to, where?
> This point is my centre . . .
>
> With this earth and this ocean
> To rise to the infinite:
> One ray more of the sun. (Trans. by J. M. Cohen.)

[38] Cf. *Aion,* Ch. IV.

in its deeper layers is of a collective nature, it cannot be distinguished from that of another individual. As a result, it continually creates that ubiquitous *participation mystique* which is the unity of many, the *one* man in all men. This psychological fact forms the basis for the archetype of the ἄνθρωπος, the Son of Man, the *homo maximus,* the *vir unus,* purusha, etc.[39] Because the unconscious, in fact and by definition, cannot be discriminated as such, the most we can hope to do is to infer its nature from the empirical material. Certain unconscious contents are undoubtedly personal and individual and cannot be attributed to any other individual. But, besides these, there are numerous others that can be observed in almost identical form in many different individuals in no way connected with one another. These experiences suggest that the unconscious has a collective aspect. It is therefore difficult to understand how people today can still doubt the existence of a collective unconscious. After all, nobody would dream of regarding the instincts or human morphology as personal acquisitions or personal caprices. The unconscious is the universal mediator among men. It is in a sense the all-embracing One, or the one psychic substratum common to all. The alchemists knew it as their Mercurius and they called him the mediator in analogy to Christ.[40] Ecclesiastical doctrine says the same thing about Christ, and so, particularly, does our hymn. Its antithetical statements could, however, be interpreted as referring just as well to Mercurius, if not better.

420 For instance, in the first verse, "I will be saved," it is not clear how far the Lord is able to say such a thing of himself, since he is the saviour (σωτήρ) par excellence. Mercurius, on the other hand, the helpful arcane substance of the alchemists, is the world-soul imprisoned in matter and, like the Original Man who fell into the embrace of Physis, is in need of salvation through the labours of the artifex. Mercurius is set free ("loosed") and redeemed; as *aqua permanens* he is also the

39 The universality of this figure may explain why its epiphanies take so many different forms. For instance, it is related in the Acts of John (James, p. 251) that Drusiana saw the Lord once "in the likeness of John" and another time "in that of a youth." The disciple James saw him as a child, but John as an adult. John saw him first as "a small man and uncomely," and then again as one reaching to heaven (p. 251). Sometimes his body felt "material and solid," but sometimes "the substance was immaterial and as if it existed not at all" (p. 252).

40 "The Spirit Mercurius," pt. 2, ch. 9.

classical solvent. "I will be wounded, and I will wound" is clearer: it refers to the wound in Christ's side and to the divisive sword. But Mercurius too, as the arcane substance, is divided or pierced through with the sword (*separatio* and *penetratio*), and wounds himself with the sword or *telum passionis,* the dart of love. The reference to Christ is less clear in the words "I will be begotten, and I will beget." The first statement refers essentially to him in so far as the Son was begotten by the Holy Ghost and not created, but the "begetting" is generally held to be the property of the Holy Ghost and not of Christ as such. It certainly remains a moot point whether Mercurius as the world-soul was begotten or created, but he is unquestionably "vivifying," and in his ithyphallic form as Hermes Kyllenios he is actually the symbol of generation. "Eating" as compared with "being eaten" is not exactly characteristic of Christ, but rather of the devouring dragon, the corrosive Mercurius, who, as the uroboros, also eats himself, like Zosimos's homunculus.

421 "I will be thought," if evangelical at all, is an exclusively Johannine, post-apostolic speculation concerning the nature of the Logos. Hermes was very early considered to be Nous and Logos, and Hermes Trismegistus was actually the Nous of revelation. Mercurius, until well into the seventeenth century, was thought of as the *veritas* hidden in the human body, i.e., in matter, and this truth had to be known by meditation, or by *cogitatio,* reflection. Meditation is an idea that does not occur at all in the New Testament.[41] The *cogitatio* which might possibly correspond to it usually has a negative character and appears as the wicked *cogitatio cordis* of Genesis 6:5 (and 8:21): "Cuncta cogitatio cordis intenta ad malum" (DV: ". . . all the thought of their heart was bent upon evil at all times"; AV: ". . . every imagination of the thoughts of his heart . . ."). In I Peter 4:1 ἔννοια is given as "cogitatio" (DV: ". . . arm yourselves with the same intent"; AV: "same mind"; RSV: "same thought"). "Cogitare" has a more positive meaning in II Corinthians 10:7, where it really means to "bethink oneself," "remember by reflection": "hoc cogitet iterum apud se" ("τοῦτο λογιζέσθω πάλιν ἐφ' ἑαυτοῦ"; DV: "let him reflect within himself";

41 "Haec meditare" (ταῦτα μελέτα) in I Tim. 4:15 has more the meaning of 'see to' or 'attend to' these things. [Both DV and AV have "meditate on these things," but RSV has "practise these duties."—TRANS.]

AV: "let him of himself think this again"; RSV: "let him remind himself"). But this positive thinking in us is of God (II Cor. 3:5: "non quod sufficientes simus cogitare aliquid a nobis, quasi ex nobis"; "οὐχ ὅτι ἀφ' ἑαυτῶν ἱκανοί ἐσμεν λογίσασθαί τι ὡς ἐξ ἑαυτῶν, ἀλλ' ἡ ἱκανότης ἡμῶν ἐκ τοῦ θεοῦ"; DV: "Not that we are sufficient of ourselves to think anything, as from ourselves, but our sufficiency is from God"). The only place where *cogitatio* has the character of a meditation culminating in enlightenment is Acts 10:19: "Petro autem cogitante de visione, dixit Spiritus ei" ("Τοῦ δὲ Πέτρου διενθυμουμένου περὶ τοῦ ὁράματος εἶπεν τὸ πνεῦμα αὐτῷ"; DV: "But while Peter was pondering over the vision, the spirit said to him . . .").

422 Thinking, in the first centuries of our era, was more the concern of the Gnostics than of the Church, for which reason the great Gnostics, such as Basilides and Valentinus, seem almost like Christian theologians with a bent for philosophy. With John's doctrine of the Logos, Christ came to be regarded simultaneously as the Nous and the object of human thought; the Greek text says literally: "Νοηθῆναι θέλω νοῦς ὢν ὅλος" [42] (I will be thought, being wholly spirit). Similarly, the Acts of Peter say of Christ: "Thou art perceived of the spirit only." [43]

423 The "washing" refers to the *purificatio,* or to baptism, and equally to the washing of the dead body. The latter idea lingered on into the eighteenth century, as the alchemical washing of the "black corpse," an *opus mulierum.* The object to be washed was the black *prima materia:* it, the washing material (*sapo sapientum!*), and the washer were—all three of them—the selfsame Mercurius in different guises. But whereas in alchemy the *nigredo* and sin were identical concepts (since both needed washing), in Christian Gnosticism there are only a few hints of Christ's possible identity with the darkness. The λούσασθαι ("I will be washed") in our text is one of them.

424 The "ogdoad," being a double quaternity, belongs to the symbolism of the mandala. It obviously represents the archetype of the round dance in the "supra-celestial place," since it sings in harmony. The same applies to the number Twelve, the zodiacal archetype of the twelve disciples, a cosmic idea that still

[42] Lipsius and Bonnet, eds., *Acta Apostolorum Apocrypha,* I, p. 197.
[43] James, p. 335.

echoes in Dante's *Paradiso,* where the saints form shining constellations.

425 Anyone who does not join in the dance, who does not make the circumambulation of the centre (Christ and Anthropos), is smitten with blindness and sees nothing. What is described here as an outward event is really a symbol for the inward turning towards the centre in each of the disciples, towards the archetype of man, towards the self—for the dance can hardly be understood as an historical event. It should be understood, rather, as a sort of paraphrase of the Eucharist, an amplifying symbol that renders the mystery more assimilable to consciousness, and it must therefore be interpreted as a psychic phenomenon. It is an act of conscious realization on a higher level, establishing a connection between the consciousness of the individual and the supraordinate symbol of totality.

426 The "Acts of Peter" says of Christ:

> Thou art unto me father, thou my mother, thou my brother, thou my friend, thou my bondsman, thou my steward. Thou art All and All is in thee; thou Art, and there is naught else that IS save thee only.
>
> Unto him therefore do ye also, brethren, flee, and if ye learn that in him alone ye exist, ye shall obtain those things whereof he saith unto you: "Which neither eye hath seen nor ear heard, neither have they entered into the heart of man." [44]

427 The words "I will be united" must be understood in this sense, as meaning that subjective consciousness is united with an objective centre, thus producing the unity of God and man represented by Christ. The self is brought into actuality through the concentration of the many upon the centre, and the self wants this concentration. It is the subject and the object of the process. Therefore it is a "lamp" to those who "perceive" it. Its light is invisible if it is not perceived; it might just as well not exist. It is as dependent on being perceived as the act of perception is on light. This brings out once again the paradoxical subject-object nature of the unknowable. Christ, or the self, is a "mirror": on the one hand it reflects the subjective consciousness of the disciple, making it visible to him, and on the other hand it "knows" Christ, that is to say it does not merely

44 James, p. 335.

reflect the empirical man, it also shows him as a (transcendental) whole. And, just as a "door" opens to one who "knocks" on it, or a "way" opens out to the wayfarer who seeks it, so, when you relate to your own (transcendental) centre, you initiate a process of conscious development which leads to oneness and wholeness. You no longer see yourself as an isolated point on the periphery, but as the One in the centre. Only subjective consciousness is isolated; when it relates to its centre it is integrated into wholeness. Whoever joins in the dance sees himself in the reflecting centre, and his suffering is the suffering which the One who stands in the centre "wills to suffer." The paradoxical identity and difference of ego and self could hardly be formulated more trenchantly.

428 As the text says, you would not be able to understand what you suffer unless there were that Archimedean point outside, the objective standpoint of the self, from which the ego can be seen as a phenomenon. Without the objectivation of the self the ego would remain caught in hopeless subjectivity and would only gyrate round itself. But if you can see and understand your suffering without being subjectively involved, then, because of your altered standpoint, you also understand "how not to suffer," for you have reached a place beyond all involvements ("you have me as a bed, rest upon me"). This is an unexpectedly psychological formulation of the Christian idea of overcoming the world, though with a Docetist twist to it: "Who I am, you shall know when I depart. What now I am seen to be, I am not." [45] These statements are clarified by a vision in which John sees the Lord "standing in the midst of the cave and illuminating it." He says to John:

429 John, for the multitude below in Jerusalem I am being crucified and pierced with lances and staves, and vinegar and gall are given me to drink. But to you I speak, and what I say, hear: I put it into your mind to go up on this mountain, that you might hear those things which a disciple must learn from his master and a man from his God. And with these words he showed me a cross of light, and about the cross a great multitude that had no form [μίαν μορφὴν μὴ ἔχοντα], and in the cross there was one form and one appearance. And above [ἐπάνω] the cross I saw the Lord himself, and he had no outward shape [σχῆμα], but only a voice, and a voice not

[45] Ibid., p. 254.

such as we knew, but one sweet and kind and truly [that] of [a] God, which spoke to me: John, one man must hear this from me, for I require one that shall hear. For your sakes this cross of light was named by me now Logos, now Nous, now Jesus, now Christ, now Door, now Way, now Bread, now Seed [σπόρος], now Resurrection, now Son, now Father, now Pneuma, now Life, now Truth, now Faith [πίστις], now Grace. So is it called for men; but in itself and in its essence, as spoken of to you, it is the Boundary of all things, and the composing of things unstable,[46] and the harmony of wisdom, and the wisdom that is in harmony. For there are [places] of the right and of the left, Powers, Authorities, Archons, Daemons, Workings, Threatenings, Wraths, Devils, Satan, and the Nether Root whence proceeded the nature of whatever comes to be. And so it is this cross which joined all things together through the Word, and which separated the things that are from those that are below, and which caused all things to flow forth from the One.

But this is not the cross of wood which you will see when you go down from here; neither am I he that is on the cross, whom now you do not see, but only hear his voice. I passed for that which I am not, for I am not what I was to many others. But what they will say of me is vile and not worthy of me. Since, then, the place of rest is neither seen nor named, how much less will they see and name me, their Lord!

Now the formless multitude about the cross is of the lower nature. And if those whom you see in the cross have not one form, then not all the parts of him who descended have yet been recollected. But when the nature of man has been taken up and a generation of men that obey my voice draws near to me, he that now hears me shall be united with them and shall no longer be what he now is, but shall stand above them, as I do now. For so long as you call not yourself mine, I am not what I was. But if you understand me, you shall be in your understanding as I am, and I shall be what I was when I have you with me. For this you are through me. . . .

Behold, what you are, I have shown you. But what I am, I alone know, and no man else. Therefore let me have what is mine, but behold what is thine through me. And behold me truly, not as I have said I am, but as you, being akin to me, know me.[47]

430 Our text throws some doubt on the traditional view of Docetism. Though it is perfectly clear from the texts that Christ only seemed to have a body, which only seemed to suffer, this

46 Ἀνάγγη βιάβα uncertain.

47 Based on James, pp. 254ff., and the author's modified version of Hennecke, ed., *Neutestamentliche Apokryphen,* pp. 186ff.

is Docetism at its grossest. The Acts of John are more subtle, and the argument used is almost epistemological: the historical facts are real enough, but they reveal no more than is intelligible to the senses of the ordinary man. Yet even for the knower of divine secrets the act of crucifixion is a mystery, a symbol that expresses a parallel psychic event in the beholder. In the language of Plato it is an event which occurs in a "supra-celestial place," i.e., on a "mountain" and in a "cave" where a cross of light is set up, its many synonyms signifying that it has many aspects and many meanings. It expresses the unknowable nature of the "Lord," the supraordinate personality and *τέλειος ἄνθρωπος*, and since it is a quaternity, a whole divided into four parts, it is the classic symbol of the self.

431 Understood in this sense, the Docetism of the Acts of John appears more as a completion of the historical event than a devaluation of it. It is not surprising that the common people should have failed to appreciate its subtlety, though it is plain enough from a psychological point of view. On the other hand, the educated public of those days were by no means unfamiliar with the parallelism of earthly and metaphysical happenings, only it was not clear to them that their visionary symbols were not necessarily metaphysical realities but were perceptions of intrapsychic or subliminal processes that I have called "phenomena of assimilation." The contemplation of Christ's sacrificial death in its traditional form and cosmic significance constellated analogous psychic processes which in their turn gave rise to a wealth of symbols, as I have shown elsewhere.[48] This is, quite obviously, what has happened here, and it took the form of a visible split between the historical event down below on earth, as perceived by the senses, and its ideal, visionary reflection on high, the cross appearing on the one hand as a wooden instrument of torture and on the other as a glorious symbol. Evidently the centre of gravity has shifted to the ideal event, with the result that the psychic process is involuntarily given the greater importance. Although the emphasis on the pneuma detracts from the meaning of the concrete event in a rather one-sided and debatable way, it cannot be dismissed as superfluous, since a concrete event by itself can never create meaning, but is largely dependent for this on the manner in which it is understood.

48 Cf. *Aion*.

Interpretation is necessary before the meaning of a thing can be grasped. The naked facts by themselves "mean" nothing. So one cannot assert that the Gnostic attempts at interpretation were entirely lacking in merit, even though it went far beyond the framework of early Christian tradition. One could even venture to assert that it was already implicit in that tradition, since the cross and the crucified are practically synonymous in the language of the New Testament.[49]

432 The text shows the cross as the antithesis of the formless multitude: it is, or it has, "form" and its meaning is that of a central point defined by the crossing of two straight lines. It is identical with the Kyrios (Lord) and the Logos, with Jesus and with Christ. How John could "see" the Lord above the cross, when the Lord is described as having no "outward shape," must remain a mystery. He only hears an explanatory voice, and this may indicate that the cross of light is only a visualization of the unknowable, whose voice can be heard apart from the cross. This seems to be confirmed by the remark that the cross was named Logos and so on "for your sakes."

433 The cross signifies order as opposed to the disorderly chaos of the formless multitude. It is, in fact, one of the prime symbols of order, as I have shown elsewhere. In the domain of psychological processes it functions as an organizing centre, and in states of psychic disorder [50] caused by an invasion of unconscious contents it appears as a mandala divided into four. No doubt this was a frequent phenomenon in early Christian times, and not only in Gnostic circles.[51] Gnostic introspection could hardly fail, therefore, to perceive the numinosity of this archetype and be duly impressed by it. For the Gnostics the cross had exactly the same function that the atman or Self has always had for the East. This realization is one of the central experiences of Gnosticism.

49 The quaternity, earlier hinted at in the vision of Ezekiel, is patently manifest in the pre-Christian Book of Enoch. (Cf. "Answer to Job," below, pars. 662ff.) In the Apocalypse of Sophonias [Zephaniah], Christ appears surrounded by a garland of doves (Stern, "Die koptische Apokalypse des Sophonias," p. 124). Cf. also the mosaic of St. Felix at Nola, showing a cross surrounded by doves. There is another in San Clemente, Rome (Wickhoff, "Das Apsismosaik in der Basilica des H. Felix zu Nola," pp. 158ff.; and Rossi, *Musaici Cristiani delle Chiese di Roma anteriori al secolo XV*, pl. XXIX).

50 Symbolized by the formless multitude.

51 Cf. "speaking with tongues" and glossolalia.

434 The definition of the cross or centre as διορισμός, the "boundary" of all things, is exceedingly original, for it suggests that the limits of the universe are not to be found in a nonexistent periphery but in its centre. There alone lies the possibility of transcending this world. All instability culminates in that which is unchanging and quiescent, and in the self all disharmonies are resolved in the "harmony of wisdom."

435 As the centre symbolizes the idea of totality and finality, it is quite appropriate that the text should suddenly start speaking of the dichotomy of the universe, polarized into right and left, brightness and darkness, heaven and the "nether root," the *omnium genetrix*. This is a clear reminder that everything is contained in the centre and that, as a result, the Lord (i.e., the cross) unites and composes all things and is therefore "nirdvanda," free from the opposites, in conformity with Eastern ideas and also with the psychology of this archetypal symbol. The Gnostic Christ-figure and the cross are counterparts of the typical mandalas spontaneously produced by the unconscious. They are *natural symbols* and they differ fundamentally from the dogmatic figure of Christ, in whom all trace of darkness is expressly lacking.

436 In this connection mention should be made of Peter's valedictory words, which he spoke during his martyrdom (he was crucified upside down, at his own request):

> O name of the cross, hidden mystery! O grace ineffable that is pronounced in the name of the cross! O nature of man, that cannot be separated from God! O love unspeakable and indivisible, that cannot be shown forth by unclean lips! I grasp thee now, I that am at the end of my earthly course. I will declare thee as thou art, I will not keep silent the mystery of the cross which was once shut and hidden from my soul. You that hope in Christ, let not the cross be for you that which appears; for it is another thing, and different from that which appears, this suffering which is in accordance with Christ's. And now above all, because you that can hear are able to hear it of me, who am at the last and farewell hour of my life, hearken: separate your souls from everything that is of the senses, from everything that appears to be but in truth is not. Lock your eyes, close your ears, shun those happenings which are seen! Then you shall perceive that which was done to Christ, and the whole mystery of your salvation. . . .

Learn the mystery of all nature and the beginning of all things, as it was. For the first man, of whose race I bear the likeness, fell head downwards, and showed forth a manner of birth such as had not existed till then, for it was dead, having no motion. And being pulled downwards, and having also cast his origin upon the earth, he established the whole disposition of things; for, being hanged up in the manner appointed, he showed forth the things of the right as those of the left, and the things of the left as those of the right, and changed about all the marks of their nature, so that things that were not fair were perceived to be fair, and those that were in truth evil were perceived to be good. Wherefore the Lord says in a mystery: "Except ye make the things of the right as those of the left, and those of the left as those of the right, and those that are above as those below, and those that are behind as those that are before, ye shall not have knowledge of the kingdom."

This understanding have I brought you, and the figure in which you now see me hanging is the representation of that first man who came to birth.

437 In this passage, too, the symbolical interpretation of the cross is coupled with the problem of opposites, first in the unusual idea that the creation of the first man caused everything to be turned upside down, and then in the attempt to unite the opposites by identifying them with one another. A further point of significance is that Peter, crucified head downwards, is identical not only with the first created man, but with the cross:

For what else is Christ but the word, the sound of God? So the word is this upright beam on which I am crucified; and the sound is the beam which crosses it, the nature of man; but the nail which holds the centre of the crossbeam to the upright is man's conversion and repentance (μετάνοια).[52]

438 In the light of these passages it can hardly be said that the author of the Acts of John—presumably a Gnostic—has drawn the necessary conclusions from his premises or that their full implications have become clear to him. On the contrary, one gets the impression that the light has swallowed up everything dark. Just as the enlightening vision appears high above the actual scene of crucifixion, so, for John, the enlightened one stands high above the formless multitude. The text says: "Therefore care not for the many, and despise those that are outside

52 Based on James, pp. 334f.

the mystery!"[53] This overweening attitude arises from an inflation caused by the fact that the enlightened John has identified with his own light and confused his ego with the self. Therefore he feels superior to the darkness in him. He forgets that light only has a meaning when it illuminates something dark and that his enlightenment is no good to him unless it helps him to recognize his own darkness. If the powers of the left are as real as those of the right, then their union can only produce a third thing that shares the nature of both. Opposites unite in a new energy potential: the "third" that arises out of their union is a figure "free from the opposites," beyond all moral categories. This conclusion would have been too advanced for the Gnostics. Recognizing the danger of Gnostic irrealism, the Church, more practical in these matters, has always insisted on the concretism of the historical events despite the fact that the original New Testament texts predict the ultimate deification of man in a manner strangely reminiscent of the words of the serpent in the Garden of Eden: "Ye shall be as gods."[54] Nevertheless, there was some justification for postponing the elevation of man's status until after death, as this avoided the danger of Gnostic inflation.[55]

439 Had the Gnostic not identified with the self, he would have been bound to see how much darkness was in him—a realization that comes more naturally to modern man but causes him no less difficulties. Indeed, he is far more likely to assume that he himself is wholly of the devil than to believe that God could ever indulge in paradoxical statements. For all the ill consequences of his fatal inflation, the Gnostic did, however, gain an insight into religion, or into the psychology of religion, from which we can still learn a thing or two today. He looked deep into the background of Christianity and hence into its future developments. This he could do because his intimate connection with pagan Gnosis made him an "assimilator" that helped to integrate the Christian message into the spirit of the times.

440 The extraordinary number of synonyms piled on top of one another in an attempt to define the cross have their analogy in the Naassene and Peratic symbols of Hippolytus, all pointing to

53 Ibid., p. 255. 54 Genesis 3:5.

55 The possibility of inflation was brought very close indeed by Christ's words: "Ye are gods" (John 10:34).

this one centre. It is the ἓν τὸ πᾶν of alchemy, which is on the one hand the heart and governing principle of the macrocosm, and on the other hand its reflection in a point, in a microcosm such as man has always been thought to be. He is of the same essence as the universe, and his own mid-point is its centre. This inner experience, shared by Gnostics, alchemists, and mystics alike, has to do with the nature of the unconscious—one could even say that it *is* the experience of the unconscious; for the unconscious, though its objective existence and its influence on consciousness cannot be doubted, is in itself undifferentiable and therefore unknowable. Hypothetical germs of differentiation may be conjectured to exist in it, but their existence cannot be proved, because everything appears to be in a state of mutual contamination. The unconscious gives the impression of multiplicity and unity at once. However overwhelmed we may be by the vast quantity of things differentiated in space and time, we know from the world of the senses that the validity of its laws extends to immense distances. We therefore believe that it is one and the same universe throughout, in its smallest part as in its greatest. On the other hand the intellect always tries to discern differences, because it cannot discriminate without them. Consequently the unity of the cosmos remains, for it, a somewhat nebulous postulate which it doesn't rightly know what to do with. But as soon as introspection starts penetrating into the psychic background it comes up against the unconscious, which, unlike consciousness, shows only the barest traces of any definite contents, surprising the investigator at every turn with a confusing medley of relationships, parallels, contaminations, and identifications. Although he is forced, for epistemological reasons, to postulate an indefinite number of distinct and separate archetypes, yet he is constantly overcome by doubt as to how far they are really distinguishable from one another. They overlap to such a degree and have such a capacity for combination that all attempts to isolate them conceptually must appear hopeless. In addition the unconscious, in sharpest contrast to consciousness and its contents, has a tendency to personify itself in a uniform way, just as if it possessed only one shape or one voice. Because of this peculiarity, the unconscious conveys an experience of unity, to which are due all those qualities enumerated by the Gnostics and alchemists, and a lot more besides.

41 As can plainly be seen from Gnosticism and other spiritual movements of the kind, people are naïvely inclined to take all the manifestations of the unconscious at their face value and to believe that in them the essence of the world itself, the ultimate truth, has been unveiled. This assumption does not seem to me quite as unwarranted as it may look at first sight, because the spontaneous utterances of the unconscious do after all reveal a psyche which is not identical with consciousness and which is, at times, greatly at variance with it. These utterances occur as a natural psychic activity that can neither be learnt nor controlled by the will. The manifestation of the unconscious is therefore a revelation of the unknown in man. We have only to disregard the dependence of dream language on environment and substitute "eagle" for "aeroplane," "dragon" for "automobile" or "train," "snake-bite" for "injection," and so forth, in order to arrive at the more universal and more fundamental language of mythology. This gives us access to the primordial images that underlie all thinking and have a considerable influence even on our scientific ideas.[56]

42 In these archetypal forms, something, presumably, is expressing itself that must in some way be connected with the mysterious operation of a natural psyche—in other words, with a cosmic factor of the first order. To save the honour of the objective psyche, which the contemporary hypertrophy of consciousness has done so much to depreciate, I must again emphasize that without the psyche we could not establish the existence of any world at all, let alone know it. But, judging by all we do know, it is certain that the original psyche possesses no consciousness of itself. This only comes in the course of development, a development that falls mostly within the historical epoch.[57] Even today we know of primitive tribes whose level of consciousness is not so far removed from the darkness of the primordial psyche, and numerous vestiges of this state can still be found among civilized people. It is even probable, in view of its potentialities for further differentiation, that our modern consciousness is still on a relatively low level. Nevertheless, its development so

56 Cf. Pauli, "The Influence of Archetypal Ideas on Kepler's Scientific Theories."

57 Cf. the remarkable account of developing consciousness in an ancient Egyptian text, translated, with commentary, by Jacobsohn, entitled "Das Gespräch eines Lebensmüden mit seinem Ba."

far has made it emancipated enough to forget its dependence on the unconscious psyche. It is not a little proud of this emancipation, but it overlooks the fact that although it has apparently got rid of the unconscious it has become the victim of its own verbal concepts. The devil is cast out with Beelzebub. Our dependence on words is so strong that a philosophical brand of "existentialism" had to restore the balance by pointing to a reality that exists in spite of words—at considerable risk, however, of concepts such as "existence," "existential," etc. turning into more words which delude us into thinking that we have caught a reality. One can be—and is—just as dependent on words as on the unconscious. Man's advance towards the Logos was a great achievement, but he must pay for it with loss of instinct and loss of reality to the degree that he remains in primitive dependence on mere words. Because words are substitutes for things, which of course they cannot be in reality, they take on intensified forms, become eccentric, outlandish, stupendous, swell up into what schizophrenic patients call "power words." A primitive word-magic develops, and one is inordinately impressed by it because anything out of the ordinary is felt to be especially profound and significant. Gnosticism in particular affords some very instructive examples of this. Neologisms tend not only to hypostatize themselves to an amazing degree, but actually to replace the reality they were originally intended to express.

443 This rupture of the link with the unconscious and our submission to the tyranny of words have one great disadvantage: the conscious mind becomes more and more the victim of its own discriminating activity, the picture we have of the world gets broken down into countless particulars, and the original feeling of unity, which was integrally connected with the unity of the unconscious psyche, is lost. This feeling of unity, in the form of the correspondence theory and the sympathy of all things, dominated philosophy until well into the seventeenth century and is now, after a long period of oblivion, looming up again on the scientific horizon, thanks to the discoveries made by the psychology of the unconscious and by parapsychology. The manner in which the unconscious forcibly obtrudes upon the conscious by means of neurotic disturbances is not only

reminiscent of contemporary political and social conditions but even appears as an accompanying phenomenon. In both cases there is an analogous dissociation: in the one case a splitting of the world's consciousness by an "iron curtain," and in the other a splitting of the individual personality. This dissociation extends throughout the entire world, so that a psychological split runs through vast numbers of individuals who, in their totality, call forth the corresponding mass phenomena. In the West it was chiefly the mass factor, and in the East technology, that undermined the old hierarchies. The cause of this development lay principally in the economic and psychological uprootedness of the industrial masses, which in turn was caused by the rapid technological advance. But technology, it is obvious, is based on a specifically rationalistic differentiation of consciousness which tends to repress all irrational psychic factors. Hence there arises, in the individual and nation alike, an unconscious counterposition which in time grows strong enough to burst out into open conflict.

444 The same situation in reverse was played out on a smaller scale and on a spiritual plane during the first centuries of our era, when the spiritual disorientation of the Roman world was compensated by the irruption of Christianity. Naturally, in order to survive, Christianity had to defend itself not only against its enemies but also against the excessive pretensions of some of its adherents, including those of the Gnostics. Increasingly it had to rationalize its doctrines in order to stem the flood of irrationality. This led, over the centuries, to that strange marriage of the originally irrational Christian message with human reason, which is so characteristic of the Western mentality. But to the degree that reason gradually gained the upper hand, the intellect asserted itself and demanded autonomy. And just as the intellect subjugated the psyche, so also it subjugated Nature and begat on her an age of scientific technology that left less and less room for the natural and irrational man. Thus the foundations were laid for an inner opposition which today threatens the world with chaos. To make the reversal complete, all the powers of the underworld now hide behind reason and intellect, and under the mask of rationalistic ideology a stubborn faith seeks to impose itself by fire and sword, vying with the darkest aspects

of a church militant. By a strange enantiodromia,[58] the Christian spirit of the West has become the defender of the irrational, since, in spite of having fathered rationalism and intellectualism, it has not succumbed to them so far as to give up its belief in the rights of man, and especially the freedom of the individual. But this freedom guarantees a recognition of the irrational principle, despite the lurking danger of chaotic individualism. By appealing to the eternal rights of man, faith binds itself inalienably to a higher order, not only on account of the historical fact that Christ has proved to be an ordering factor for many hundreds of years, but also because the self effectively compensates chaotic conditions no matter by what name it is known: for the self is the Anthropos above and beyond this world, and in him is contained the freedom and dignity of the individual man. From this point of view, disparagement and vilification of Gnosticism are an anachronism. Its obviously psychological symbolism could serve many people today as a bridge to a more living appreciation of Christian tradition.

445 These historical changes have to be borne in mind if we wish to understand the Gnostic figure of Christ, because the sayings in the Acts of John concerning the nature of the Lord only become intelligible when we interpret them as expressing an experience of the original unity as contrasted with the formless multiplicity of conscious contents. This Gnostic Christ, of whom we hear hints even in the Gospel according to St. John, symbolizes man's original unity and exalts it as the saving goal of his development. By "composing the unstable," by bringing order into chaos, by resolving disharmonies and centring upon the mid-point, thus setting a "boundary" to the multitude and focusing attention upon the cross, consciousness is reunited with the unconscious, the unconscious man is made one with his centre, which is also the centre of the universe, and in this wise the goal of man's salvation and exaltation is reached.

446 Right as this intuition may be, it is also exceedingly dangerous, for it presupposes a coherent ego-consciousness capable of resisting the temptation to identify with the self. Such an ego-consciousness seems to be comparatively rare, as history shows;

58 [Cf. *Psychological Types,* Def. 18, and *Two Essays on Analytical Psychology,* par. 111.—EDITORS.]

usually the ego identifies with the inner Christ, and the danger is increased by an *imitatio Christi* falsely understood. The result is inflation, of which our text affords eloquent proof. In order to exorcise this danger, the Church has not made too much of the "Christ within," but has made all it possibly could of the Christ whom we "have seen, heard, and touched with hands," in other words, with the historical event "below in Jerusalem." This is a wise attitude, which takes realistic account of the primitiveness of man's consciousness, then as now. For the less mindful it is of the unconscious, the greater becomes the danger of its identification with the latter, and the greater, therefore, the danger of inflation, which, as we have experienced to our cost, can seize upon whole nations like a psychic epidemic. If Christ is to be "real" for this relatively primitive consciousness, then he can be so only as an historical figure and a metaphysical entity, but not as a psychic centre in all too perilous proximity to a human ego. The Gnostic development, supported by scriptural authority, pushed so far ahead that Christ was clearly recognized as an inner, psychic fact. This also entailed the relativity of the Christ-figure, as expressively formulated in our text: "For so long as you call not yourself mine, I am not what I was. . . . I shall be what I was when I have you with me." From this it follows unmistakably that although Christ was whole once upon a time, that is, before time and consciousness began, he either lost this wholeness or gave it away to mankind [59] and can only get it back again through man's integration. His wholeness depends on man: "You shall be in your understanding as I am"—this ineluctable conclusion shows the danger very clearly. The ego is dissolved in the self; unbeknown to itself, and with all its inadequacy and darkness, it has become a god and deems itself superior to its unenlightened fellows. It has identified with its own conception of the "higher man," quite regardless of the fact that this figure consists of "Places of the right and left, Authorities, Archons, Daemons" etc., and the devil himself. A figure like this is simply not to be comprehended, an awesome

59 This view may be implicit in the *kenosis* passage (Philippians 2:5f.): "Have this mind in you which was also in Christ Jesus, who though he was by nature God, did not consider being equal to God a thing to be clung to, but emptied himself [ἐκένωσεν, *exinanivit*], taking the nature of a slave and being made like unto man" (DV).

mystery with which one had better not identify if one has any sense. It is sufficient to know that such a mystery exists and that somewhere man can feel its presence, but he should take care not to confuse his ego with it. On the contrary, the confrontation with his own darkness should not only warn him against identification but should inspire him with salutary terror on beholding just what he is capable of becoming. He cannot conquer the tremendous polarity of his nature on his own resources; he can only do so through the terrifying experience of a psychic process that is independent of him, that works *him* rather than he *it*.

447 If such a process exists at all, then it is something that can be experienced. My own personal experience, going back over several decades and garnered from many individuals, and the experience of many other doctors and psychologists, not to mention the statements—terminologically different, but essentially the same—of all the great religions,[60] all confirm the existence of a compensatory ordering factor which is independent of the ego and whose nature transcends consciousness. The existence of such a factor is no more miraculous, in itself, than the orderliness of radium decay, or the attunement of a virus to the anatomy and physiology of human beings,[61] or the symbiosis of plants and animals. What is miraculous in the extreme is that man can have conscious, reflective knowledge of these hidden processes, while animals, plants, and inorganic bodies seemingly lack it. Presumably it would also be an ecstatic experience for a radium atom to know that the time of its decay is exactly determined, or for the butterfly to recognize that the flower has made all the necessary provisions for its propagation.

448 The numinous experience of the individuation process is, on the archaic level, the prerogative of shamans and medicine men; later, of the physician, prophet, and priest; and finally, at the civilized stage, of philosophy and religion. The shaman's experience of sickness, torture, death, and regeneration implies, at a higher level, the idea of being made whole through sacrifice, of being changed by transubstantiation and exalted to the

60 Including shamanism, whose widespread phenomenology anticipates the alchemist's individuation symbolism on an archaic level. For a comprehensive account see Eliade, *Shamanism*.

61 Cf. Portmann, "Die Bedeutung der Bilder in der lebendigen Energiewandlung."

pneumatic man—in a word, of apotheosis. The Mass is the summation and quintessence of a development which began many thousands of years ago and, with the progressive broadening and deepening of consciousness, gradually made the isolated experience of specifically gifted individuals the common property of a larger group. The underlying psychic process remained, of course, hidden from view and was dramatized in the form of suitable "mysteries" and "sacraments," these being reinforced by religious teachings, exercises, meditations, and acts of sacrifice which plunge the celebrant so deeply into the sphere of the mystery that he is able to become conscious of his intimate connection with the mythic happenings. Thus, in ancient Egypt, we see how the experience of "Osirification," [62] originally the prerogative of the Pharaohs, gradually passed to the aristocracy and finally, towards the end of the Old Kingdom, to the single individual as well. Similarly, the mystery religions of the Greeks, originally esoteric and not talked about, broadened out into collective experience, and at the time of the Caesars it was considered a regular sport for Roman tourists to get themselves initiated into foreign mysteries. Christianity, after some hesitation, went a step further and made celebration of the mysteries a public institution, for, as we know, it was especially concerned to introduce as many people as possible to the experience of the mystery. So, sooner or later, the individual could not fail to become conscious of his own transformation and of the necessary psychological conditions for this, such as confession and repentance of sin. The ground was prepared for the realization that, in the mystery of transubstantiation, it was not so much a question of magical influence as of psychological processes—a realization for which the alchemists had already paved the way by putting their *opus operatum* at least on a level with the ecclesiastical mystery, and even attributing to it a cosmic significance since, by its means, the divine world-soul could be liberated from imprisonment in matter. As I think I have shown, the "philosophical" side of alchemy is nothing less than a symbolic anticipation of certain psychological insights, and these—to judge by the example of Gerhard Dorn—were pretty far advanced by the end of the sixteenth century.[63] Only our in-

[62] Cf. Neumann, *The Origins and History of Consciousness,* pp. 220ff.
[63] *Aion,* pp. 162ff.

tellectualized age could have been so deluded as to see in alchemy nothing but an abortive attempt at chemistry, and in the interpretative methods of modern psychology a mere "psychologizing," i.e., annihilation, of the mystery. Just as the alchemists knew that the production of their stone was a miracle that could only happen "Deo concedente," so the modern psychologist is aware that he can produce no more than a description, couched in scientific symbols, of a psychic process whose real nature transcends consciousness just as much as does the mystery of life or of matter. At no point has he explained the mystery itself, thereby causing it to fade. He has merely, in accordance with the spirit of Christian tradition, brought it a little nearer to individual consciousness, using the empirical material to set forth the individuation process and show it as an actual and experienceable fact. To treat a metaphysical statement as a psychic process is not to say that it is "merely psychic," as my critics assert—in the fond belief that the word "psychic" postulates something known. It does not seem to have occurred to people that when we say "psyche" we are alluding to the densest darkness it is possible to imagine. The ethics of the researcher require him to admit where his knowledge comes to an end. This end is the beginning of true wisdom.

III

SHORTER ESSAYS

PSYCHOTHERAPISTS OR THE CLERGY [1]

88 It is far more the urgent psychic problems of patients, rather than the curiosity of research workers, that have given effective impetus to the recent developments in medical psychology and psychotherapy. Medical science—almost in defiance of the patients' needs—has held aloof from all contact with strictly psychic problems, on the partly justifiable assumption that psychic problems belong to other fields of study. But it has been compelled to widen its scope so as to include experimental psychology, just as it has been driven time and time again—out of regard for the biological unity of the human being—to borrow from such outlying branches of science as chemistry, physics, and biology.

89 It was natural that the branches of science adopted by medicine should be given a new direction. We can characterize the change by saying that instead of being regarded as ends in themselves they were valued for their practical application to human beings. Psychiatry, for example, helped itself out of the treasure-chest of experimental psychology and its methods, and funded its borrowings in the inclusive body of knowledge that we call

1 [First given as a lecture before the Alsatian Pastoral Conference at Strasbourg in May 1932; published as a pamphlet, *Die Beziehungen der Psychotherapie zur Seelsorge* (Zurich, 1932). Previously translated by W. S. Dell and Cary F. Baynes in *Modern Man in Search of a Soul* (London and New York, 1933).—EDITORS.]

psychopathology—a name for the study of complex psychic phenomena. Psychopathology is built for one part on the findings of psychiatry in the strict sense of the term, and for the other part on the findings of neurology—a field of study which originally embraced the so-called psychogenic neuroses, and still does so in academic parlance. In practice, however, a gulf has opened out in the last few decades between the trained neurologist and the psychotherapist, especially after the first researches in hypnotism. This rift was unavoidable, because neurology, strictly speaking, is the science of organic nervous diseases, whereas the psychogenic neuroses are not organic diseases in the usual sense of the term. Nor do they fall within the realm of psychiatry, whose particular field of study is the psychoses, or mental diseases—for the psychogenic neuroses are not mental diseases as this term is commonly understood. Rather do they constitute a special field by themselves with no hard and fast boundaries, and they show many transitional forms which point in two directions: towards mental disease on the one hand, and diseases of the nerves on the other.

490 The unmistakable feature of the neuroses is the fact that their causes are psychic, and that their cure depends entirely upon psychic methods of treatment. The attempts to delimit and explore this special field—both from the side of psychiatry and from that of neurology—led to a discovery which was very unwelcome to the science of medicine: namely, the *discovery of the psyche* as an aetiological or causal factor in disease. In the course of the nineteenth century medicine had become, in its methods and theory, one of the disciplines of natural science, and it cherished the same basically philosophical assumption of *material causation*. For medicine, the psyche as a mental "substance" did not exist, and experimental psychology also did its best to constitute itself a psychology without a psyche.

491 Investigation, however, has established beyond a doubt that the crux of the psychoneuroses is the psychic factor, that this is the essential cause of the pathological state, and must therefore be recognized in its own right along with other admitted pathogenic factors such as inheritance, disposition, bacterial infection, and so forth. All attempts to explain the psychic factor in terms of more elementary physical factors were doomed to failure. There was more promise in the attempt to reduce it to the con-

cept of the drive or instinct—a concept taken over from biology. It is well known that instincts are observable physiological urges based on the functioning of the glands, and that, as experience shows, they condition or influence psychic processes. What could be more plausible, therefore, than to seek the specific cause of the psychoneuroses not in the mystical notion of the "soul," but in a disturbance of the instincts which might possibly be curable in the last resort by medicinal treatment of the glands?

492 Freud's theory of the neuroses is based on this standpoint: it explains them in terms of disturbances of the sexual instinct. Adler likewise resorts to the concept of the drive, and explains the neuroses in terms of disturbances of the urge to power, a concept which, we must admit, is a good deal more psychic than that of the physiological sexual instinct.

493 The term "instinct" is anything but well defined in the scientific sense. It applies to a biological phenomenon of immense complexity, and is not much more than a border-line concept of quite indefinite content standing for an unknown quantity. I do not wish to enter here upon a critical discussion of instinct. Instead I will consider the possibility that the psychic factor is just a combination of instincts which for their part may again be reduced to the functioning of the glands. We may even consider the possibility that everything "psychic" is comprised in the sum total of instincts, and that the psyche itself is therefore only an instinct or a conglomerate of instincts, being in the last analysis nothing but a function of the glands. A psychoneurosis would then be a glandular disease.

494 There is, however, no proof of this statement, and no glandular extract that will cure a neurosis has yet been found. On the other hand, we have been taught by all too many mistakes that organic therapy fails completely in the treatment of neuroses, while psychic methods cure them. These psychic methods are just as effective as we might suppose the glandular extracts would be. So far, then, as our present knowledge goes, neuroses are to be influenced or cured by approaching them not from the proximal end, i.e., from the functioning of the glands, but from the distal end, i.e., from the psyche, just as if the psyche were itself a substance. For instance, a suitable explanation or a comforting word to the patient can have something like a healing

effect which may even influence the glandular secretions. The doctor's words, to be sure, are "only" vibrations in the air, yet their special quality is due to a particular psychic state in the doctor. His words are effective only in so far as they convey a meaning or have significance. It is this that makes them work. But "meaning" is something mental or spiritual. Call it a fiction if you like. Nevertheless this fiction enables us to influence the course of the disease far more effectively than we could with chemical preparations. Indeed, we can even influence the biochemical processes of the body. Whether the fiction forms itself in me spontaneously or reaches me from outside via human speech, it can make me ill or cure me. Fictions, illusions, opinions are perhaps the most intangible and unreal things we can think of; yet they are the most effective of all in the psychic and even the psychophysical realm.

495 It was by recognizing these facts that medicine discovered the psyche, and it can no longer honestly deny the psyche's reality. It has been shown that the instincts are a condition of psychic activity, while at the same time psychic processes seem to condition the instincts.

496 The reproach levelled at the Freudian and Adlerian theories is not that they are based on instincts, but that they are one-sided. It is psychology without the psyche, and this suits people who think they have no spiritual needs or aspirations. But here both doctor and patient deceive themselves. Even though the theories of Freud and Adler come much nearer to getting at the bottom of the neuroses than any earlier approach from the medical side, their exclusive concern with the instincts fails to satisfy the deeper spiritual needs of the patient. They are too much bound by the premises of nineteenth-century science, too matter of fact, and they give too little value to fictional and imaginative processes. In a word, they do not give enough meaning to life. And it is only meaning that liberates.

497 Ordinary reasonableness, sound human judgment, science as a compendium of common sense, these certainly help us over a good part of the road, but they never take us beyond the frontiers of life's most commonplace realities, beyond the merely average and normal. They afford no answer to the question of psychic suffering and its profound significance. A psychoneurosis must be understood, ultimately, as the suffering of a soul

which has not discovered its meaning. But all creativeness in the realm of the spirit as well as every psychic advance of man arises from the suffering of the soul, and the cause of the suffering is spiritual stagnation, or psychic sterility.

498 With this realization the doctor sets foot on territory which he enters with the greatest caution. He is now confronted with the necessity of conveying to his patient the healing fiction, the meaning that quickens—for it is this that the sick person longs for, over and above everything that reason and science can give him. He is looking for something that will take possession of him and give meaning and form to the confusion of his neurotic soul.

499 Is the doctor equal to this task? To begin with, he will probably hand his patient over to the clergyman or philosopher, or abandon him to that vast perplexity which is the special note of our day. As a doctor he is not required to have a finished outlook on life, and his professional conscience does not demand it of him. But what will he do when he sees only too clearly why his patient is ill; when he sees that he has no love, but only sexuality; no faith, because he is afraid to grope in the dark; no hope, because he is disillusioned by the world and by life; and no understanding, because he has failed to read the meaning of his own existence?

500 There are many well-educated patients who flatly refuse to consult a clergyman. Still less will they listen to a philosopher, for the history of philosophy leaves them cold, and intellectual problems seem to them more barren than the desert. And where are the great and wise men who do not merely talk about the meaning of life and of the world, but really possess it? One cannot just think up a system or truth which would give the patient what he needs in order to live, namely faith, hope, love, and understanding.

501 These four highest achievements of human endeavour are so many gifts of grace, which are neither to be taught nor learned, neither given nor taken, neither withheld nor earned, since they come through experience, which is an irrational datum not subject to human will and caprice. Experiences cannot be *made*. They happen—yet fortunately their independence of man's activity is not absolute but relative. We can draw closer to them—that much lies within our human reach. There

are ways which bring us nearer to living experience, yet we should beware of calling these ways "methods." The very word has a deadening effect. The way to experience, moreover, is anything but a clever trick; it is rather a venture which requires us to commit ourselves with our whole being.

502 Thus, in trying to meet the therapeutic demands made upon him, the doctor is confronted with a question which seems to contain an insuperable difficulty. How can he help the sufferer to attain the liberating experience which will bestow upon him the four great gifts of grace and heal his sickness? We can, of course, advise the patient with the best intentions that he should have true love, or true faith, or true hope; and we can admonish him with the phrase: "Know thyself." But how is the patient to obtain beforehand that which only experience can give him?

503 Saul owed his conversion neither to true love, nor to true faith, nor to any other truth. It was solely his hatred of the Christians that set him on the road to Damascus, and to that decisive experience which was to alter the whole course of his life. He was brought to this experience by following out, with conviction, his own worst mistake.

504 This opens up a problem which we can hardly take too seriously. And it confronts the psychotherapist with a question which brings him shoulder to shoulder with the clergyman: the question of good and evil.

505 It is in reality the priest or the clergyman, rather than the doctor, who should be most concerned with the problem of spiritual suffering. But in most cases the sufferer consults the doctor in the first place, because he supposes himself to be physically ill, and because certain neurotic symptoms can be at least alleviated by drugs. But if, on the other hand, the clergyman is consulted, he cannot persuade the sick man that the trouble is psychic. As a rule he lacks the special knowledge which would enable him to discern the psychic factors of the disease, and his judgment is without the weight of authority.

506 There are, however, persons who, while well aware of the psychic nature of their complaint, nevertheless refuse to turn to the clergyman. They do not believe that he can really help them. Such persons distrust the doctor for the same reason, and rightly so, for the truth is that both doctor and clergyman stand before them with empty hands, if not—what is even worse—

with empty words. We can hardly expect the doctor to have anything to say about the ultimate questions of the soul. It is from the clergyman, not from the doctor, that the sufferer should expect such help. But the Protestant clergyman often finds himself face to face with an almost impossible task, for he has to cope with practical difficulties that the Catholic priest is spared. Above all, the priest has the authority of his Church behind him, and his economic position is secure and independent. This is far less true of the Protestant clergyman, who may be married and burdened with the responsibility of a family, and cannot expect, if all else fails, to be supported by the parish or taken into a monastery. Moreover the priest, if he is also a Jesuit, is *au fait* with the most up-to-date developments in psychology. I know, for instance, that my own writings were seriously studied in Rome long before any Protestant theologian thought them worthy of a glance.

507 We have come to a serious pass. The exodus from the German Protestant Church is only one of many symptoms which should make it plain to the clergy that mere admonitions to believe, or to perform acts of charity, do not give modern man what he is looking for. The fact that many clergymen seek support or practical help from Freud's theory of sexuality or Adler's theory of power is astonishing, inasmuch as both these theories are, at bottom, hostile to spiritual values, being, as I have said, psychology without the psyche. They are rationalistic methods of treatment which actually hinder the realization of meaningful experience. By far the larger number of psychotherapists are disciples of Freud or of Adler. This means that the great majority of patients are necessarily alienated from a spiritual standpoint—a fact which cannot be a matter of indifference to one who has the fate of the psyche at heart. The wave of interest in psychology which at present is sweeping over the Protestant countries of Europe is far from receding. It is coincident with the mass exodus from the Church. Quoting a Protestant minister, I may say: "Nowadays people go to the psychotherapist rather than to the clergyman."

508 I am convinced that this statement is true only of relatively educated persons, not of mankind in the mass. However, we must not forget that it takes about twenty years for the ordinary run of people to begin thinking the thoughts of the educated

person of today. For instance, Büchner's work *Force and Matter*[2] became one of the most widely read books in German public libraries some twenty years after educated persons had forgotten all about it. I am convinced that the psychological needs of the educated today will be the interests of the people tomorrow.

509 I should like to call attention to the following facts. During the past thirty years, people from all the civilized countries of the earth have consulted me. Many hundreds of patients have passed through my hands, the greater number being Protestants, a lesser number Jews, and not more than five or six believing Catholics. Among all my patients in the second half of life—that is to say, over thirty-five—there has not been one whose problem in the last resort was not that of finding a religious outlook on life. It is safe to say that every one of them fell ill because he had lost what the living religions of every age have given to their followers, and none of them has been really healed who did not regain his religious outlook. This of course has nothing whatever to do with a particular creed or membership of a church.

510 Here, then, the clergyman stands before a vast horizon. But it would seem as if no one had noticed it. It also looks as though the Protestant clergyman of today were insufficiently equipped to cope with the urgent psychic needs of our age. It is indeed high time for the clergyman and the psychotherapist to join forces to meet this great spiritual task.

511 Here is a concrete example which goes to show how closely this problem touches us all. A little more than a year ago the leaders of the Christian Students' Conference at Aarau [Switzerland] laid before me the question whether people in spiritual distress prefer nowadays to consult the doctor rather than the clergyman, and what are the causes of their choice. This was a very direct and very practical question. At the time I knew nothing more than the fact that my own patients obviously had consulted the doctor rather than the clergyman. It seemed to me to be open to doubt whether this was generally the case or not. At any rate, I was unable to give a definite reply. I therefore set on foot an inquiry, through acquaintances of mine, among people

2 [Ludwig Büchner (1824–99), German materialistic philosopher. His *Kraft und Stoff* was pub. 1855.—EDITORS.]

whom I did not know personally; I sent out a questionnaire which was answered by Swiss, German, and French Protestants, as well as by a few Catholics. The results are very interesting, as the following general summary shows. Those who decided for the doctor represented 57 per cent of the Protestants and only 25 per cent of the Catholics, while those who decided for the clergyman formed only 8 per cent of the Protestants as against 58 per cent of the Catholics. These were the unequivocal decisions. The remaining 35 per cent of the Protestants could not make up their minds, while only 17 per cent of the Catholics were undecided.

512 The main reasons given for not consulting the clergyman were, firstly, his lack of psychological knowledge and insight, and this covered 52 per cent of the answers. Some 28 per cent were to the effect that he was prejudiced in his views and showed a dogmatic and traditional bias. Curiously enough, there was even one clergyman who decided for the doctor, while another made the irritated retort: "Theology has nothing to do with the treatment of human beings." All the relatives of clergymen who answered my questionnaire pronounced themselves against the clergy.

513 So far as this inquiry was restricted to educated persons, it is only a straw in the wind. I am convinced that the uneducated classes would have reacted differently. But I am inclined to accept these sample results as a more or less valid indication of the views of educated people, the more so as it is a well-known fact that their indifference in matters of the Church and religion is steadily growing. Nor should we forget the above-mentioned truth of social psychology: that it takes about twenty years for the general outlook and problems of the educated to percolate down to the uneducated masses. Who, for instance, would have dared to prophesy twenty years ago, or even ten, that Spain, the most Catholic of European countries, would undergo the tremendous mental revolution we are witnessing today? [3] And yet it has broken out with the violence of a cataclysm.

514 It seems to me that, side by side with the decline of religious life, the neuroses grow noticeably more frequent. There are as

3 [Under the second republic, established in 1931 and later overthrown by the Franco forces.—EDITORS.]

yet no statistics with actual figures to prove this increase. But of one thing I am sure, that everywhere the mental state of European man shows an alarming lack of balance. We are living undeniably in a period of the greatest restlessness, nervous tension, confusion, and disorientation of outlook. Among my patients from many countries, all of them educated persons, there is a considerable number who came to see me not because they were suffering from a neurosis but because they could find no meaning in their lives or were torturing themselves with questions which neither our philosophy nor our religion could answer. Some of them perhaps thought I knew of a magic formula, but I soon had to tell them that I didn't know the answer either. And this brings us to practical considerations.

515 Let us take for example that most ordinary and frequent of questions: What is the meaning of my life, or of life in general? Today people believe that they know only too well what the clergyman will—or rather must—say to this. They smile at the very thought of the philosopher's answer, and in general do not expect much of the physician. But from the psychotherapist who analyses the unconscious—from him one might at last learn something. Perhaps he has dug up from the abstruse depths of his mind, among other things, some meaning which could even be bought for a fee! It must be a relief to every serious-minded person to hear that the psychotherapist also does not know what to say. Such a confession is often the beginning of the patient's confidence in him.

516 I have found that modern man has an ineradicable aversion for traditional opinions and inherited truths. He is a Bolshevist for whom all the spiritual standards and forms of the past have somehow lost their validity, and who therefore wants to experiment with his mind as the Bolshevist experiments with economics. Confronted with this attitude, every ecclesiastical system finds itself in an awkward situation, be it Catholic, Protestant, Buddhist, or Confucianist. Among these moderns there are of course some of those negative, destructive, and perverse natures —degenerates and unbalanced eccentrics—who are never satisfied anywhere, and who therefore flock to every new banner, much to the hurt of these movements and undertakings, in the hope of finding something *for once* which will compensate at low cost for their own ineptitude. It goes without saying that,

in my professional work, I have come to know a great many modern men and women, including of course their pathological hangers-on. But these I prefer to leave aside. Those I am thinking of are by no means sickly eccentrics, but are very often exceptionally able, courageous, and upright persons who have repudiated traditional truths for honest and decent reasons, and not from wickedness of heart. Every one of them has the feeling that our religious truths have somehow become hollow. Either they cannot reconcile the scientific and the religious outlook, or the Christian tenets have lost their authority and their psychological justification. People no longer feel redeemed by the death of Christ; they cannot believe—for although it is a lucky man who *can* believe, it is not possible to compel belief. Sin has become something quite relative: what is evil for one man is good for another. After all, why should not the Buddha be right too?

517 There is no one who is not familiar with these questions and doubts. Yet Freudian analysis would brush them all aside as irrelevant, for in its view, it is basically a question of repressed sexuality, which the philosophical or religious doubts only serve to mask. If we closely examine an individual case of this sort, we do discover peculiar disturbances in the sexual sphere as well as in the sphere of unconscious impulses in general. Freud sees in the presence of these disturbances an explanation of the psychic disturbance as a whole; he is interested only in the causal interpretation of the sexual symptoms. He completely overlooks the fact that, in certain cases, the supposed causes of the neurosis were always present, but had no pathological effect until a disturbance of the conscious attitude set in and led to a neurotic upset. It is as though, when a ship was sinking because of a leak, the crew interested itself in the chemical constitution of the water that was pouring in, instead of stopping the leak. The disturbance of the instinctual sphere is not a primary but a secondary phenomenon. When conscious life has lost its meaning and promise, it is as though a panic had broken loose: "Let us eat and drink, for tomorrow we die!" It is this mood, born of the meaninglessness of life, that causes the disturbance in the unconscious and provokes the painfully curbed instincts to break out anew. The causes of a neurosis lie in the present as much as in the past, and only a cause actually existing in the

present can keep a neurosis active. A man is not tubercular because he was infected twenty years ago with bacilli, but because active foci of infection are present *now*. The questions when and how the infection occurred are totally irrelevant. Even the most accurate knowledge of the previous history cannot cure the tuberculosis. And the same holds true of the neuroses.

518 That is why I regard the religious problems which the patient puts before me as authentic and as possible causes of the neurosis. But if I take them seriously, I must be able to confess to the patient: "Yes, I agree, the Buddha may be just as right as Jesus. Sin is only relative, and it is difficult to see how we can feel ourselves in any way redeemed by the death of Christ." As a doctor I can easily admit these doubts, while it is hard for the clergyman to do so. The patient feels my attitude to be one of understanding, while the parson's hesitation strikes him as a traditional prejudice, and this estranges them from one another. He asks himself: "What would the parson say if I began to tell him of the painful details of my sexual disturbances?" He rightly suspects that the parson's moral prejudice is even stronger than his dogmatic bias. In this connection there is a good story about the American president, "silent Cal" Coolidge. When he returned after an absence one Sunday morning his wife asked him where he had been. "To church," he replied. "What did the minister say?" "He talked about sin." "And what did he say about sin?" "He was against it."

519 It is easy for the doctor to show understanding in this respect, you will say. But people forget that even doctors have moral scruples, and that certain patients' confessions are hard even for a doctor to swallow. Yet the patient does not feel himself accepted unless the very worst in him is accepted too. No one can bring this about by mere words; it comes only through reflection and through the doctor's attitude towards himself and his own dark side. If the doctor wants to guide another, or even accompany him a step of the way, he must *feel* with that person's psyche. He never feels it when he passes judgment. Whether he puts his judgments into words, or keeps them to himself, makes not the slightest difference. To take the opposite position, and to agree with the patient offhand, is also of no use, but estranges him as much as condemnation. Feeling comes only through unprejudiced objectivity. This sounds almost like

a scientific precept, and it could be confused with a purely intellectual, abstract attitude of mind. But what I mean is something quite different. It is a human quality—a kind of deep respect for the facts, for the man who suffers from them, and for the riddle of such a man's life. The truly religious person has this attitude. He knows that God has brought all sorts of strange and inconceivable things to pass and seeks in the most curious ways to enter a man's heart. He therefore senses in everything the unseen presence of the divine will. This is what I mean by "unprejudiced objectivity." It is a moral achievement on the part of the doctor, who ought not to let himself be repelled by sickness and corruption. We cannot change anything unless we accept it. Condemnation does not liberate, it oppresses. I am the oppressor of the person I condemn, not his friend and fellow-sufferer. I do not in the least mean to say that we must never pass judgment when we desire to help and improve. But if the doctor wishes to help a human being he must be able to accept him as he is. And he can do this in reality only when he has already seen and accepted himself as he is.

520 Perhaps this sounds very simple, but simple things are always the most difficult. In actual life it requires the greatest art to be simple, and so acceptance of oneself is the essence of the moral problem and the acid test of one's whole outlook on life. That I feed the beggar, that I forgive an insult, that I love my enemy in the name of Christ—all these are undoubtedly great virtues. What I do unto the least of my brethren, that I do unto Christ. But what if I should discover that the least amongst them all, the poorest of all beggars, the most impudent of all offenders, yea the very fiend himself—that these are within me, and that I myself stand in need of the alms of my own kindness, that I myself am the enemy who must be loved—what then? Then, as a rule, the whole truth of Christianity is reversed: there is then no more talk of love and long-suffering; we say to the brother within us "Raca," and condemn and rage against ourselves. We hide him from the world, we deny ever having met this least among the lowly in ourselves, and had it been God himself who drew near to us in this despicable form, we should have denied him a thousand times before a single cock had crowed.

521 Anyone who uses modern psychology to look behind the

scene not only of his patients' lives but more especially of his own life—and the modern psychotherapist must do this if he is not to be merely an unconscious fraud—will admit that to accept himself in all his wretchedness is the hardest of tasks, and one which it is almost impossible to fulfil. The very thought can make us sweat with fear. We are therefore only too delighted to choose, without a moment's hesitation, the complicated course of remaining in ignorance about ourselves while busying ourselves with other people and their troubles and sins. This activity lends us a perceptible air of virtue, by means of which we benevolently deceive ourselves and others. God be praised, we have escaped from ourselves at last! There are countless people who can do this with impunity, but not everyone can, and these few break down on the road to their Damascus and succumb to a neurosis. How can I help these people if I myself am a fugitive, and perhaps also suffer from the *morbus sacer* of a neurosis? Only he who has fully accepted himself has "unprejudiced objectivity." But no one is justified in boasting that he has fully accepted himself. We can point to Christ, who sacrificed his historical bias to the god within him, and lived his individual life to the bitter end without regard for conventions or for the moral standards of the Pharisees.

522 We Protestants must sooner or later face this question: Are we to understand the "imitation of Christ" in the sense that we should copy his life and, if I may use the expression, ape his stigmata; or in the deeper sense that we are to live our own proper lives as truly as he lived his in its individual uniqueness? It is no easy matter to live a life that is modelled on Christ's, but it is unspeakably harder to live one's own life as truly as Christ lived his. Anyone who did this would run counter to the conditions of his own history, and though he might thus be fulfilling them, he would none the less be misjudged, derided, tortured, and crucified. He would be a kind of crazy Bolshevist who deserved the cross. We therefore prefer the historically sanctioned and sanctified imitation of Christ. I would never disturb a monk in the practice of this identification, for he deserves our respect. But neither I nor my patients are monks, and it is my duty as a physician to show my patients how they can live their lives without becoming neurotic. Neurosis is an inner cleavage—the state of being at war with oneself.

Everything that accentuates this cleavage makes the patient worse, and everything that mitigates it tends to heal him. What drives people to war with themselves is the suspicion or the knowledge that they consist of two persons in opposition to one another. The conflict may be between the sensual and the spiritual man, or between the ego and the shadow. It is what Faust means when he says: "Two souls, alas, are housed within my breast." A neurosis is a splitting of personality.

523 Healing may be called a religious problem. In the sphere of social or national relations, the state of suffering may be civil war, and this state is to be cured by the Christian virtue of forgiveness and love of one's enemies. That which we recommend, with the conviction of good Christians, as applicable to external situations, we must also apply inwardly in the treatment of neurosis. This is why modern man has heard enough about guilt and sin. He is sorely enough beset by his own bad conscience, and wants rather to know how he is to reconcile himself with his own nature—how he is to love the enemy in his own heart and call the wolf his brother.

524 The modern man does not want to know in what way he can imitate Christ, but in what way he can live his own individual life, however meagre and uninteresting it may be. It is because every form of imitation seems to him deadening and sterile that he rebels against the force of tradition that would hold him to well-trodden ways. All such roads, for him, lead in the wrong direction. He may not know it, but he behaves as if his own individual life were God's special will which must be fulfilled at all costs. This is the source of his egoism, which is one of the most tangible evils of the neurotic state. But the person who tells him he is too egoistic has already lost his confidence, and rightly so, for that person has driven him still further into his neurosis.

525 If I wish to effect a cure for my patients I am forced to acknowledge the deep significance of their egoism. I should be blind, indeed, if I did not recognize it as a true will of God. I must even help the patient to prevail in his egoism; if he succeeds in this, he estranges himself from other people. He drives them away, and they come to themselves—as they should, for they were seeking to rob him of his "sacred" egoism. This must be left to him, for it is his strongest and healthiest power; it is,

as I have said, a true will of God, which sometimes drives him into complete isolation. However wretched this state may be, it also stands him in good stead, for in this way alone can he get to know himself and learn what an invaluable treasure is the love of his fellow beings. It is, moreover, only in the state of complete abandonment and loneliness that we experience the helpful powers of our own natures.

526 When one has several times seen this development at work one can no longer deny that what was evil has turned to good, and that what seemed good has kept alive the forces of evil. The archdemon of egoism leads us along the royal road to that ingathering which religious experience demands. What we observe here is a fundamental law of life—*enantiodromia* or conversion into the opposite; and it is this that makes possible the reunion of the warring halves of the personality and thereby brings the civil war to an end.

527 I have taken the neurotic's egoism as an example because it is one of his most common symptoms. I might equally well have taken any other characteristic symptom to show what attitude the physician must adopt towards the shortcomings of his patients, in other words, how he must deal with the problem of evil.

528 No doubt this also sounds very simple. In reality, however, the acceptance of the shadow-side of human nature verges on the impossible. Consider for a moment what it means to grant the right of existence to what is unreasonable, senseless, and evil! Yet it is just this that the modern man insists upon. He wants to live with every side of himself—to know what he is. That is why he casts history aside. He wants to break with tradition so that he can experiment with his life and determine what value and meaning things have in themselves, apart from traditional presuppositions. Modern youth gives us astonishing examples of this attitude. To show how far this tendency may go, I will instance a question addressed to me by a German society. I was asked if incest is to be reprobated, and what facts can be adduced against it!

529 Granted such tendencies, the conflicts into which people may fall are not hard to imagine. I can well understand that one would like to do everything possible to protect one's fellow beings from such adventures. But curiously enough we find our-

selves without means to do this. All the old arguments against unreasonableness, self-deception, and immorality, once so potent, have lost their attraction. We are now reaping the fruit of nineteenth-century education. Throughout that period the Church preached to young people the merit of blind faith, while the universities inculcated an intellectual rationalism, with the result that today we plead in vain whether for faith or reason. Tired of this warfare of opinions, the modern man wishes to find out for himself how things are. And though this desire opens the door to the most dangerous possibilities, we cannot help seeing it as a courageous enterprise and giving it some measure of sympathy. It is no reckless adventure, but an effort inspired by deep spiritual distress to bring meaning once more into life on the basis of fresh and unprejudiced experience. Caution has its place, no doubt, but we cannot refuse our support to a serious venture which challenges the whole of the personality. If we oppose it, we are trying to suppress what is best in man—his daring and his aspirations. And should we succeed, we should only have stood in the way of that invaluable experience which might have given a meaning to life. What would have happened if Paul had allowed himself to be talked out of his journey to Damascus?

530 The psychotherapist who takes his work seriously must come to grips with this question. He must decide in every single case whether or not he is willing to stand by a human being with counsel and help upon what may be a daring misadventure. He must have no fixed ideas as to what is right, nor must he pretend to know what is right and what not—otherwise he takes something from the richness of the experience. He must keep in view what actually happens—for only that which acts is actual.[4] If something which seems to me an error shows itself to be more effective than a truth, then I must first follow up the error, for in it lie power and life which I lose if I hold to what seems to me true. Light has need of darkness—otherwise how could it appear as light?

531 It is well known that Freudian psychoanalysis limits itself to the task of making conscious the shadow-side and the evil within

4 [A more literal translation, which brings out the meaning more clearly while losing the play on words, would be: "He must keep in view only what is real (for the patient). But a thing is 'real' (*wirklich*) if it 'works' (*wirkt*)."—TRANS.]

us. It simply brings into action the civil war that was latent, and lets it go at that. The patient must deal with it as best he can. Freud has unfortunately overlooked the fact that man has never yet been able single-handed to hold his own against the powers of darkness—that is, of the unconscious. Man has always stood in need of the spiritual help which his particular religion held out to him. The opening up of the unconscious always means the outbreak of intense spiritual suffering; it is as when a flourishing civilization is abandoned to invading hordes of barbarians, or when fertile fields are exposed by the bursting of a dam to a raging torrent. The World War was such an invasion which showed, as nothing else could, how thin are the walls which separate a well-ordered world from lurking chaos. But it is the same with the individual and his rationally ordered world. Seeking revenge for the violence his reason has done to her, outraged Nature only awaits the moment when the partition falls so as to overwhelm the conscious life with destruction. Man has been aware of this danger to the psyche since the earliest times, even in the most primitive stages of culture. It was to arm himself against this threat and to heal the damage done that he developed religious and magical practices. This is why the medicine-man is also the priest; he is the saviour of the soul as well as of the body, and religions are systems of healing for psychic illness. This is especially true of the two greatest religions of humanity, Christianity and Buddhism. Man is never helped in his suffering by what he thinks of for himself; only suprahuman, revealed truth lifts him out of his distress.

532 Today the tide of destruction has already reached us and the psyche has suffered damage. That is why patients force the psychotherapist into the role of the priest and expect and demand of him that he shall free them from their suffering. That is why we psychotherapists must occupy ourselves with problems which, strictly speaking, belong to the theologian. But we cannot leave these questions for theology to answer; challenged by the urgent psychic needs of our patients, we are directly confronted with them every day. Since, as a rule, every concept and every point of view handed down from the past proves futile, we must first tread with the patient the path of his illness—the path of his mistake that sharpens his conflicts and increases his

loneliness till it becomes unbearable—hoping that from the psychic depths which cast up the powers of destruction the rescuing forces will also come.

533 When I first took this path I did not know where it would lead. I did not know what lay hidden in the depths of the psyche—that region which I have since called the "collective unconscious" and whose contents I designate as "archetypes." Since time immemorial, invasions of the unconscious have occurred, and ever and again they repeat themselves. For consciousness did not exist from the beginning; in every child it has to be built up anew in the first years of life. Consciousness is very weak in this formative period, and the same is true of the psychic history of mankind—the unconscious easily seizes power. These struggles have left their mark. To put it in scientific terms: instinctive defence-mechanisms have been built up which automatically intervene when the danger is greatest, and their coming into action during an emergency is represented in fantasy by helpful images which are ineradicably imprinted on the human psyche. Science can only establish the existence of these psychic factors and attempt a rationalistic explanation by offering an hypothesis as to their source. This, however, only thrusts the problem a stage further back without solving the riddle. We thus come to those ultimate questions: Where does consciousness come from? What is the psyche? At this point all science ends.

534 It is as though, at the climax of the illness, the destructive powers were converted into healing forces. This is brought about by the archetypes awaking to independent life and taking over the guidance of the psychic personality, thus supplanting the ego with its futile willing and striving. As a religious-minded person would say: guidance has come from God. With most of my patients I have to avoid this formulation, apt though it is, for it reminds them too much of what they had to reject in the first place. I must express myself in more modest terms and say that the psyche has awakened to spontaneous activity. And indeed this formulation is better suited to the observable facts, as the transformation takes place at that moment when, in dreams or fantasies, motifs appear whose source in consciousness cannot be demonstrated. To the patient it is nothing less than a revelation when something altogether strange rises up to confront him

from the hidden depths of the psyche—something that is not his ego and is therefore beyond the reach of his personal will. He has regained access to the sources of psychic life, and this marks the beginning of the cure.

535 In order to illustrate this process, I ought really to discuss it with the help of examples. But it is almost impossible to give a convincing example offhand, for as a rule it is an extremely subtle and complicated matter. Often it is simply the deep impression made on the patient by the independent way the dreams deal with his problem. Or it may be that his fantasy points to something for which his conscious mind was quite unprepared. But in most cases it is contents of an archetypal nature, or the connections between them, that exert a strong influence of their own whether or not they are understood by the conscious mind. This spontaneous activity of the psyche often becomes so intense that visionary pictures are seen or inner voices heard—a true, primordial experience of the spirit.

536 Such experiences reward the sufferer for the pains of the labyrinthine way. From now on a light shines through the confusion; more, he can accept the conflict within him and so come to resolve the morbid split in his nature on a higher level.

*

537 The fundamental problems of modern psychotherapy are so important and far-reaching that their discussion in an essay precludes any presentation of details, however desirable this might be for clarity's sake. I hope nevertheless that I have succeeded in my main purpose, which was to set forth the attitude of the psychotherapist to his work. This may be found more rewarding than precepts and pointers to methods of treatment, which in any case never work properly unless they are applied with right understanding. The attitude of the psychotherapist is infinitely more important than the theories and methods of psychotherapy, and that is why I was particularly concerned to make this attitude known. I believe I have given an honest account and have, at the same time, imparted information which will allow you to decide how far and in what way the clergyman can join with the psychotherapist in his aspirations and endeavours. I believe, also, that the picture I have drawn of the spiritual outlook of modern man corresponds to the true state

of affairs, though I make no claim to infallibility. In any case, what I have had to say about the cure of neurosis, and the problems involved, is the unvarnished truth. We doctors would naturally welcome the sympathetic understanding of the clergy in our endeavours to heal psychic suffering, but we are also fully aware of the fundamental difficulties which stand in the way of co-operation. My own position is on the extreme left wing in the parliament of Protestant opinion, yet I would be the first to warn people against uncritical generalizations of their own point of view. As a Swiss I am an inveterate democrat, yet I recognize that Nature is aristocratic and, what is even more, esoteric. "Quod licet Jovi, non licet bovi" is an unpleasant but eternal truth. Who are forgiven their many sins? Those who have loved much. But as to those who love little, their few sins are held against them. I am firmly convinced that a vast number of people belong to the fold of the Catholic Church and nowhere else, because they are most suitably housed there. I am as much persuaded of this as of the fact, which I have myself observed, that a primitive religion is better suited to primitive people than Christianity, which is so incomprehensible to them and so foreign to their blood that they can only ape it in the most disgusting way. I believe, too, that there must be protestants against the Catholic Church, and also protestants against Protestantism—for the manifestations of the spirit are truly wondrous, and as varied as Creation itself.

38 The living spirit grows and even outgrows its earlier forms of expression; it freely chooses the men who proclaim it and in whom it lives. This living spirit is eternally renewed and pursues its goal in manifold and inconceivable ways throughout the history of mankind. Measured against it, the names and forms which men have given it mean very little; they are only the changing leaves and blossoms on the stem of the eternal tree.

PSYCHOANALYSIS AND THE CURE OF SOULS [1]

539 The question of the relations between psychoanalysis and the pastoral cure of souls is not easy to answer, because the two are concerned with essentially different things. The cure of souls as practised by the clergyman or priest is a religious influence based on a Christian confession of faith. Psychoanalysis, on the other hand, is a medical intervention, a psychological technique whose purpose it is to lay bare the contents of the unconscious and integrate them into the conscious mind. This definition of psychoanalysis applies, however, only to the methods employed by Freud's school and mine. The Adlerian method is not an analysis in this sense, nor does it pursue the aim stated above. It is chiefly pedagogical in intent, and works directly upon the conscious mind without, as it were, considering the unconscious. It is a further development of the French "rééducation de la volonté" and of Dubois' "psychic orthopedics." The normalization of the individual at which Adlerian pedagogics aim, and his adaptation to the collective psyche, represent a different goal from that pursued by the pastoral cure of souls, which has for its aim the salvation of the soul and its deliverance from the snares of this world. Normalization and adaptation may, under certain circumstances, even be aims which are diametrically

1 [First published as "Psychoanalyse und Seelsorge," in *Ethik: Sexual- und Gesellschafts-Ethik* (Halle), V (1928): 1, 7–12.—EDITORS.]

opposed to the Christian ideal of detachment from the world, submission to the will of God, and the salvation of the individual. The Adlerian method and the pastoral cure of souls, whether Protestant or Catholic, have only one thing in common, and that is the fact that they both apply themselves to the conscious mind, and in so doing appeal to a person's insight and will.

540 Freudian psychoanalysis, on the other hand, appeals in the first place neither to insight nor to the will, but seeks to lead the contents of the unconscious over into the conscious mind, thereby destroying the roots of the disturbances or symptoms. Freud seeks, therefore, to remove the disturbance of adaptation by an undermining of the symptoms, and not through treatment of the conscious mind. That is the aim of his psychoanalytic technique.

541 My difference with Freud begins with the interpretation of unconscious material. It stands to reason that you cannot integrate anything into consciousness without some measure of comprehension, i.e., insight. In order to make the unconscious material assimilable or understandable, Freud employs his famous sexual theory, which conceives the material brought to light through analysis mainly as sexual tendencies (or other immoral wishes) that are incompatible with the conscious attitude. Freud's standpoint here is based on the rationalistic materialism of the scientific views current in the late nineteenth century (of which his book *The Future of an Illusion* affords the plainest possible demonstration). With these views a fairly far-reaching recognition of the animal nature of man can be effected without too much difficulty, for the moral conflict is then apparently limited to easily avoidable collisions with public opinion or the penal code. At the same time Freud speaks of "sublimation," which he understands as an application of libido in desexualized form. I cannot enter here into a criticism of this very delicate subject, but would merely point out that not everything that comes out of the unconscious can be "sublimated."

542 For anyone who, whether by temperament, or for philosophical or religious reasons, cannot adopt the standpoint of scientific materialism, the realization of unconscious contents is in every respect a serious problem. Fortunately an instinctive

resistance protects us from realizations that would take us too far; hence one can often content onself with a moderate increase of consciousness. This is particularly so in the case of simple, uncomplicated neuroses, or rather, with people who are simple and uncomplicated (a neurosis is never more complicated than the person who has it). Those, on the other hand, with more refined natures suffer mostly from a passion for consciousness far exceeding their instinctive resistance. They want to see, know, and understand. For these people the answer given by the Freudian art of interpretation is unsatisfying. Here the Church's means of grace, especially as entrusted to the Catholic priest, are likely to come to the aid of understanding, for their form and meaning are suited at the outset to the nature of unconscious contents. That is why the priest not only hears the confession, but also asks questions—indeed, it is incumbent on him to ask them. What is more, he can ask about things which would otherwise only come to the ears of the doctor. In view of the means of grace at his disposal, the priest's intervention cannot be regarded as exceeding his competence, seeing that he is also empowered to lay the storm which he has provoked.

43 For the Protestant minister the problem is not so simple. Apart from common prayer and Holy Communion, he has no ritual ceremonies at his disposal, no spiritual exercises, rosaries, pilgrimages, etc., with their expressive symbolism. He is therefore compelled to take his stand on moral ground, which puts the instinctual forces coming up from the unconscious in danger of a new repression. Any sacral action, in whatever form, works like a vessel for receiving the contents of the unconscious. Puritan simplification has deprived Protestantism of just this means of acting on the unconscious; at any rate it has dispossessed the clergyman of his quality as a priestly mediator, which is so very necessary to the soul. Instead, it has given the individual responsibility for himself and left him alone with his God. Herein lies the advantage and also the danger of Protestantism. From this, too, comes its inner unrest, which in the course of a few centuries has begotten more than four hundred Protestant denominations—an indubitable symptom of individualism run riot.

44 There can be no doubt that the psychoanalytical unveiling of the unconscious has a great effect. Equally, there can be no

doubt of the tremendous effect of Catholic confession, especially when it is not just a passive hearing, but an active intervention. In view of this, it is truly astonishing that the Protestant Churches have not long since made an effort to revive the institution of confession as the epitome of the pastoral bond between the shepherd and his flock. For the Protestant, however, there is—and rightly so—no going back to this primitive Catholic form; it is too sharply opposed to the nature of Protestantism. The Protestant minister, rightly seeing in the cure of souls the real purpose of his existence, naturally looks round for a new way that will lead to the souls, and not merely to the ears, of his parishioners. Analytical psychology seems to him to provide the key, for the meaning and purpose of his ministry are not fulfilled with the Sunday sermon, which, though it reaches the ears, seldom penetrates to the heart, much less to the soul, the most hidden of all things hidden in man. The cure of souls can only be practised in the stillness of a colloquy, carried on in the healthful atmosphere of unreserved confidence. Soul must work on soul, and many doors be unlocked that bar the way to the innermost sanctuary. Psychoanalysis possesses the means of opening doors otherwise tightly closed.

545 The opening of these doors, however, is often very like a surgical operation, where the doctor, with knife poised, must be prepared for anything the moment the cut is made. The psychoanalyst, likewise, can discover unforeseen things that are very unpleasant indeed, such as latent psychoses and the like. Although these things, given time, often come to the surface entirely of their own accord, the blame nevertheless falls on the analyst, who, by his intervention, releases the disturbance prematurely. Only a thorough knowledge of psychiatry and its specialized techniques can protect the doctor from such blunders. A lay analyst should therefore always work in collaboration with a doctor.

546 Fortunately, the unlucky accidents I have just mentioned occur relatively seldom. But what psychoanalysis brings to light is, in itself, difficult enough to cope with. It brings the patient face to face with his life problem, and hence with some of the ultimate, serious questions which he has hitherto evaded. As human nature is very far from innocent, the facts that come up are usually quite sufficient to explain why the patient avoided

them: he felt instinctively that he did not know a satisfactory answer to these questions. Accordingly he expects it from the analyst. The analyst can now safely leave certain critical questions open—and to the patient's own advantage; for no sensible patient will expect from him anything more than *medical* help. More is expected from the clergyman, namely the solution of *religious* questions.

547 As already said, the Catholic Church has at her disposal ways and means which have served since olden times to gather the lower, instinctual forces of the psyche into symbols and in this way integrate them into the hierarchy of the spirit. The Protestant minister lacks these means, and consequently often stands perplexed before certain facts of human nature which no amount of admonition, or insight, or goodwill, or heroic self-castigation can subdue. In Protestantism good and evil are flatly and irreconcilably opposed to one another. There is no visible forgiveness; the human being is left alone with his sin. And God, as we know, only forgives the sins we have conquered ourselves. For the Protestant clergy it is a momentous psychological difficulty that they possess no forms which would serve to catch the lower instincts of psychic life. It is precisely the problem of the unconscious conflict brought to light by psychoanalysis that requires solving. The doctor can—on the basis of scientific materialism—treat the problem with medical discretion, that is to say he can regard the ethical problems of his patient as lying outside his competence as a doctor. He can safely retire behind a regretful "There you must make out as best you can." But the Protestant clergyman cannot, in my opinion, wash his hands in innocence; he must accompany the soul of the person who confides in him on its dark journey. The reductive standpoint of psychoanalysis is of little use to him here, for any development is a building up and not a breaking down. Good advice and moral exhortation are little if any help in serious cases because, if followed, they dispel that intense darkness which precedes the coming of the light. As a wise saying of the East puts it: It is better to do good than to eschew evil. He who is wise, therefore, will play the part of beggar, king, or criminal, and be mindful of the gods.

548 It is easier for the Catholic clergy to employ the elements of psychological analysis than it is for the Protestant. The latter

are faced with the harder task. Not only do the Catholics possess a ready-made pastoral technique in the historically sanctioned form of confession, penance, and absolution, but they also have at their command a rich and palpably ritualistic symbolism which fully satisfies the demands as well as the obscure passions of simpler minds. The Protestants need a psychological technique to an even greater degree since they lack all essential forms of ritual. I therefore hold that psychological interest on the part of the Protestant clergy is entirely legitimate and even necessary. Their possible encroachment upon medical territory is more than balanced by medical incursions into religion and philosophy, to which doctors naïvely believe themselves entitled (witness the explanation of religious processes in terms of sexual symptoms or infantile wish-fantasies). The doctor and the clergyman undoubtedly clash head-on in analytical psychology. This collision should lead to co-operation and not to enmity.

49 Owing to the absence of ritual forms, the Protestant (as opposed to the Catholic) cure of souls develops into a personal discussion in the sense of an "I-Thou" relationship. It cannot translate the fundamental problem of the transference into something impersonal, as the Catholic can, but must handle it with confidence as a personal experience. Any contact with the unconscious that goes at all deep leads to transference phenomena. Whenever, therefore, the clergyman penetrates any distance into the psychic background, he will provoke a transference (with men as well as with women). This involves him personally, and on top of that he has no form which he could substitute for his own person, as the Catholic priest can, or rather must do. In this way he finds himself drawn into the most personal participation for the sake of his parishioner's spiritual welfare, more so even than the analyst, for whom the specific salvation of the patient's soul is not necessarily a matter of burning importance. At all events he can resort to plausible excuses which the clergyman, somewhat nervously, must repudiate for higher reasons. Hence he stands, and must stand, in constant danger of involving himself in serious psychic conflicts which, to put it mildly, are not conducive to the parochial peace of mind. This danger is no trifling one, but it has the great advantage of drawing the responsible pastor back into real life and, at the same time, of exposing him to the tribulations of the

early Church (cf. the gossip against which Paul had to defend himself).

550 The pastor must make up his mind how far his public position, his stipend, and considerations for his family keep him from setting forth on the perilous mission of curing souls. I would not think ill of him if he decided not to follow the advice that Tertullian gave his catechumens, namely, that they should deliberately visit the arena. Real pastoral work that is based on modern psychology can easily expose the clergyman to the martyrdom of public misinterpretation. Public position and regard for the family, though worldly considerations, counsel a wise reserve (for the children of this world are, as we know, wiser than the children of light). Nevertheless, the eyes of the soul turn longingly to those who, regardless of their worldly welfare, can throw everything into the scales for the sake of something better. Nothing, certainly, is ever won by childish enthusiasm; yet only with daring—a daring which never leaves the firm ground of the real and the possible, and which shrinks from no suffering—can anything of greater worth be achieved.

551 Thus it is the Protestant minister's lack of ritual equipment which holds him back from closer contact with the world, and at the same time drives him towards a greater adventure—because it moves him right into the firing line. I hope that the Protestant will not be found wanting in courage for this task.

552 All intelligent psychotherapists would be glad if their endeavours were supported and supplemented by the work of the clergy. Certainly the problems of the human soul, approached from opposite ends by cleric and doctor, will cause considerable difficulties for both, not least on account of the difference in standpoint. But it is just from this encounter that we may expect the most fruitful stimulation for both sides.

BROTHER KLAUS [1]

74 Before me lies a little book by Father Alban Stoeckli on the Visions of the Blessed Brother Klaus.[2] Let the reader not be alarmed. Though a psychiatrist takes up his pen, it does not necessarily mean that he is going to set about this venerable figure with the profane instrument of psychopathology. Psychiatrists have committed enough sins already and have put their science to the most unsuitable uses. Nothing of the kind is to happen here: no diagnosis or analysis will be undertaken, no significant hints of pathological possibilities will be dropped, and no attempt will be made to bring the Blessed Nicholas of Flüe anywhere near a psychiatric clinic. Hence it must seem all the stranger to the reader that the reviewer of the book is a physician. I admit this fact is difficult to explain to anyone who does not know my unfashionable view on visions and the like. In this respect I am a good deal less sophisticated and more conservative than the so-called educated public, who in their philosophical embarrassment heave a sigh of relief when visions are equated with hallucinations, delusional ideas, mania, and schizo-

1 [First published as a review in the *Neue Schweizer Rundschau* (Zurich), new series, I (1933) : 4, 223–29. Previously trans. by Horace Gray in the *Journal of Nervous and Mental Diseases* (New York, Richmond, London), CIII (1946) : 4, 359–77. In 1947 Nicholas of Flüe, "Bruder Klaus," was canonized by Pope Pius XII and declared patron saint of Switzerland.—EDITORS.]

2 [*Die Visionen des seligen Bruder Klaus* (Einsiedeln, 1933).—EDITORS.]

phrenia, or whatever else these morbid things may be called, and are reduced to the right denominator by some competent authority. Medically, I can find nothing wrong with Brother Klaus. I see him as a somewhat unusual but in no wise pathological person, a man after my own heart: my brother Klaus. Rather remote, to be sure, at this distance of more than four hundred years, separated by culture and creed, by those fashionable trifles which we always think constitute a world. Yet they amount to no more than linguistic difficulties, and these do not impede understanding of the essentials. So little, in fact, that I was able to converse, in the primitive language of inward vision, with a man who in every way was even further removed from me than Brother Klaus—a Pueblo Indian, my friend Ochwiabiano ("Mountain Lake").[2a] For what interests us here is not the historical personage, not the well-known figure at the Diet of Stans,[3] but the "friend of God," who appeared but a few times on the world stage, yet lived a long life in the realms of the soul. Of what he there experienced he left behind only scant traces, so few and inarticulate that it is hard for posterity to form any picture of his inner life.

475 It has always intrigued me to know what a hermit does with himself all day long. Can we still imagine a real spiritual anchorite nowadays, one who has not simply crept away to vegetate in misanthropic simplicity? A solitary fellow, like an old elephant who resentfully defies the herd instinct? Can we imagine a normal person living a sensible, vital existence by himself, with no visible partner?

476 Brother Klaus had a house, wife, and children, and we do not know of any external factors which could have induced him to become a hermit. The sole reason for this was his singular inner life; experiences for which no merely natural grounds can be adduced, decisive experiences which accompanied him from youth up. These things seemed to him of more value than ordinary human existence. They were probably the object of his daily interest and the source of his spiritual vitality. It

2a [See *Memories, Dreams, Reflections,* ch. 9, sec. ii.]

3 [The Diet of Stans was a meeting in 1481 of representatives of the Swiss cantons at which disputes between the predominantly rural and the predominantly urban cantons were regulated, and as a result of which—largely through the intervention of Nicholas—Fribourg and Solothurn joined the Confederation.—EDITORS.]

sounds rather like an anecdote from the life of a scholar who is completely immersed in his studies when the so-called "Pilgrim's Tract" [4] relates: "And he [Brother Klaus] began to speak again and said to me, 'If it does not trouble you, I would like to show you my book, in which I am learning and seeking the art of this doctrine.' And he brought me a figure, drawn like a wheel with six spokes." So evidently Brother Klaus studied some mysterious "doctrine" or other; he sought to understand and interpret the things that happened to him. That the hermit's activity was a sort of study must also have occurred to Gundolfingen,[5] one of the oldest writers on our subject. He says: "Did he not likewise learn in that High School of the Holy Ghost the representation of the wheel, which he caused to be painted in his chapel, and through which, as in a clear mirror, was reflected the entire essence of the Godhead?" From the same "High School" he derived "his kindness, his doctrine, and his science." [5a]

477 Here we are concerned with the so-called Trinity Vision, which was of the greatest significance for the hermit's inner life. According to the oldest reports, it was an apparition of light, of surpassing intensity, in the form of a human face. The first-hand reports make no mention of a "wheel." This seems to have been a subsequent addition for the purpose of clarifying the vision. Just as a stone, falling into calm water, produces wave after wave of circles, so a sudden and violent vision of this kind has long-lasting after-effects, like any shock. And the stranger and more impressive the initial vision was, the longer it will take to be assimilated, and the greater and more persevering will be the efforts of the mind to master it and render it intelligible to human understanding. Such a vision is a tremendous "irruption" in the most literal sense of the word, and it has therefore always been customary to draw rings round it like those made by the falling stone when it breaks the smooth surface of the water.

[4] *Ein nutzlicher und loblicher Tractat von Bruder Claus und einem Bilger* (Nürnberg, 1488). Cited in Stoeckli, p. 41.

[5] Heinrich Gundolfingen (Gundelfingen or Gundelfinger), *c.* 1444–90, priest and professor of humanistic studies at the University of Fribourg, knew Klaus probably around the year 1480, and wrote his biography.

[5a] Durrer, *Bruder Klaus,* I, p. 434.

478 Now what has "irrupted" here, and wherein lies its mighty "impression"? The oldest source, Wölflin's biography,[6] narrates the following on this score:

> All who came to him were filled with terror at the first glance. As to the cause of this, he himself used to say that he had seen a piercing light resembling a human face. At the sight of it he feared that his heart would burst into little pieces. Overcome with terror, he instantly turned his face away and fell to the ground. And that was the reason why his face was now terrible to others.

This is borne out by the account which the humanist Karl Bovillus (Charles de Bouelles) gave to a friend in 1508 (some twenty years after the death of Brother Klaus):

> I wish to tell you of a vision which appeared to him in the sky, on a night when the stars were shining and he stood in prayer and contemplation. He saw the head of a human figure with a terrifying face, full of wrath and threats.[7]

So we shall not go wrong in surmising that the vision was terrifying in the extreme. When we consider that the mental attitude of that age, and in particular that of Brother Klaus, allowed no other interpretation than that this vision represented God himself, and that God signified the *summum bonum,* Absolute Perfection, then it is clear that such a vision must, by its violent contrast, have had a profound and shattering effect, whose assimilation into consciousness required years of the most strenuous spiritual effort. Through subsequent elaboration this vision then became the so-called Trinity Vision. As Father Stoeckli rightly conjectures, the "wheel" or circles were formed on the basis of, and as parallels to, the illustrated devotional books that were read at the time. As mentioned above, Brother Klaus even seems to have possessed such a book himself. Later, as a result of further mental elaboration, there were added the spokes of the wheel and the six secondary circles, as shown in the old picture of the vision in the parish church at Sachseln.

6 Heinrich Wölflin, also called by the Latin form Lupulus, born 1470, humanist and director of Latin studies at Bern.

7 *Ein gesichte Bruder Clausen ynn Schweytz und seine deutunge* (Wittenberg, 1528), p. 5. Cited in Stoeckli, p. 34, and Durrer, I, p. 560.

479 The vision of light was not the only one which Brother Klaus had. He even thought that, while still in his mother's womb, he had seen a star that outshone all others in brightness, and later, in his solitude, he saw a very similar star repeatedly. The vision of light had, therefore, occurred several times before in his life. Light means illumination; it is an illuminating idea that "irrupts." Using a very cautious formulation, we could say that the underlying factor here is a considerable tension of psychic energy, evidently corresponding to some very important unconscious content. This content has an overpowering effect and holds the conscious mind spellbound. The tremendous power of the "objective psychic" has been named "demon" or "God" in all epochs with the sole exception of the recent present. We have become so bashful in matters of religion that we correctly say "unconscious," because God has in fact become unconscious to us. This is what always happens when things are interpreted, explained, and dogmatized until they become so encrusted with man-made images and words that they can no longer be seen. Something similar seems to have happened to Brother Klaus, which is why the immediate experience burst upon him with appalling terror. Had his vision been as charming and edifying as the present picture at Sachseln, no such terror would ever have emanated from it.

480 "God" is a primordial experience of man, and from the remotest times humanity has taken inconceivable pains either to portray this baffling experience, to assimilate it by means of interpretation, speculation, and dogma, or else to deny it. And again and again it has happened, and still happens, that one hears too much about the "good" God and knows him too well, so that one confuses him with one's own ideas and regards them as sacred because they can be traced back a couple of thousand years. This is a superstition and an idolatry every bit as bad as the Bolshevist delusion that "God" can be educated out of existence. Even a modern theologian like Gogarten [8] is quite sure that God *can only be good.* A good man does not terrify me—what then would Gogarten have made of the Blessed Brother Klaus? Presumably he would have had to explain to him that he had seen the devil in person.

8 [Friedrich Gogarten (b. 1887), recently professor of systematic theology at Göttingen; author of *Die Kirche in der Welt* (1948).—EDITORS.]

481 And here we are in the midst of that ancient dilemma of how such visions are to be evaluated. I would suggest taking every genuine case at its face value. If it was an overwhelming experience for so worthy and shrewd a man as Brother Klaus, then I do not hesitate to call it a true and veritable experience of God, even if it turns out not quite right dogmatically. Great saints were, as we know, sometimes great heretics, so it is probable that anyone who has immediate experience of God is a little bit outside the organization one calls the Church. The Church itself would have been in a pretty pass if the Son of God had remained a law-abiding Pharisee, a point one tends to forget.

482 There are many indubitable lunatics who have experiences of God, and here too I do not contest the genuineness of the experience, for I know that it takes a complete and a brave man to stand up to it. Therefore I feel sorry for those who go under, and I shall not add insult to injury by saying that they tripped up on a mere psychologism. Besides, one can never know in what form a man will experience God, for there are very peculiar things just as there are very peculiar people—like those, for instance, who think that one can make anything but a conceptual distinction between the individual experience of God and God himself. It would certainly be desirable to make this distinction, but to do so one would have to know what God is in and for himself, which does not seem to me possible.

483 Brother Klaus's vision was a genuine primordial experience, and it therefore seemed to him particularly necessary to submit it to a thorough dogmatic revision. Loyally and with great efforts he applied himself to this task, the more so as he was smitten with terror in every limb so that even strangers took fright. The unconscious taint of heresy that probably clings to all genuine and unexpurgated visions is only hinted at in the Trinity Vision, but in the touched-up version it has been successfully eliminated. All the affectivity, the very thing that made the strongest impression, has vanished without a trace, thus affording at least a negative proof of our interpretation.

484 Brother Klaus's elucidation of his vision with the help of the three circles (the so-called "wheel") is in keeping with age-old human practice, which goes back to the Bronze Age sun-wheels (often found in Switzerland) and to the mandalas depicted in the Rhodesian rock-drawings. These sun-wheels may

possibly be paleolithic;[9] we find them in Mexico, India, Tibet, and China. The Christian mandalas probably date back to St. Augustine and his definition of God as a circle. Presumably Henry Suso's notions of the circle, which were accessible to the "Friends of God," were derived from the same source. But even if this whole tradition had been cut off and no little treatise with mandalas in the margin had ever come to light, and if Brother Klaus had never seen the rose-window of a church, he would still have succeeded in working his great experience into the shape of a circle, because this is what has always happened in every part of the world and still goes on happening today.[10]

485 We spoke above of heresy. In Father Stoeckli's newly found fragment describing the vision, there is another vision which contains an interesting parallelism. I put the two passages side by side for the sake of comparison:

There came a handsome majestic man through the palace, with a shining colour in his face, and in a white garment. And he laid both arms on his shoulders and pressed him close and thanked him with all the fervent love of his heart, because he had stood by his son and helped him in his need.	There came a beautiful majestic woman through the palace, also in a white garment. . . . And she laid both arms on his shoulders and pressed him close to her heart with an overflowing love, because he had stood so faithfully by her son in his need.[11]

486 It is clear that this is a vision of God the Father and Son, and of the Mother of God. The palace is heaven, where "God the Father" dwells, and also "God the Mother." In pagan form they are unmistakably God and Goddess, as their absolute parallelism shows. The androgyny of the divine Ground is characteristic of mystic experience. In Indian Tantrism the masculine Shiva and the feminine Shakti both proceed from

9 [Documentation of the Rhodesian sun-wheels has not been possible, though such rock-carved forms are noted in Angola and South Africa. Their dating is in doubt. Cf. supra, par. 100, n. 43. Also Jung's "Tavistock Lectures," Lecture 2 (par. 81, n. 5).—EDITORS.]

10 More on this in Zimmer, *Kunstform und Yoga*, and in my "Commentary on *The Secret of the Golden Flower,*" pars. 31–45.

11 Stoeckli, pp. 20f.

Brahman, which is devoid of qualities. Man as the son of the Heavenly Father and Heavenly Mother is an age-old conception which goes back to primitive times, and in this vision the Blessed Brother Klaus is set on a par with the Son of God. The Trinity in this vision—Father, Mother, and Son—is very undogmatic indeed. Its nearest parallel is the exceedingly unorthodox Gnostic Trinity: God, Sophia, Christ. The Church, however, has expunged the feminine nature of the Holy Ghost, though it is still suggested by the symbolic dove.

487 It is nice to think that the only outstanding Swiss mystic received, by God's grace, unorthodox visions and was permitted to look with unerring eye into the depths of the divine soul, where all the creeds of humanity which dogma has divided are united in *one* symbolic archetype. As I hope Father Stoeckli's little book will find many attentive readers, I shall not discuss the Vision of the Well, nor the Vision of the Man with the Bearskin,[12] although from the standpoint of comparative symbolism they offer some very interesting aspects—for I do not want to deprive the reader of the pleasure of finding out their meaning by himself.

[12] Cf. also Franz, *Die Visionen des Niklaus von Fluë*.

LETTER TO PÈRE LACHAT[1]

Küsnacht, 27 March 1954

Dear Sir,

532 It was very kind of you to send me your booklet[2] on the reception and action of the Holy Spirit. I have read it with special interest since the subject of the Holy Spirit seems to me one of current importance. I remember that the former Archbishop of York, Dr. Temple, admitted, in conversation with me, that the Church has not done all that it might to develop the idea of the Holy Spirit. It is not difficult to see why this is so, for *τὸ πνεῦμα πνεῖ ὅπου θέλει*[3]—a fact which an institution may find very inconvenient! In the course of reading your little book a number of questions and thoughts have occurred to me, which I set out below, since my reactions may perhaps be of some interest to you.

533 I quite agree with your view that one pauses before entrusting oneself to the "unforeseeable action" of the Holy Spirit. One feels afraid of it, not, I think, without good reason. Since there is a marked difference between the God of the Old Testament and the God of the New, a definition is desirable. You nowhere explain your idea of God. Which God have you in mind: The New Testament God, or the Old? The latter is a paradox; good and demonlike, just and unjust at the same time, while the God of the New Testament is by definition perfect, good, the Summum Bonum even, without any element of the dark or the demon in him. But if you identify these two Gods, different as they are, the fear and resistance one feels in entrusting oneself unconditionally to the Holy Spirit are easy to understand. The divine action is so unforeseeable that it may well be really disastrous. That being so, the prudence of the serpent counsels us not to approach the Holy Spirit too closely.

534 If, on the other hand, it is the New Testament God you have in mind, one can be absolutely certain that the risk is more apparent

[1] [(Translated from the French by A.S.B.G.) See Jung's letters of 18 Jan. and 29 June 1955 to Père William Lachat in *Letters,* ed. G. Adler, vol. 2.]

[2] [*La Réception et l'action du Saint-Esprit dans la vie personnelle et communautaire* (Neuchâtel, 1953).]

[3] ["The spirit bloweth where it listeth." John 3:8.]

than real since the end will always be good. In that event the experiment loses its venturesome character; it is not really dangerous. It is then merely foolish not to give oneself up entirely to the action of the Holy Spirit. Rather one should seek him day by day, and one will easily lay hold of him, as Mr. Horton[4] assures us. In the absence of a formal statement on your part, I assume that you identify the two Gods. In that case the Holy Spirit would not be easy to apprehend; it would even be highly dangerous to attract the divine attention by specially pious behaviour (as in the case of Job and some others). In the Old Testament Satan still has the Father's ear, and can influence him even against the righteous. The Old Testament furnishes us with quite a number of instances of this kind, and they warn us to be very careful when we are dealing with the Holy Spirit. The man who is not particularly bold and adventurous will do well to bear these examples in mind and to thank God that the Holy Spirit does not concern himself with us overmuch. One feels much safer under the shadow of the Church, which serves as a fortress to protect us against God and his Spirit. It is very comforting to be assured by the Catholic Church that it "possesses" the Spirit, who assists regularly at its rites. Then one knows that he is well chained up. Protestantism is no less reassuring in that it represents the Spirit to us as something to be sought for, to be easily "drunk," even to be possessed. We get the impression that he is something passive, which cannot budge without us. He has lost his dangerous qualities, his fire, his autonomy, his power. He is represented as an innocuous, passive, and purely beneficent element, so that to be afraid of him would seem just stupid.

1535 This characterization of the Holy Spirit leaves out of account the terrors of YHWH. It does not tell us what the Holy Spirit is, since it has failed to explain to us clearly what it has done with the *Deus absconditus*. Albert Schweitzer naïvely informs us that he takes the side of the ethical God and avoids the *absconditus,* as if a mortal man had the ability to hide himself when faced with an almighty God or to take the other, less risky side. God can implicate him in unrighteousness whenever he chooses.

1536 I also fail to find a definition of Christ; one does not know whether he is identical with the Holy Spirit, or different from him. Everyone talks about Christ; but who is this Christ? When talking to a Catholic or Anglican priest, I am in no doubt. But when I

[4] [Unidentified.]

am talking to a pastor of the Reformed Church, it may be that Christ is the Second Person of the Trinity and God in his entirety, or a divine man (the "supreme authority," as Schweitzer has it, which doesn't go too well with the error of the parousia), or one of those great founders of ethical systems like Pythagoras, Confucius, and so on. It is the same with the idea of God. What is Martin Buber talking about when he discloses to us his intimate relations with "God"? YHWH? The olden Trinity, or the modern Trinity, which has become something more like a Quaternity since the Sponsa has been received into the Thalamus?[5] Or the rather misty God of Protestantism? Do you think that everyone who says that he is surrendering himself to Christ has really surrendered himself to Christ? Isn't it more likely that he has surrendered himself to the image of Christ which he has made for himself, or to that of God the Father or the Holy Spirit? Are they all the same Christ—the Christ of the Synoptics, of the *Exercitia Spiritualia,* of a mystic of Mount Athos, of Count Zinzendorf,[6] of the hundred sects, of Caux[7] and Rudolf Steiner, and—last but not least—of St. Paul? Do you really believe that anyone, be he who he may, can bring about the real presence of one of the Sacred Persons by an earnest utterance of their name? I can be certain only that someone has called up a psychic image, but it is impossible for me to confirm the real presence of the Being evoked. It is neither for us nor for others to decide *who* has been invoked by the holy name and to whom one has surrendered oneself. Has it not happened that the invocation of the Holy Spirit has brought the devil on the scene? What are invoked are in the first place images, and that is why images have a special importance. I do not for a moment deny that the deep emotion of a true prayer may reach transcendence, but it is above our heads. There would not even be any transcendence if our images and metaphors were more than anthropomorphism and the words themselves had a magical effect. The Catholic Church protects itself against this insinuation *expressis verbis,* insisting on its teaching that God cannot go back on his own institutions. He is morally obliged to maintain them by his Holy Spirit or his

[5] [*Apostolic Constitution ("Munificentissimus Deus") of Pius XII* (1950), sec. 33: ". . . on this day the Virgin Mother was taken up to her heavenly bridal-chamber." Cf. "Answer to Job" (C.W., vol. 11), par. 743, n. 4.]

[6] [Count Nikolaus Ludwig von Zinzendorf (1700–60), founder of the Herrnhuter Brüdergemeinde, a community of Moravian Brethren.]

[7] [Caux-sur-Montreux, Switzerland, a conference centre of the Moral Re-Armament movement. A World Assembly was held there in 1949.]

grace. All theological preaching is a mythologem, a series of archetypal images intended to give a more or less exact description of the unimaginable transcendence. It is a paradox, but it is justified. The totality of these archetypes corresponds to what I have called the *collective unconscious. We are concerned here with empirical facts, as I have proved.* (Incidentally, you don't seem to be well informed about either the nature of the unconscious or my psychology. The idea that the unconscious is the abyss of all the horrors is a bit out of date. The collective unconscious is neutral; it is only nature, both spiritual and chthonic. To impute to my psychology the idea that the Holy Spirit is "only a projection of the human soul" is false. He is a transcendental fact which presents itself to us under the guise of an archetypal image (e.g, [ ][8], or are we to believe that he is really "breathed forth" by the Father and the Son?). There is no guarantee that this image corresponds exactly to the transcendental entity.

1537 The unconscious is ambivalent; it can produce both good and evil effects. So the image of God also has two sides, like YHWH or the God of Clement of Rome with two hands; the right is Christ, the left Satan, and it is with these two hands that he rules the world.[9] Nicholas of Cusa calls God a *complexio oppositorum* (naturally under the apotropaic condition of the *privatio boni*!). YHWH's paradoxical qualities are continued in the New Testament. In these circumstances it becomes very difficult to know what to make of *prayer*. Can we address our prayer to the good God to the exclusion of the demon, as Schweitzer recommends? Have we the power of dissociating God like the countrywoman who said to the child Jesus, when he interrupted her prayer to the Virgin: "Shhh, child, I'm talking to your mother"? Can we really put on one side the God who is dangerous to us? Do we believe that God is so powerless that we can say to him: "Get out, I'm talking to your better half?" Or can we ignore the *absconditus?* Schweitzer invites us to do just this; we're going to have our bathe in the river, and never mind the crocodiles. One can, it seems, brush them aside. Who is there who can produce this "simple faith"?

1538 Like God, then, the unconscious has two aspects; one good, favourable, beneficent, the other evil, malevolent, disastrous. The unconscious is the immediate source of our religious experiences. This psychic nature of all experience does not mean that the tran-

8 [Lacuna in the file copy of the letter.]

9 [Cf. *Aion*, C.W., vol. 9, ii, pars. 99ff.]

scendental realities are also psychic; the physicist does not believe that the transcendental reality represented by his psychic model is also psychic. He calls it *matter,* and in the same way the psychologist in no wise attributes a psychic nature to his images or archetypes. He calls them "psychoids"[10] and is convinced that they represent transcendental realities. He even knows of "simple faith" as that *conviction which one cannot avoid.* It is vain to seek for it; it comes when it wills, for it is the gift of the Holy Spirit. There is only one divine spirit—an immediate presence, often terrifying and in no degree subject to our choice. There is no guarantee that it may not just as well be the devil, as happened to St. Ignatius Loyola in his vision of the *serpens oculatus,* interpreted at first as Christ or God and later as the devil.[11] Nicholas of Flüe had his terrifying vision of the *absconditus,* and transformed it later into the kindly Trinity of the parish church of Sachseln.[12]

1539 Surrender to God is a formidable adventure, and as "simple" as any situation over which man has no control. He who can risk himself wholly to it finds himself directly in the hands of God, and is there confronted with a situation which makes "simple faith" a vital necessity; in other words, the situation becomes so full of risk or overtly dangerous that the deepest instincts are aroused. An experience of this kind is always numinous, for it unites all aspects of totality. All this is wonderfully expressed in Christian religious symbolism: the divine will incarnate in Christ urges towards the fatal issue, the catastrophe followed by the fact or hope of resurrection, while Christian faith insists on the deadly danger of the adventure; but the Churches assure us that God protects us against all danger and especially against the fatality of our character. Instead of taking up our cross, we are told to cast it on Christ. He will take on the burden of our anguish and we can enjoy our "simple faith" at Caux. We take flight into the Christian collectivity where we can forget even the will of God, for in society we lose the feeling of personal responsibility and can swim with the current. One feels safe in the multitude, and the Church does everything to reassure us against the fear of God, as if it did not believe that He could bring about a serious situation. On the other hand psychology is painted as black as possible, because it teaches, in full agreement

10 [Cf. *Mysterium Coniunctionis,* C.W., vol. 14, pars. 786f.]

11 [Cf. "On the Nature of the Psyche" (C.W., vol. 8), par. 395.]

12 [Cf. "Brother Klaus" (C.W., vol. 11) and "Archetypes of the Collective Unconscious" (C.W., vol. 9, i), pars. 12ff.]

with the Christian creed, that no man can ascend unless he has first descended. A professor of theology once accused me publicly that "in flagrant contradiction to the words of Christ" I had criticized as *childish* the man who remains an infant retaining his early beliefs. I had to remind him of the fact that Christ never said "remain children" but "become like children." This is one small example of the way in which Christian experience is falsified; it is prettied up, its sombre aspects are denied, its dangers are hidden. But the action of the Holy Spirit does not meet us in the atmosphere of a normal, bourgeois (or proletarian!), sheltered, regular life, but only in the insecurity outside the human economy, in the infinite spaces where one is alone with the *providentia Dei.* We must never forget that Christ was an innovator and revolutionary, *executed with criminals.* The reformers and great religious geniuses were *heretics.* It is there that you find the footprints of the Holy Spirit, and no one asks for him or receives him *without having to pay a high price.* The price is so high that no one today would dare to suggest that he possesses or is possessed by the Holy Spirit, or he would be too close to the psychiatric clinic. The danger of making oneself ridiculous is too real, not to mention the risk of offending our real god: *respectability.* There one even becomes very strict, and it would not be at all allowable for God and his Spirit to permit themselves to give advice or orders as in the Old Testament. Certainly everyone would lay his irregularities to the account of the unconscious. One would say: God is faithful, he does not forsake us, God does not lie, he will keep his word, and so on. We know it isn't true, but we go on repeating these lies ad infinitum. It is quite understandable that we should seek to hold the truth at arm's length, because it seems impossible to give oneself up to a God who doesn't even respect his own laws when he falls victim to one of his fits of rage or forgets his solemn oath. When I allow myself to mention these well-attested facts the theologians accuse me of blasphemy, unwilling as they are to admit the ambivalence of the divine nature, the demonic character of the God of the Bible and even of the Christian God. Why was that cruel immolation of the Son necessary if the anger of the "deus ultionum" is not hard to appease? One doesn't notice much of the Father's goodness and love during the tragic end of his Son.

1540 True, we ought to abandon ourselves to the divine will as much as we can, but admit that to do so is difficult and dangerous, so dangerous indeed that I would not dare to advise one of my clients to "take" the Holy Spirit or to abandon himself to him until I had first made him realize the risks of such an enterprise.

541 Permit me here to make a few comments. On pp. 11f.: The Holy Spirit is to be feared. He is revolutionary *especially* in religious matters (not at all "perhaps even religious," p. 11 bottom). Ah, yes, one does well to refuse the Holy Spirit, because people would like to palm him off on us without telling us what this sacred fire is which killeth and maketh to live. One may get through a battle without being wounded, but there are some unfortunates who do not know how to avoid either mutilation or death. Perhaps one is among their number. One can hardly take the risk of that without the most convincing necessity. It is quite normal and reasonable to refuse oneself to the Holy Spirit. Has M. Boegner's[13] life been turned upside down? Has he taken the risk of breaking with convention (e.g., eating with Gentiles when one is an orthodox Jew, or even better with women of doubtful reputation), or been immersed in darkness like Hosea, making himself ridiculous, overturning the traditional order, etc.? It is deeds that are needed, not words.

542 p. 13. It is very civil to say that the Holy Spirit is "uncomfortable and sometimes upsetting," but very characteristic.

543 p. 16. It is clear that the Holy Spirit is concerned in the long run with the collectivity (*ecclesia*), but in the first place with the individual, and to create him he isolates him from his environment, just as Christ himself was thought mad by his own family.

544 p. 19. The Holy Spirit, "the accredited bearer of the holiness of God." But who will recognize him as such? Everyone will certainly say that he is drunk or a heretic or mad. To the description "bearer of the holiness" needs to be added the holiness which God himself sometimes sets on one side (Ps. 89).

545 p. 21. It is no use for Mr. Horton to believe that receiving the Holy Spirit is quite a simple business. It is so to the degree that we do not realize what is at issue. We are surrendering ourselves to a Spirit with two aspects. That is why we are not particularly ready to "drink" of him, or to "thirst" for him. We hope rather that God is going to pass us by, that we are protected against his injustice and his violence. Granted, the New Testament speaks otherwise, but when we get to the Apocalypse the style changes remarkably and approximates to that of older times. Christ's kingdom has been provisional; the world is left thereafter for another aeon to Antichrist and to all the horrors that can be envisaged by a pitiless

[13] [Unidentified.]

and loveless imagination. This witness in favour of the god with two faces represents the last and tragic chapter of the New Testament which would like to have set up a god exclusively good and made only of love. This Apocalypse—was it a frightful gaffe on the part of those Fathers who drew up the canon? I don't think so. They were still too close to the hard reality of things and of religious traditions to share our mawkish interpretations and prettily falsified opinions.

1546 p. 23. "Surrender without the least reserve." Would Mr. Horton advise us to cross the Avenue de l'Opéra blindfold? His belief in the good God is so strong that he has forgotten the fear of God. For Mr. Horton God is dangerous no longer. But in that case—what is the Apocalypse all about? He asks nevertheless, "To what interior dynamism is one surrendering oneself, natural or supernatural?" When he says, "I surrender myself wholly to God," how does he know what is "whole"? Our wholeness is an unconscious fact, whose extent we cannot establish. God alone can judge of human wholeness. We can only say humbly: "As wholly as possible."

1547 There is no guarantee that it is really *God* when we say "god." It is perhaps a word concealing a demon or a void, or it is an act of grace coincident with our prayer.

1548 This total surrender is disturbing. Nearly twenty years ago I gave a course at the Ecole Polytechnique Suisse for two semesters on the *Exercitia Spiritualia* of St. Ignatius.[14] On that occasion I received a profound impression of this total surrender, in relation to which one never knows whether one is dealing with sanctity or with spiritual pride. One sees too that the god to whom one surrenders oneself is a clear and well-defined prescription given by the director of the Exercises. This is particularly evident in the part called the "colloquium," where there is only one who speaks, and that is the initiand. One asks oneself what God or Christ would say if it were a real dialogue, but no one expects God to reply.

1549 p. 26. The identity of Christ with the Holy Spirit seems to me to be questionable, since Christ made a very clear distinction between himself and the paraclete, even if the latter's function resembles Christ's. The near-identity of the Holy Spirit with Christ in St. John's Gospel is characteristic of the evangelist's Gnosticism.

14 [Lectures at the Federal Polytechnic Institute (ETH), Zurich, June 1939 to March 1940. Privately issued.]

It seems to me important to insist on the chronological sequence of the Three Persons, for there is an evolution in three stages:

1. The Father. The opposites not yet differentiated; Satan is still numbered among the "sons of God." Christ then is only hinted at.

2. God is incarnated as the "Son of Man." Satan has fallen from heaven. He is the other "son." The opposites are differentiated.

3. The Holy Spirit is One, his prototype is the Ruach Elohim, an emanation, an active principle, which proceeds (as quintessence) *a Patre Filioque*. Inasmuch as he proceeds also from the Son he is different from the Ruach Elohim, who represents the active principle of Yahweh (not incarnate, with only angels in place of a son). The angels are called "sons," they are not begotten and there is no mother of the angels. Christ on the other hand shares in human nature, he is even man by definition. In this case it is evident that the Holy Spirit proceeding from the Son does not arise from the divine nature only, that is, from the second Person, but also from the human nature. Thanks to this fact, human nature is included in the mystery of the Trinity. Man forms part of it.

550 This "human nature" is only figuratively human, for it is exempt from original sin. This makes the "human" element definitely doubtful inasmuch as man without exception, save for Christ and his mother, is begotten and born bearing the stamp of the *macula peccati*. That is why Christ and his mother enjoy a nature divine rather than human. For the Protestant there is no reason to think of Mary as a goddess. Thus he can easily admit that on his mother's side Christ was contaminated by original sin; this makes him all the more human, at least so far as the *filioque* of the Protestant confession does not exclude the true man from the "human" nature of Christ. On the other hand it becomes evident that the Holy Spirit necessarily proceeds *from the two natures* of Christ, not only from the God in him, but also from the man in him.

551 There were very good reasons why the Catholic Church has carefully purified Christ and his mother from all contamination by the *peccatum originale*. Protestantism was more courageous, even daring or—perhaps?—more oblivious of the consequences, in not denying—*expressis verbis*—the human nature (in part) of Christ and (wholly) of his mother. *Thus the ordinary man became a source of the Holy Spirit,* though certainly not the only one. It is like lightning, which issues not only from the clouds but also

from the peaks of the mountains. This fact signifies the continued and progressive divine incarnation. Thus man is received and integrated into the divine drama. He seems destined to play a decisive part in it; that is why he must receive the Holy Spirit. I look upon the receiving of the Holy Spirit as a highly revolutionary fact which cannot take place until the ambivalent nature of the Father is recognized. If God is the *summum bonum,* the incarnation makes no sense, for a good god could never produce such hate and anger that his only son had to be sacrificed to appease it. A Midrash says that the Shofar is still sounded on the Day of Atonement to remind YHWH of his act of injustice towards Abraham (by compelling him to slay Isaac) and to prevent him from repeating it. A conscientious clarification of the idea of God would have consequences as upsetting as they are necessary. They would be indispensable for an interior development of the trinitarian drama and of the role of the Holy Spirit. The Spirit is destined to be incarnate in man or to choose him as a transitory dwelling-place. "Non habet nomen proprium," says St. Thomas;[15] because he will receive the name of man. That is why he must not be identified with Christ. We cannot receive the Holy Spirit unless we have accepted our own individual life as Christ accepted his. Thus we become the "sons of god" fated to experience the conflict of the divine opposites, represented by the crucifixion.

1552 Man seems indispensable to the divine drama. We shall understand this role of man's better if we consider the paradoxical nature of the Father. As the Apocalypse has alluded to it (*evangelium aeternum*) and Joachim of Flora[16] has expressed it, the Son would seem to be the intermediary between the Father and the Holy Spirit. We could repeat what Origen said of the Three Persons, that the Father is the greatest and the Holy Spirit the least. This is true inasmuch as the Father by descending from the cosmic immensity became the least by incarnating himself within the narrow bounds of the human soul (cult of the child-god, Angelus Silesius). Doubtless the presence of the Holy Spirit enlarges human nature by divine attributes. Human nature is the divine vessel and as such the union of the Three. This results in a kind of quaternity which always signifies *totality,* while the triad is rather a process, but never the natural division of the *circle,* the natural symbol of wholeness. The quaternity as union of the Three seems to be aimed at by the

15 ["He has no proper name." *Summa theologica,* I, xxvi, art. 1.]

16 [The "everlasting gospel" in Rev. 14:7 is "Fear God." For Joachim's view, see *Aion,* pars. 137ff.]

Assumption of Mary. This dogma adds the feminine element to the masculine Trinity, the terrestrial element (*virgo terra!*) to the spiritual, and thus sinful man to the Godhead. For Mary in her character of *omnium gratiarum mediatrix* intercedes for the sinner before the judge of the world. (She is his "paraclete.") She is φιλανθρωπος like her prefiguration, the Sophia of the Old Testament.[17] Protestant critics have completely overlooked the symbolic aspect of the new dogma and its emotional value, which is a capital fault.

553 The "littleness" of the Holy Spirit stems from the fact that God's pneuma dissolves into the form of little flames, remaining none the less intact and whole. His dwelling in a certain number of human individuals and their transformation into υἱῷ τοῦ θεοῦ signifies a very important step forward beyond "Christocentrism." Anyone who takes up the question of the Holy Spirit seriously is faced with the question whether Christ is identical with the Holy Spirit or different from him. With dogma, I prefer the independence of the Holy Spirit. The Holy Spirit is *one,* a *complexio oppositorum,* in contrast to YHWH after the separation of the divine opposites symbolized by God's two sons, Christ and Satan. On the level of the Son there is no answer to the question of good and evil; there is only an incurable separation of the opposites. The annulling of evil by the *privatio boni* (declaring to be μὴ ὄν) is a *petitio principii* of the most flagrant kind and no solution whatever.[18] It seems to me to be the Holy Spirit's task and charge to reconcile and reunite the opposites in the human individual through a special development of the human soul. The soul is paradoxical like the Father; it is black and white, divine and demon-like, in its primitive and natural state. By the discriminative function of its conscious side it separates opposites of every kind, and especially those of the moral order personified in Christ and Devil. Thereby the soul's spiritual development creates an enormous tension, from which man can only suffer. Christ promised him redemption. But in what exactly does this consist? The *imitatio Christi* leads us to Calvary and to the annihilation of the "body," that is, of biological life, and if we take this death as symbolic it is a state of suspension between the opposites, that is to say, an unresolved conflict. That is exactly what Przywara has named the "rift,"[19] the gulf separating good from evil, the latent and apparently incurable dualism of

[17] [Cf. "Answer to Job," pars. 613ff.]

[18] [Cf. *Aion,* pars. 89ff.]

[19] [Erich Przywara, *Deus semper maior,* I, pp. 71f.]

Christianity, the eternity of the devil and of damnation. (Inasmuch as good is real so also is evil.)

1554 To find the answer to this question we can but trust to our mental powers on the one hand and on the other to the functioning of the unconscious, that spirit which we cannot control. It can only be hoped that it is a "holy" spirit. The cooperation of conscious reasoning with the data of the unconscious is called the "transcendent function" (cf. *Psychological Types,* par. 828).[20] This function progressively unites the opposites. Psychotherapy makes use of it to heal neurotic dissociations, but this function had already served as the basis of Hermetic philosophy for seventeen centuries. Besides this, it is a natural and spontaneous phenomenon, part of the process of individuation. Psychology has no proof that this process does not unfold itself at the instigation of God's will.

1555 The Holy Spirit will manifest himself in any case in the psychic sphere of man and will be presented as a psychic experience. He thus becomes the object of empirical psychology, which he will need in order to translate his symbolism into the possibilities of this world. Since his intention is the incarnation, that is, the realization of the divine being in human life, he cannot be a light which the darkness comprehendeth not. On the contrary, he needs the support of man and his understanding to comprehend the *mysterium iniquitatis* which began in paradise before man existed. (The serpent owes his existence to God and by no means to man. The idea: *omne bonum a Deo, omne malum ab homine* is an entirely false one.) YHWH is inclined to find the cause of evil in men, but he evidently represents a moral antinomy accompanied by an almost complete lack of reflection. For example, he seems to have forgotten that he created his son Satan and kept him among the other "sons of God" until the coming of Christ—a strange oversight!

1556 The data of the collective unconscious favour the hypothesis of a paradoxical creator such as YHWH. An entirely good Father seems to have very little probability; such a character is difficult to admit, seeing that Christ himself endeavoured to reform his Father. He didn't completely succeed, even in his own logia. Our unconscious resembles this paradoxical God. That is why man is faced with a psychological condition which does not let him differentiate himself from the image of God (YHWH). Naturally we can believe that God is different from the image of him that we possess, but it must be admitted on the other side that the Lord

20 [Cf. also "The Transcendent Function" (C.W., vol. 8).]

himself, while insisting on the Father's perfect goodness, has given a picture of him which fits in badly with the idea of a perfectly moral being. (A father who tempts his children, who did not prevent the error of the immediate parousia, who is so full of wrath that the blood of his only son is necessary to appease him, who left the crucified one to despair, who proposes to devastate his own creation and slay the millions of mankind to save a very few of them, and who before the end of the world is going to replace his Son's covenant by another gospel and complement the love by the fear of God.) It is interesting, or rather tragic, that God undergoes a complete relapse in the last book of the New Testament. But in the case of an antinomian being we could expect no other development. The opposites are kept in balance, and so the kingdom of Christ is followed by that of Antichrist. In the circumstances the Holy Spirit, the third form of God, becomes of extreme importance, for it is thanks to him that the man of good will is drawn towards the divine drama and mingled in it, and the Spirit is *one*. In him the opposites are separated no longer.

57 Begging you to excuse the somewhat heretical character of my thoughts as well as their imperfect presentation, I remain, dear monsieur, yours sincerely,

C. G. JUNG

ON RESURRECTION[1]

558 You are quite right: I have never dealt with all aspects of the Christ-figure for the simple reason that it would have been too much. I am not a theologian and I have had no time to acquire all the knowledge that is wanted in order to attempt the solution of such problems as that of the Resurrection.

559 Indubitably resurrection is one of the most—if not the most—important item in the myth or the biography of Christ and in the history of the primitive church.

1. Resurrection as a historical fact in the biography of Jesus

560 Three Gospels have a complete report about the postmortal events after the Crucifixion. Mark, however, mentions only the open and empty tomb and the presence of the angel, while the apparition of the visible body of Christ has been reported by a later hand in an obvious addendum. The first report about the resurrected Christ is made by Mary Magdalene, from whom Christ had driven out seven devils. This annotation has a peculiarly cursory character (cf. in particular Mark 11:19),[2] as if somebody had realized that Mark's report was altogether too meagre and that the usual things told about Christ's death ought to be added for the sake of completeness.

561 The earliest source about the Resurrection is St. Paul, and he is no eyewitness, but he strongly emphasizes the absolute and vital importance of resurrection as well as the authenticity of the reports. (Cf. I Cor. 15:14ff and 15:5ff.) He mentions Cephas (Peter) as the first witness, then the twelve, then the five hundred, then James,

1 [Written in English, 19 Feb. 1954, in reply to an inquiry from Martha Dana, Peggy Gerry, and Marian Reith, members of a seminar on Jung's *Aion* led by Dr. James Kirsch, Los Angeles, 1953–54, during which (Dr. Kirsch has stated) "every line of the book was read and commented upon. While the seminar was in progress Mrs. Dana, Mrs. Gerry, and Mrs. Reith became curious about the fact that in all of the writings of Jung they had not found any commentary on the idea of Resurrection . . . [which] seemed to be the central event in the Christ story, and they therefore wondered why Jung had not said anything about it."]

2 [Evidently an error for 16:9ff.]

then the apostles, and finally himself. This is interesting, since his experience was quite clearly an understandable vision, while the later reports insist upon the material concreteness of Christ's body (particularly Luke 24:42 and John 20:24ff.). The evangelical testimonies agree with each other only about the emptiness of the tomb, but not at all about the chronology of the eyewitnesses. There the tradition becomes utterly unreliable. If one adds the story about the end of Judas, who must have been a very interesting object to the hatred of the Christians, our doubts of the Resurrection story are intensified: there are two absolutely different versions of the way of his death.

1562 *The fact of the Resurrection is historically doubtful.* If we extend the *beneficium dubii* to those contradictory statements we could consider the possibility of an individual as well as collective vision (less likely of a materialization).

1563 The conclusion drawn by the ancient Christians—since Christ has risen from the dead so shall we rise in a new and incorruptible body—is of course just what St. Paul has feared most,[3] viz., invalid and as vain as the expectation of the immediate parousia, which has come to naught.

1564 As the many shocking miracle-stories in the Gospels show, spiritual reality could not be demonstrated to the uneducated and rather primitive population in any other way but by crude and tangible "miracles" or stories of such kind. Concretism was unavoidable with all its grotesque implications—for example, the believers in Christ were by the grace of God to be equipped with a glorified body at their resurrection, and the unbelievers and unredeemed sinners were too, so that they could be plagued in hell or purgatory for any length of time. An incorruptible body was necessary for the latter performance, otherwise damnation would have come to an end in no time.

1565 Under those conditions, resurrection as a historical and concrete fact cannot be maintained, whereas the vanishing of the corpse could be a real fact.

2. *Resurrection as a psychological event*

1566 The facts here are perfectly clear and well documented: The life of the God-man on earth comes to an end with his resurrection and transition to heaven. This is firm belief since the beginning

[3] "If Christ be not risen, then is our preaching vain, and your faith is also vain" (I Cor. 15:14).

of Christianity. In mythology it belongs to the hero that he conquers death and brings back to life his parents, tribal ancestors, etc. He has a more perfect, richer, and stronger personality than the ordinary mortal. Although he is also mortal himself, death does not annihilate his existence: he continues living in a somewhat modified form. On a higher level of civilization he approaches the type of the dying and resurrected god, like Osiris, who becomes the greater personality in every individual (like the Johannine Christ), viz., his τέλειος ἄνθρωπος, the complete (or perfect) man, the self.

567 The self as an archetype represents a numinous wholeness, which can be expressed only by symbols (e.g., mandala, tree, etc.). As a collective image it reaches beyond the individual in time and space[4] and is therefore not subjected to the corruptibility of *one* body: the realization of the self is nearly always connected with the feeling of timelessness, "eternity," or immortality. (Cf. the personal and superpersonal ātman.) We do not know what an archetype is (i.e., consists of), since the nature of the psyche is inaccessible to us, but we know that archetypes exist and work.

568 From this point of view it is no longer difficult to see to what degree the story of the Resurrection represents the projection of an indirect realization of the self that had appeared in the figure of a certain man, Jesus of Nazareth, of whom many rumors were circulating.[5] In those days the old gods had ceased to be significant. Their power had already been replaced by the concrete one of the visible god, the Caesar, whose sacrifices were the only obligatory ones. But this substitution was as unsatisfactory as that of God by the communistic state. It was a frantic and desperate attempt to create—out of no matter how doubtful material—a spiritual monarch, a *pantokrator,* in opposition to the concretized divinity in Rome. (What a joke of the *esprit d'escalier* of history—the substitution for the Caesar of the pontifical office of St. Peter!)

569 Their need of a spiritual authority then became so particularly urgent, because there was only one divine individual, the Caesar, while all the others were anonymous and hadn't even private gods listening to their prayers.[6] They took therefore to magic of all kinds.

[4] Cf. the so-called parapsychological phenomena.

[5] Cf. the passage about Christ in the Church Slavonic text of Josephus, *The Jewish War,* in G.R.S. Mead, *The Gnostic John the Baptizer,* pp. 97ff. [=ch. III: "The Slavonic Josephus' Account of the Baptist and Jesus," pp. 106ff.]

[6] Their condition was worse than that of the Egyptians in the last pre-Christian centuries: these had already acquired an individual Osiris. As a matter of fact, Egypt turned Christian at once with no hesitation.

Our actual situation is pretty much the same: we are rapidly becoming the slaves of an anonymous state as the highest authority ruling our lives. Communism has realized this ideal in the most perfect way. Unfortunately our democracy has nothing to offer in the way of different ideals; it also believes in the concrete power of the state. There is no spiritual authority comparable to that of the state anywhere. We are badly in need of a spiritual counterbalance to the ultimately bolshevistic concretism. It is again the case of the "witnesses" against the Caesar.

1570 The gospel writers were as eager as St. Paul to heap miraculous qualities and spiritual significances upon that almost unknown young rabbi, who after a career lasting perhaps only one year had met with an untimely end. What they made of him we know, but we don't know to what extent this picture has anything to do with the truly historical man, smothered under an avalanche of projections. Whether he was the eternally living Christ and Logos, we don't know. It makes no difference anyhow, since the image of the God-man lives in everybody and has been incarnated (i.e., projected) in the man Jesus, to make itself visible, so that people could realize him as their own interior *homo,* their self.

1571 Thus they had regained their human dignity: everybody had divine nature. Christ had told them: *Dii estis:* "ye are gods"; and as such they were his brethren, of his nature, and had overcome annihilation either through the power of the Caesar or through physical death. They were "resurrected with Christ."

1572 Since we are psychic beings and not entirely dependent upon space and time, we can easily understand the central importance of the resurrection idea: we are not completely subjected to the powers of annihilation because our psychic totality reaches beyond the barrier of space and time. Through the progressive integration of the unconscious we have a reasonable chance to make experiences of an archetypal nature providing us with the feeling of continuity before and after our existence. The better we understand the archetype, the more we participate in its life and the more we realize its eternity or timelessness.

1573 As roundness signifies completeness or perfection, it also expresses rotation (the rolling movement) or progress on an endless circular way, an identity with the sun and the stars (hence the beautiful confession in the "Mithraic Liturgy"; *ἐγώ εἰμι σύμπλανος ὑμῖν ἀστήρ* ("I am a Star following his way like you"). The realization of the self also means a re-establishment of Man as the microcosm, i.e., man's cosmic relatedness. Such realizations are frequently accompanied by synchronistic events. (The prophetic experience of vocation belongs to this category.)

574 To the primitive Christians as to all primitives, the Resurrection had to be a concrete, materialistic event to be seen by the eyes and touched by the hands, as if the spirit had no existence of its own. Even in modern times people cannot easily grasp the reality of a psychic event, unless it is concrete at the same time. Resurrection as a psychic event is certainly not concrete, it is just a psychic experience. It is funny that the Christians are still so pagan that they understand spiritual existence only as a body and as a physical event. I am afraid our Christian churches cannot maintain this shocking anachronism any longer, if they don't want to get into intolerable contradictions. As a concession to this criticism, certain theologians have explained St. Paul's glorified (subtle) body given back to the dead on the day of judgment as the authentic individual "form," viz., a spiritual idea sufficiently characteristic of the individual that the material body could be skipped. It was the evidence for man's survival after death and the hope to escape eternal damnation that made resurrection in the body the mainstay of Christian faith. We know positively only of the fact that space and time are relative to the psyche.

IV

JUNG AND RELIGIOUS BELIEF

JUNG AND RELIGIOUS BELIEF[1]

1. Questions to Jung and His Answers[2]

QUESTION 1. *You say that religion is psychically healthy and often for the latter part of life essential, but is it not psychically healthy only if the religious person believes that his religion is true?*

Do you think that in your natural wish to keep to the realm of psychology you have tended to underestimate man's search for truth and the ways in which he might reach this as, for example, by inference?

584 Nobody is more convinced of the importance of the search for truth than I am. But when I say: something transcendental is true, my critique begins. If I call something true, it does not mean that it is absolutely true. It merely seems to be true to myself and/or to other people. If I were not doubtful in this respect it would mean that I implicitly assume that I am able to state an absolute truth. This is an obvious hybris. When Mr. Erich Fromm[3] criticizes

1 [Extracts from H. L. Philp, *Jung and the Problem of Evil* (London, 1958). The book consists of correspondence between the author and Jung in the form of questions and answers (in English), and an extended critical attack of 175 pages on Jung's writings on religion, with particular reference to *Answer to Job*. It concludes with Jung's answers to questions sent by another correspondent, the Rev. David Cox (author of *Jung and St. Paul,* 1959). In both cases the answers are reproduced here with minor stylistic revisions and additional footnotes. The bibliographical references to Jung's works have been brought up to date. For other letters from Jung to Philp, see *Letters,* ed. G. Adler, vol. 2.]

2 [Philp, pp. 8–21. (9 Nov. 1956.)]

3 [In his question, Philp quoted the following passage from Fromm, *Psychoanalysis and Religion,* pp. 23f.: "Before I present Jung's analysis of religion a critical examination of these methodological premises seems warranted. Jung's use of the concept of truth is not tenable. He states that 'truth is a fact and not a judgment,' that 'an elephant is true because it exists.' But he forgets that truth always and necessarily refers to a judgment and not to a description of a phenomenon which we perceive with our senses and which we denote with a word symbol. Jung then states that an idea is 'psychologically true inasmuch as it exists.' But an idea 'exists' regardless of whether it is a delusion or whether it corresponds to fact. The existence of an idea does

me for having a wrong idea and quotes Judaism, Christianity, and Buddhism he demonstrates how illogical his standpoint is, as are the views of those religions themselves, i.e., their truths contradict each other. Judaism has a morally ambivalent God; Christianity a Trinity and Summum Bonum; Buddhism has no God but has interior gods. Their truth is relative and not an absolute truth—if you put them on the same level, as Mr. Fromm does. I naturally admit, and I even strongly believe, that it is of the highest importance to state a "truth." I should be prepared to make transcendental statements, but on one condition: that I state at the same time the possibility of their being untrue. For instance "God is," i.e., is as I think he is. But as I know that I could not possibly form an adequate idea of an all-embracing eternal being, my idea of him is pitifully incomplete; thus the statement "God is not" (so) is equally true and necessary. To make absolute statements is beyond man's reach, although it is ethically indispensable that he give all the credit to his subjective truth, which means that he admits being bound by his conviction to apply it as a principle of his actions. Any human judgment, no matter how great its subjective conviction, is liable to error, particularly judgments concerning transcendental subjects. Mr. Fromm's philosophy has not transcended yet—I am afraid—the level of the twentieth century; but the power-drive of man and his hybris are so great that he believes in an absolutely valid judgment. No scientifically minded person with a sense of intellectual responsibility can allow himself such arrogance. These are the reasons why I insist upon the criterion of *existence,* both in the realm of science and in the realm of religion, and upon immediate and primordial *experience*. Facts are facts and contain no falsity. It is our judgment that introduces the element of deception. To my mind it is more important that an idea exists than that it is true. This despite the fact that it makes a great deal of difference subjectively whether an idea seems to

not make it 'true' in any sense. Even the practising psychiatrist could not work were he not concerned with the truth of an idea, that is, with its relation to the phenomena it tends to portray. Otherwise, he could not speak of a delusion or a paranoid system. But Jung's approach is not only untenable from a psychiatric standpoint; he advocates a standpoint of relativism which though on the surface more friendly to religion than Freud's, is in its spirit fundamentally opposed to religions like Judaism, Christianity, and Buddhism. These consider the striving for truth as one of man's cardinal virtues and obligations and insist that their doctrines whether arrived at by revelation or only by the power of reason are subject to the criterion of truth."]

me to be true or not, though this is a secondary consideration since there is no way of establishing the truth or untruth of a transcendental statement other than by a subjective belief.

QUESTION 2. *Is it possible that you depreciate consciousness through an overvaluation of the unconscious?*

585 I have never had any tendency to depreciate consciousness by insisting upon the importance of the unconscious. If such a tendency is attributed to me it is due to a sort of optical illusion. Consciousness is the "known," but the unconscious is very little known and my chief efforts are devoted to the elucidation of our unconscious psyche. The result of this is, naturally, that I talk more about the unconscious than about the conscious. Since everybody believes or, at least, tries to believe in the unequivocal superiority of rational consciousness, I have to emphasize the importance of the unconscious irrational forces, to establish a sort of balance. Thus to superficial readers of my writings it looks as if I were giving the unconscious a supreme significance, disregarding consciousness. As a matter of fact the emphasis lies on consciousness as the *conditio sine qua non* of apperception of unconscious contents, and the supreme arbiter in the chaos of unconscious possibilities. My book about *Types* is a careful study of the empirical structure of consciousness. If we had an inferior consciousness, we should all be crazy. The ego and ego-consciousness are of paramount importance. It would be superfluous to emphasize consciousness if it were not in a peculiar compensatory relationship with the unconscious.

586 People like Demant[4] start from the prejudiced idea that the unconscious is something more or less nasty and archaic that one should get rid of. This is not vouched for by experience. The unconscious is neutral, rather like nature. If it is destructive on the one side, it is as constructive on the other side. It is the source of all sorts of evils and also the matrix of all divine experience and—paradoxical as it may sound—it has brought forth and brings forth consciousness. Such a statement does not mean that the source *originates,* i.e., that the water is created just at the spot where you see the source of a river; it comes from deep down in the mountain and runs along its secret ways before it reaches daylight. When I say, "Here is the source," I only mean the spot where the water becomes visible. The water-simile expresses rather aptly the nature and importance of the unconscious. Where there is no water nothing

[4] [Cf. *The Religious Prospect,* pp. 188ff., quoted by Philp in his question.]

lives; where there is too much of it everything drowns. It is the task of consciousness to select the right place where you are not too near and not too far from water; but the water is indispensable. An unfavourable opinion about the unconscious does not enable proper Christians, like Demant, to realize that religious experience, so far as the human mind can grasp it, cannot be distinguished from the experience of so-called unconscious phenomena. A metaphysical being does not as a rule speak through the telephone to you; it usually communicates with man through the medium of the soul, in other words, our unconscious, or rather through its transcendental "psychoid" basis.[5] If one depreciates the unconscious one blocks the channels through which the *aqua gratiae* flows, but one certainly does not incapacitate the devil by this method. Creating obstacles is just his métier.

1587 When St. Paul had the vision of Christ, that vision was a psychic phenomenon—if it was anything. I don't presume to know what the psyche is; I only know that there is a psychic realm in which and from which such manifestations start. It is the place where the *aqua gratiae* springs forth, but it comes, as I know quite well, from the immeasurable depths of the mountain and I don't pretend to know about the secret ways and places the water flows through before it reaches the surface.

1588 As the general manifestations of the unconscious are ambivalent or even ambiguous ("It is a fearful thing to fall into the hands of the living God," Heb. 10:31), decision and discriminating judgment are all-important. We see that particularly clearly in the development of the individuation process, when we have to prevent the patient from either rejecting blindly the data of the unconscious or submitting to them without criticism. (Why has Jacob to fight the angel of the Lord? Because he would be killed if he did not defend his life.) There is no development at all but only a miserable death in a thirsty desert if one thinks one can rule the unconscious by our arbitrary rationalism. That is exactly what the German principle, "Where there is a will, there is a way," tried to do, and you know with what results.

QUESTION 3. *In your "Answer to Job" you state, page 463 (Collected Works, Vol. 11): "I have been asked so often whether I believe in the existence of God or not that I am somewhat concerned lest I be taken for an adherent of 'psychologism' far more*

[5] [Cf. "On the Nature of the Psyche" (C.W., vol. 8), par. 368.]

commonly than I suspect." You go on to say, "God is an obvious psychic and non-physical fact," but I feel in the end you do not actually answer the question as to whether or not you believe in the existence of God other than as an archetype. Do you?

This question is important because I should like to answer the kind of objection raised by Glover in his Freud or Jung, *page 163: "Jung's system is fundamentally irreligious. Nobody is to care whether God exists, Jung least of all. All that is necessary is to 'experience' an "attitude' because it 'helps one to live.' "*

589 An archetype—so far as we can establish it empirically—is an *image*. An image, as the very term denotes, is a picture of something. An archetypal image is like the portrait of an unknown man in a gallery. His name, his biography, his existence in general are unknown, but we assume nevertheless that the picture portrays a once living subject, a man who was real. We find numberless images of God, but we cannot produce the original. There is no doubt in my mind that there is an original behind our images, but it is inaccessible. We could not even be aware of the original since its translation into psychic terms is necessary in order to make it perceptible at all. How would Kant's *Critique of Pure Reason* look when translated into the psychic imagery of a cockroach? And I assume that the difference between man and the creator of all things is immeasurably greater than between a cockroach and man. Why should we be so immodest as to suppose that we could catch a universal being in the narrow confines of our language? We know that God-images play a great role in psychology, but we cannot prove the physical existence of God. As a responsible scientist I am not going to preach my personal and subjective convictions which I cannot prove. I add nothing to cognition or to a further improvement and extension of consciousness when I confess my personal prejudices. I simply go as far as my mind can reach, but to venture opinions beyond my mental reach would be immoral from the standpoint of my intellectual ethics. If I should say, "I believe in such and such a God," it would be just as futile as when a Negro states his firm belief that the tin-box he found on the shore contains a powerful fetish. If I keep to a statement which I think I can prove, this does not mean that I deny the existence of anything else that might exist beyond it. It is sheer malevolence to accuse me of an atheistic attitude simply because I try to be honest and disciplined. Speaking for myself, the question whether God exists or not is futile. I am sufficiently convinced of the effects

man has always attributed to a divine being. If I should express a belief beyond that or should assert the existence of God, it would not only be superfluous and inefficient, it would show that I am not basing my opinion on facts. When people say that they believe in the existence of God, it has never impressed me in the least. Either I know a thing and then I don't need to believe it; or I believe it because I am not sure that I know it. I am well satisfied with the fact that I know experiences which I cannot avoid calling numinous or divine.

QUESTION 4. *Do you ignore the importance of other disciplines for the psyche?*

Goldbrunner in his Individuation, *page 161, says that your treatment of "what God is in Himself" is a question which you regard as beyond the scope of psychology, and adds: "This implies a positivistic, agnostic renunciation of all metaphysics." Do you agree that your treatment amounts to that? Would you not agree that such subjects as metaphysics and history have their place in the experience of the psyche?*

1590 I do not ignore the importance of other disciplines for the psyche. When I was professor at the E.T.H. in Zurich I lectured for a whole year about Tantrism[6] and for another year about the *Spiritual Exercises* of St. Ignatius of Loyola.[7] Moreover, I have written a number of books about the peculiar spiritual discipline of the alchemists.

1591 What Goldbrunner says is quite correct. I don't know what God is in himself. I don't suffer from megalomania. Psychology to me is an honest science that recognizes its own boundaries, and I am not a philosopher or a theologian who believes in his ability to step beyond the epistemological barrier. Science is made by man, which does not mean that there are not occasionally acts of grace permitting transgression into realms beyond. I don't depreciate or deny such facts, but to me they are beyond the scope of science as pointed out above. I believe firmly in the intrinsic value of the human attempt to gain understanding, but I also recognize that the human mind cannot step beyond itself, although divine grace may and probably does allow at least glimpses into a transcendental

6 [Seminar on Buddhism and Tantric Yoga (Oct. 1938 to June 1939), in *The Process of Individuation*. Notes on Lectures at the ETH, Zurich, trans. and ed. by Barbara Hannah. Privately issued.]

7 [Exercitia Spiritualia of St. Ignatius of Loyola (June 1939 to Mar. 1940), in ibid.]

order of things. But I am neither able to give a rational account of such divine interventions nor can I prove them. Many of the analytical hours with my patients are filled with discussions of "metaphysical" intrusions, and I am in dire need of historical knowledge to meet all the problems I am asked to deal with. For the patient's mental health it is all-important that he gets some proper understanding of the numina the collective unconscious produces, and that he assigns the proper place to them. It is, however, either a distortion of the truth or lack of information when Goldbrunner calls my attitude "positivistic," which means a one-sided recognition of scientific truth. I know too well how transitory and sometimes even futile our hypotheses are, to assume their validity as durable truths and as trustworthy foundations of a *Weltanschauung* capable of giving man sure guidance in the chaos of this world. On the contrary, I rely very much on the continuous influx of the numina from the unconscious and from whatever lies behind it. Goldbrunner therefore is also wrong to speak of an "agnostic renunciation of all metaphysics." I merely hold that metaphysics cannot be an object of science, which does not mean that numinous experiences do not happen frequently, particularly in the course of an analysis or in the life of a truly religious individual.

QUESTION 5. *If my reading of your views is correct, I should judge that you think evil to be a far more active force than traditional theological views have allowed for. You appear unable to interpret the condition of the world today unless this is so. Am I correct in this? If so, is it really necessary to expect to find the dark side in the Deity? And if you believe that Satan completes the quaternity does this not mean that the Deity would be amoral?*

Victor White in his God and the Unconscious *writes at the end of his footnote on page 76: "On the other hand, we are unable to find any intelligible, let alone desirable, meaning in such fundamental Jungian conceptions as the 'assimilation of the shadow' if they are not to be understood as the supplying of some absent good (e.g., consciousness) to what is essentially valuable and of itself 'good.'"*

592 I am indeed convinced that evil is as positive a factor as good. Quite apart from everyday experience it would be extremely illogical to assume that one can state a quality without its opposite. If something is good, then there must needs be something that is evil or bad. The statement that something is good would not be

possible if one could not discriminate it from something else. Even if one says that something exists, such a statement is only possible alongside the other statement that something does not exist. Thus when the Church doctrine declares that evil is not (μὴ ὄν) or is a mere shadow, then the good is equally illusory, as its statement would make no sense.

1593 Suppose one has something 100-per-cent good, and if anything evil comes in it is diminished, say by 5 per cent. Then one possesses 95 per cent of goodness and 5 per cent is just absent. If the original good diminished by 99 per cent, one has 1 per cent good and 99 per cent is gone. If that 1 per cent also disappears, the whole possession is gone and one has nothing at all. To the very last moment one had only good and oneself was good, but on the other side there is simply nothing and nothing has happened. Evil deeds simply do not *exist*. The identification of good with *ousia* is a fallacy, because a man who is thoroughly evil does not disappear at all when he has lost his last good. But even if he has 1 per cent of good, his body and soul and his whole existence are still *thoroughly good;* for, according to the doctrine, evil is simply identical with non-existence. This is such a horrible syllogism that there must be a very strong motive for its construction. The reason is obvious: it is a desperate attempt to save the Christian faith from dualism. According to this theory [of the *privatio boni*] even the devil, the incarnate evil, must be good, because he exists, but inasmuch as he is thoroughly bad, he does not exist. This is a clear attempt to annihilate dualism in flagrant contradiction to the dogma that the devil is eternal and damnation a very real thing. I don't pretend to be able to explain the actual condition of the world, but it is plain to any unprejudiced mind that the forces of evil are dangerously near to a victory over the powers of good. Here Basil the Great would say, "Of course that is so, but all evil comes from man and not from God," forgetting altogether that the serpent in Paradise was not made by man, and that Satan is one of the sons of God, prior to man. If man were positively the origin of all evil, he would possess a power equal or almost equal to that of the good, which is God. But we don't need to inquire into the origin of Satan. We have plenty of evidence in the Old Testament that Yahweh is moral and immoral at the same time, and Rabbinic theology is fully aware of this fact. Yahweh behaves very much like an immoral being, though he is a guardian of law and order. He is unjust and unreliable according to the Old Testament. Even the God of the New Testament is still irascible and vengeful to such a degree that he needs the self-sacrifice of his son to quench his wrath. Christian theology has never denied the identity of the God of the Old Testament with that of the New Testament. Now I ask you: what would you call a judge that is a guardian of the Law and is himself unjust? One would be inclined to call such a man immoral. I would call him both immoral and moral, and I think I express the truth with this formula. Certainly the God of the Old Testament is good and evil. He is the Father or Creator of Satan as well as of Christ. Certainly if God the Father were nothing else than a loving Father, Christ's cruel sacrificial death would be thoroughly superfluous. I would not allow my son to be slaughtered in order to be reconciled to my disobedient children.

594 What Victor White writes about the assimilation of the shadow is not to be taken seriously. Being a Catholic priest he is bound hand and foot to the doctrine of his Church and has to defend every syllogism. The Church knows all about the assimilation of the shadow, i.e., how it is to be repressed and what is evil. Being a doctor I am never too certain about my moral judgments. Too often I find that something that is a virtue in one individual is a vice in another, and something that is good for the one is poison for another. On the other hand, pious feeling has invented the term of *felix culpa* and Christ preferred the sinner. Even God does not seem particularly pleased with mere righteousness.

595 Nowhere else is it more important to emphasize that we are speaking of our traditional image of God (which is not the same as the original) than in the discussion of the *privatio boni*. We don't produce God by the magic word or by representing his image. The word for us is still a fetish, and we assume that it produces the thing of which it is only an image. What God is in himself nobody knows; at least I don't. Thus it is beyond the reach of man to make valid statements about the divine nature. If we disregard the short-comings of the human mind in assuming a knowledge about God, which we cannot have, we simply get ourselves into most appalling contradictions and in trying to extricate ourselves from them we use awful syllogisms, like the *privatio boni*. Moreover our superstitious belief in the power of the word is a serious obstacle to our thinking. That is the historical reason why quite a number of shocking contradictions have been heaped up, offering facile opportunities to the enemy of religion. I strongly advocate, therefore, a revision of our religious formulas with the

aid of psychological insight. It is the great advantage of Protestantism that an intelligent discussion is possible. Protestantism should make use of this freedom. Only a thing that changes and evolves, lives, but static things mean spiritual death.[8]

2. *Final Questions and Answers*[9]

QUESTION 1. *If Christ, in His Incarnation, concentrated, as you contend, on goodness ("Answer to Job," pp. 414, 429f.) what do you mean by "Christ preferred the sinner" and "Even God does not seem particularly pleased with mere righteousness"? Is there not an inconsistency here?*

1596 Of course there is. I am just pointing it out.

QUESTION 2. *You stress the principle of the opposites and the importance of their union. You also write of enantiodromia in relation to the opposites but this (in the sense in which Heraclitus used the term) would never produce a condition of stability which could lead to the union of the opposites. So is there not a contradiction in what you say about the opposites?*

1597 "Enantiodromia" describes a certain psychological fact, i.e., I use it as a psychological concept. Of course it does not lead to a union of opposites, has—as a matter of fact—nothing to do with it. I see no contradiction anywhere.

QUESTION 3. *If the principle of enantiodromia, a perpetual swinging of the pendulum, is always present would we not have a condition in which there would be no sense of responsibility, but one of amorality and meaninglessness?*

1598 Naturally life would be quite meaningless if the enantiodromia of psychological states kept on for ever. But such an assumption would be both arbitrary and foolish.

QUESTION 4. *When we come into close contact with pharisaism, theft or murder, involving uncharitableness, ruthless and selfish treatment of others, we know that they are evil and very ugly. In*

[8] For the comprehension of the problems here mentioned, I recommend: "Answer to Job"; "A Psychological Approach to the Dogma of the Trinity" (ch. 5, "The Problem of the Fourth"); *Aion* (ch. 5, "Christ, A Symbol of the Self"); *Psychology and Alchemy* (Introduction, especially par. 36). For the biography of Satan, see R. Schärf-Kluger, *Satan in the Old Testament*.

[9] [Philp, pp. 214–25. (8 Oct. 1957.) Page references for "Answer to Job" are to C.W., vol. 11.]

actual life what we call goodness—loyalty, integrity, charitableness—does not appear as one of a pair of opposites but as the kind of behavior we want for ourselves and others. The difficulty is that we cannot judge all the motives involved in any action with certainty. We are unable to see the complete picture and so we should be cautious and charitable in our judgments. But this does not mean that what is good is not good, or what is evil is not evil. Do you not think that what you have to say about the quaternity and enantiodromia ultimately blurs the distinction between good and evil? Is not what is blurred only our capacity always to see the real moral issues clearly?

599 It only means that moral judgment is human, limited, and under no condition metaphysically valid. Within these confines good is good, and evil is evil. One must have the courage to stand up for one's convictions. We cannot imagine a state of wholeness (quaternity) which is good and evil. It is beyond our moral judgment.

QUESTION 5. *Theologians who believe in Satan have maintained that he was created good but that through the use of his free will he became evil. What necessity is there to assume that he is the inevitable principle of evil in the Godhead—the fourth member of the quaternity?*

600 Because the Three are the Summum Bonum, and the devil is the principle and personification of evil. In a Catholic quaternity the fourth would be the Mother, 99-per-cent divine. The devil would not count, being μὴ ὄν, an empty shadow owing to the *privatio boni,* in which the Bonum is equal to οὐσία.

QUESTION 6. *You build much on the existence of four functions, thinking, feeling, sensation, and intuition. Is this a final or satisfactory typology? If feeling is included, why not conation?*

1601 The four functions are a mere model for envisaging the qualities of *consciousness.* Conation is a term applicable to the creative process starting in the unconscious and ending in a conscious result, in other words a dynamic aspect of psychic life.

QUESTION 7. *By different approaches in your later writings you add Satan and the Blessed Virgin Mary to the Trinity, but this would make a quinary. Who compose the quaternity?*

1602 The quaternity can be a hypothetical structure, depicting a wholeness. It is also not a logical concept, but an empirical fact. The *quinarius* or *quinio* (in the form of 4 + 1, i.e., quincunx) does occur as a symbol of wholeness (in China and occasionally in alchemy) but relatively rarely. Otherwise the *quinio* is not a symbol of wholeness, quite the contrary (e.g., the five-rayed star of the Soviets or of U.S.A.). Rather, it is a chaotic *prima materia.*

QUESTION 8. *Would not the quaternity involve not only a revision of doctrine but of moral issues as well, for it would appear inevitably to mean complete moral relativity and so amorality having its source in the Godhead Itself?*

1603 Man cannot live without moral judgment. From the fact of the empirical quaternary structure of 3 + 1 (3 = good, 1 = evil) we can conclude that the unconscious characterizes itself as an unequal mixture of good and evil.

1604 There are also not a few cases where the structure is reversed: 1 + 3 (1 = good, 3 = evil). 3 in this case would form the so-called "lower triad." Since the quaternity as a rule appears as a unity, the opposites annul each other, which simply means that our anthropomorphic judgment is no more applicable, i.e., the divinity is beyond good and evil, or else metaphysical assertion is not valid. In so far as the human mind and its necessities issue from the hands of the Creator, we must assume that moral judgment was provided by the same source.

QUESTION 9. *What exactly are you referring to when you use the word "quaternity" in relation to religion? Are you using "quaternity" purely for images which men form of the Godhead? You sometimes give the impression that you are referring to God-images alone. At other times you write as if you have in mind the Godhead itself. This is especially so when you stress the necessity of including Satan and also the Blessed Virgin Mary in the Godhead. If you do not refer to the Godhead itself, there seems to me to be no explanation of the urgency of your words about recognizing the evil principle in God and your welcome of the promulgation of the Assumption.*

1605 I use the term "quaternity" for the mandala and similar structures that appear *spontaneously* in dreams and visions, or are "invented" (from *invenire* = to find), to express a totality (like four winds and seasons or four sons, seraphim, evangelists, gospels, fourfold path, etc.). The quaternity is of course an image or picture, which does not mean that there is no original!

1606 If the opposites were not contained in the image, it would not be an image of totality. But it is meant to be a picture of ineffable wholeness, in other words, its symbol. It has an importance for the theologian only in so far as the latter attributes significance to it. If he assumes that his images or formulations are not contents of his consciousness (which is a *contradictio in adiecto*), he can only state that they are exact replicas of the original. But who could suggest such a thing? In spite of the fact that the Church long ago discouraged the idea of a quaternity, the fact remains that Church symbolism abounds in quaternity allusions. As Three (Trinity) is only one (albeit the main) aspect of the Deity, the remaining fourth principle is wiped out of existence by the *privatio boni* syllogism. But the Catholic Church was aware that the picture without opposites is not complete. It therefore admitted (at least tentatively) the existence of a feminine factor within the precincts of the masculine Trinity (*Assumptio Beatae Virginis*). For good reasons the devil is still excluded, and even annihilated, by the *privatio boni*.

607 The admission of the *Beata Virgo* is a daring attempt, in so far as she belongs to *lubricum illud genus*[10] (St. Epiphanius), so suspect to the moralistic propensities of the said Church. However, she has been spiritually "disinfected" by the dogma of *Conceptio immaculata*. I consider the Assumption as a cautious approach to the solution of the problem of opposites, namely, to the integration of the fourth metaphysical figure into the divine totality. The Catholic Church has almost succeeded in creating a *quaternity without shadow,* but the devil is still outside. The Assumption is at least an important step forward in Christian (?) symbolism. This evolution will be completed when the dogma of the Co-Redemptrix is reached. But the main problem will not be solved, although one pair of opposites (♂ and ♀) has been smuggled into the divine wholeness. Thus the Catholic Church (in the person of the Pope) has at least seen fit to take the Marianic movement in the masses, i.e., a *psychological fact,* so seriously that he did not hesitate to give up the time-hallowed principle of apostolic authority.

608 Protestanism is free to ignore the spiritual problems raised by our time, but it will remove itself from the battlefield and thereby lose its contact with life.

609 Being a natural and spontaneous symbol, the quaternity has everything to do with human psychology, while the trinitarian symbol (though equally spontaneous) has become cold, a remote abstraction. Curiously enough, among my collection of mandalas I have only a small number of trinities and triads. They stem one

10 ["that slippery sex."]

and all from Germans![11] (Unconscious of their shadows, therefore unaware of collective guilt!)

1610 I do not know at all to what extent human formulas, whether invented or spontaneous, correspond with the original. I only know that we are profoundly concerned with them, whether people know it or not, just as you can be with an illness of which you are unaware. It makes an enormous practical difference whether your dominant idea of totality is three or four. In the former case all good comes from God, all evil from man. Then man is the devil. In the latter case man has a chance to be saved from devilish possession, in so far as he is not inflated with evil. What happened under National Socialism in Germany? What is happening under Bolshevism? With the quaternity the powers of evil, so much greater than man's, are restored to the divine wholeness, whence they originated, even according to Genesis. The serpent was not created by man.

1611 The quaternity symbol has as much to do with the Godhead as the Trinity has. As soon as I begin to think at all about the experience of "God," I have to choose from my store of images between [concepts representing him as a] monad, dyad, triad, tetrad or an indistinct multiplicity. In any serious case the choice is limited by the kind of revealed image one has received. Yahweh and Allah are monads, the Christian God a triad (historically), the modern experience presumably a tetrad, the early Persian deity a dyad. In the East you have the dyadic monad Tao and the monadic Anthropos (*purusha*), Buddha, etc.

1612 In my humble opinion all this has very much to do with psychology. We have nothing to go by but these images. Without images you could not even speak of divine experiences. You would be completely inarticulate. You only could stammer "mana" and even that would be an image. Since it is a matter of an ineffable experience the image is indispensable. I would completely agree if you should say: God approaches man in the form of symbols. But we are far from knowing whether the symbol is correct or not.

1613 The *privatio boni* cannot be compared to the quaternity, because it is not a revelation. On the contrary, it has all the earmarks of a "doctrine," a philosophical invention.

1614 It makes no difference at all whether I say "God" or "Godhead." Both are in themselves far beyond man's reach. To us they are revealed as psychic images, i.e., symbols.

1615 I am far from making any statements about God himself. I

[11] [Cf. "Flying Saucers: A Modern Myth" (C.W., vol. 10), par. 775.]

am talking about images, which it is very important to think and talk about, and to criticize, because so much depends upon the nature of our dominant ideas. It makes all the difference in the world whether I think that the source of evil or good is myself, my neighbour, the devil, or the supreme being.

616 Of course I am pleading the cause of the *thinking* man, and, inasmuch as most people do not think, of a small minority. Yet it has its place in creation and presumably it makes sense. Its contribution to the development of consciousness is considerable and since Nature has bestowed the highest premium of success on the *conscious* being, consciousness must be more precious to Nature than unconsciousness. Therefore I think that I am not too far astray in trying to understand the symbol of the Deity. My opinion is that such an attempt—whether successful or not—could be of great interest to theology which is built on the same primordial images, whether one likes it or not. At all events you will find it increasingly difficult to convince the educated layman that theology has nothing to do with psychology, when the latter acknowledges its indebtedness to the theological approach.

617 My discussion with theology starts from the fact that the naturally revealed central symbols, such as the quaternity, are not in harmony with trinitarian symbols. While the former includes the darkness in the divine totality, the Christian symbol excludes it. The Yahwistic symbol of the star of David is a *complexio oppositorum:* △, fire ▽ and water ✡, a mandala built on three, an unconscious acknowledgment of the Trinity but including the shadow. Properly so, because Satan is still among the *benê Elohim* [sons of God], though Christ saw him falling out of heaven [Luke 10:18]. This vision points to the Gnostic abscission of the shadow, mentioned by Irenaeus.[12] As I have said, it makes a great and vital difference to man whether or not he considers himself as the source of evil, while maintaining that all good stems from God. Whether he knows it or not, this fills him with satanic pride and hybris on the one side and with an abysmal feeling of inferiority on the other. But when he ascribes the immense power of the opposites to the Deity, he falls into his modest place as a small image of the Deity, not of Yahweh, in whom the opposites are unconscious, but of a quaternity consisting of the main opposites: male and female, good and evil, and reflected in human consciousness as confirmed by psychological experience and by the historical evi-

[12] [*Adversus haereses,* II, 5, 1. Cf. *Aion,* C.W., vol. 9,ii, par. 75 and n. 23.]

dence. Or have I invented the idea of Tao, the living spiritual symbol of ancient China? Or the four sons of Horus in ancient Egypt? Or the alchemical quaternity that lived for almost a thousand years? Or the Mahayana mandala which is still alive?

QUESTION 10. *One of your objections to the* privatio boni *doctrine is that it minimizes evil, but does not your view of the quaternity, which includes both good and evil, minimize evil much more surely and assume its existence for ever?*

1618 The quaternity symbol relativizes good and evil, but it does not minimize them in the least.

QUESTION 11. *You argue in "Answer to Job" (pp. 399, 430) that, because of his virgin birth, Christ was not truly man and so could not be a full incarnation in terms of human nature. Do you believe that Christ was born of a virgin? If not, the argument in "Answer to Job" falls to pieces. If you believe in the Virgin Birth, would it not be logical to accept the whole emphasis of the Christian Creeds, for they would not appear to be more difficult to believe in than the Virgin Birth?*

1619 The dogma of the Virgin Birth does not abolish the fact that "God" in the form of the Holy Ghost is Christ's father. If Yahweh is his father, then it is a matter of an *a priori* union of opposites. If the Summum Bonum is his father, then the powers of darkness are missing and the term "good" has lost its meaning and Christ has not become man, because man is afflicted with darkness.

QUESTION 12. *Christ, so the Gospel narratives assert, was born in a manger because there was no room for Him in the inn at Bethlehem; His early life included the Slaughter of the Innocents and His family lived for a time exiled in Egypt; He faced temptation in the wilderness; His ministry was carried on under such hard conditions that He "had not where to lay His head" (Matt. 8:20). He met and ministered to numerous sufferers; sinners received His sympathy and understanding; He endured an agony of suffering in the Garden of Gethsemane and this was followed by His trials, and finally the cruellest of deaths by crucifixion. On what grounds then can you argue that Christ was an incarnation of the light side of God and that He did not enter fully into the dark aspects of existence? ("Answer to Job," pp. 398f., 414, 430.) On the contrary, traditionally He has often been thought of as "a man of sorrows, and acquainted with grief."*

620 All that has nothing to do with the dark side of man. Christ is on the contrary the innocent and blameless victim without the *macula peccati,* therefore not really a human being who has to live without the benefit of the Virgin Birth and is crucified in a thousand forms.

QUESTION 13. *What do you mean when in "Answer to Job" you refer to Antichrist and his reign, and state that this was astrologically foretold?*

621 It is potentially foretold by the aeon of the Fishes (>—<) then beginning, and in fact by the Apocalypse. Cf. my argument in *Aion,* ch. VI.; also Rev. 20:7: "And when the thousand years are expired, Satan shall be loosed out of his prison."

QUESTION 14. *What do you mean by "divine unconsciousness" in "Answer to Job" (footnote on page 383)? Is God more limited than man?*

622 This is just the trouble. From Job it is quite obvious that Yahweh behaves like a man with inferior consciousness and an absolute lack of moral self-reflection. In this respect God-image is more limited than man. Therefore God must incarnate.

QUESTION 15. *One of Job's greatest problems was: Can I believe in a just God? Individuation, "the Christification of many," the solution given in "Answer to Job" [p. 470], does not do justice to Job's question. Did not Job want meaning, a good God and not simply individuation? He was concerned with metaphysical and theological issues, and the modern Job is too, and just as man cannot live by bread alone, so is he unlikly to feel that he can live by individuation alone which, at its most successful, would appear to be little more than a preparatory process enabling him to face these issues more objectively.*

623 Job wanted justice. He saw that he could not obtain it. Yahweh cannot be argued with. He is unreflecting power. What else is left to Job but to shut his mouth? He does not dream of individuation, but he knows what kind of God he is dealing with. It is certainly not Job drawing further conclusions but God. He sees that incarnation is unavoidable because man's insight is a step ahead of him. He must "empty himself of his Godhead and assume the shape of the δοῦλος,"[13] i.e., man in his lowest form of existence, in order to obtain the jewel which man possesses in his self-reflection.

13 [Cf. Philippians 2:6.]

Why is Yahweh, the omnipotent creator, so keen to have his "slave," body and soul, even to the point of admitted jealousy?

1624 Why do you say "by individuation alone"? *Individuation is the life in God,* as mandala psychology clearly shows. Have you not read my later books? You can see it in every one of them. The symbols of the self coincide with those of the Deity. The self is not the ego, it symbolizes the totality of man and he is obviously not whole without God. That seems to be what is meant by incarnation and incidentally by individuation.

3. Answers to Questions from the Rev. David Cox[14]

I

This question concerned Jung's statement in Two Essays on Analytical Psychology *(par. 327) that Western culture has no name or concept for the "union of opposites by the middle path" which could be compared to the concept of Tao. It was suggested that the Christian doctrine of justification by faith is such a concept.*

1625 Not being a theologian I cannot see a connection between the doctrine of justification and Tao. Tao is the cooperation of opposites, bright-dark, dry-humid, hot-cold, south-north, dragon-tiger, etc., and has nothing to do with moral opposites or with a reconciliation between the Summum Bonum and the devil. Christian doctrine—so far as I know—does not recognize dualism as the constitution of Tao, but Chinese philosophy does.

1626 It is certainly true that natural man always tries to increase what seems "good" to him and to abolish "evil." He depends upon his consciousness, which, however, may be crossed by "conscience" or by some unconscious intention. This factor can occasionally be stronger than consciousness, so that it cannot be fought. We are very much concerned in psychotherapy with such cases.

1627 The "Will of God" often contradicts conscious principles however good they may seem. Penitence or remorse follows the deviation from the superior will. The result is—if not a chronic conflict—a *coniunctio oppositorum* in the form of the symbol (*symbolum* = the two halves of a broken coin), the expression of totality.

1628 I did not know that you understand Christ as the new centre

[14] [Philp, pp. 226–39. (Aug. 1957.) The questions were not directly quoted because of the personal way in which some of them were framed.]

of the individual. Since this centre of the individual appears empirically as a union of opposites (usually a quaternity), Christ must be beyond moral conflict, thus representing ultimate decision. This conception coincides absolutely with my view of the self (= Tao, *nirdvandva*). But since the self includes my consciousness as well as my unconscious, my ego is an integral part of it. Is this also your view of Christ? If this should be so, I could completely agree with you. Life then becomes a dangerous adventure, because I surrender to a power beyond the opposites, to a superior or divine factor, without argument. His supreme decision may be what I call good or what I call bad, as it is unlimited. What is the difference between my behaviour and that of an animal fulfilling the will of God unreservedly? The only difference I can see is that I am conscious of, and reflect on, what I am doing. "If thou knowest what thou art doing, thou art blessed."[15] You have acted.

629 (*Unjust steward.*) This is Gnostic morality but not that of the decalogue. The true servant of God runs risks of no mean order. *Entendu!* Thus, at God's command, Hosea marries a whore. It is not beyond the bounds of possibility that such orders could be issued even in modern times. Who is ready to obey? And what about the fact that anything coming from the unconscious is expressed in a peculiar language (words, thoughts, feelings, impulses) that might be misinterpreted? These questions are not meant as arguments against the validity of your view. They merely illustrate the enormity of the risk. I ventilate them only to make sure we really believe in a Christ beyond good and evil. I am afraid of unreflecting optimism and of secret loopholes, as for instance, "Oh, you can trust in the end that everything will be all right." *Id est:* "God is good" (and not beyond good and evil). Why has God created consciousness and reason and doubt, if complete surrender and obedience to his will is the *ultima ratio?* He was obviously not content with animals only. He wants reflecting beings who are at the same time capable of surrendering themselves to the primordial creative darkness of his will, unafraid of the consequences.

630 I cannot help seeing that there is much evidence in primitive Christianity for your conception of Christ, but none in the later development of the Church. Nevertheless there are the seemingly unshakable scriptural testimonies to the essential goodness of God and Christ and there is—to my knowledge—no positive statement in favour of a beyond-good-and-evil conception, not even an implied

[51] [Codex Bezae to Luke 6:4.]

one. This seems to me to be a wholly modern and new interpretation of a revolutionary kind, at least in view of the Summum Bonum, as you add the Malum and transcend both. In this I completely agree with you. I only want to make sure that we understand each other when we reach the conclusion that man's true relation to God must include both love and fear to make it complete. If both are true, we can be sure that our relation to him is adequate. The one relativizes the other: in fear we may hope, in love we may distrust. Both conditions appeal to our consciousness, reflection, and reason. Both our gifts come into their own. But is this not a relativization of complete surrender? Or at least an acceptance after an internal struggle? Or a fight against God that can be won only if he himself is his advocate against himself, as Job understood it? And is this not a tearing asunder of God's original unity by man's stubborness? A disruption sought by God himself, or by the self itself? As I know from my professional experience, the self does indeed seek such issues because it seeks *consciousness,* which cannot exist without discrimination (differentiation, separation, opposition, contradiction, discussion). The self is empirically in a condition we call unconscious in our three-dimensional world. What it is in its transcendental condition, we do not know. So far as it becomes an object of cognition, it undergoes a process of discrimination and so does everything emanating from it. The discrimination is intellectual, emotional, ethical, etc. That means: the self is subject to our free decision thus far. But as it transcends our cognition, we are its objects or slaves or children or sheep that cannot but obey the shepherd. Are we to emphasize consciousness and freedom of judgment or lay more stress on obedience? In the former case can we fulfil the divine will to consciousness, and in the latter the primordial instinct of obedience? Thus we represent the intrinsic Yea and Nay of the *opus divinum* of *creatio continua.* We ourselves are in a certain respect "beyond good and evil." This is very dangerous indeed (cf. Nietzsche), but no argument against the truth. Yet our inadequacy, dullness, inertia, stupidity, etc. are equally true. Both are aspects of one and the same being.

1631 Accordingly the alchemists thought of their opus as a continuation and perfection of creation, whereas the modern psychological attempt confronts the opposites and submits to the tension of the conflict: "Expectans naturae operationem, quae lentissima est, aequo animo,"[16] to quote an old master. We know that a

[16] ["Patiently awaiting a work of nature, which is very slow."]

tertium quid develops out of an opposition, partly aided by our conscious effort, partly by the co-operation of the unconscious effort, partly by the co-operation of the unconscious (the alchemists add: *Deo concedente*). The result of this opus is the *symbol,* in the last resort the self. The alchemists understood it to be as much physical as spiritual, being the *filius macrocosmi,* a parallel to Christ, the υἵος τοῦ ἀνθρώπου. The Gnostics understood the serpent in paradise to be the λόγος, and in the same way the alchemists believed that their *filius philosophorum* was the chthonic *serpens mercurialis* transformed (taking the serpent on the σταυρός [cross] as an *allegoria ad Christum spectans*).[17] Their naïveté shows a hesitation (which I feel too) to identify the self with Christ. Their symbol is the *lapis.* It is incorruptible, *semel factus* (from the *increatum,* the primordial chaos), everlasting, our tool and master at the same time ("artifex non est magister lapidis, sed potius eius minister"),[18] the redeemer of creation in general, of minerals, plants, animals, and of man's physical imperfection. Hence its synonyms: panacea, *alexipharmacum, medicina catholica,* etc. (and hellebore, because it heals insanity).

632 Of course if you understand Christ by definition as a *complexio oppositorum,* the equation is solved. But you are confronted with a terrific historical counter-position. As it concerns a point of supreme importance, I wanted to clarify the problem beyond all doubt. This may explain and excuse my long-winded argument.

II

In "Answer to Job" Jung claims that Jesus "incarnates only the light" side of God. This may represent the way in which Jesus is thought of by the majority of Western men and women today, but is it not false to the New Testament and to Christian thought over the centuries?

633 You must consider that I am an alienist and practical psychologist, who has to take things as they *are* understood, not as they *could* or *should* be understood. Thus the Gnostics thought that Christ had cut off his shadow, and I have never heard that he embodies evil as Yahweh explicitly does. Catholic as well as Protestant teaching insists that Christ is without sin. As a scientist I am chiefly concerned with what is generally believed, although I can't help being impressed by the fact that the ecclesiastical doctrines

17 [Cf. *Psychology and Alchemy,* C.W., vol. 12, fig. 217.]

18 ["The artifex is not the master of the stone, but rather its minister."]

do not do justice to certain facts in the New Testament. I have however to consider the *consensus omnium* that Christ is without the *macula peccati*. If I should say that Christ contains some evil I am sure to have the Churches against me. As a psychologist I cannot deal with the theological conception of truth. My field is people's common beliefs.

1634 Since I am not chiefly concerned with theology but rather with the layman's picture of theological concepts (a fact you must constantly bear in mind), I am liable to make many apparent contradictions (like the medieval mind acquainted with funny stories about Jesus, as you rightly point out). The Gospels do indeed give many hints pointing to the dark side, but this has not affected the picture of the *lumen de lumine,* which is the general view. I am thinking—as a psychologist—about all sorts of erroneous notions which do exist in spite of higher criticism and accurate exegesis and all the achievements of theological research. My object is the general condition of the Christian mind, and not theology, where I am wholly incompetent. Because the *lumen de lumine* idea is paramount in the layman's mind, I dare to point to certain scriptural evidence (accessible to the layman) showing another picture of Christ. I am certain that your conception of Christ would have a hard time getting through certain thick skulls. It is the same with the idea of evil contained in God. I am concerned with dogmas, prejudices, illusions, and errors and every kind of doubt in the layman's mind, and I try to get a certain order into that chaos by the means accessible to a layman, i.e., to myself as a representative of the humble "ignoramus."

III

This question deals with the relationship between faith and projection. Has Jung, in his writing, treated faith as being connected with an outward form of religion?

1635 This I do not properly understand. Of course "faith" is a relationship to projected contents. But I cannot see how that "corresponds for all practical purposes to a withdrawal of the projection." Faith on the contrary—as it seems to me—maintains the conviction that the projection is a reality. For instance, I project saintly qualities on to somebody. My faith maintains and enhances this projection and creates a worshipful attitude on my part. But it is quite possible that the bearer of the projection is nothing of the kind, perhaps he is even an unpleasant hypocrite. Or I may project, i.e., hypostatize, a religious conviction of a certain kind which I maintain with faith and fervour. Where is the "withdrawal of the projection"?

36 In case of doubt you had better refer to *Symbols of Transformation*. Once I was at the beginning of things, at the time when I separated from Freud in 1912. I found myself in great inner difficulties, as I had no notion of the collective unconscious or of archetypes. My education was based chiefly on science, with a modest amount of the humanities. It was a time of *Sturm und Drang*. The so-called *Psychology of the Unconscious*[19] was an intuitive leap into the dark and contains no end of inadequate formulations and unfinished thoughts.

37 I make a general distinction between "religion" and a "creed" for the sake of the layman, since it is chiefly he who reads my books and not the academic scholar. He (the scholar) is not interested in the layman's mind. As a rule he nurses resentments against psychology. I must repeat again: I am a psychologist and thus people's minds interest me in the first place, although I am keen to learn the truth the specialist produces. The layman identifies religion with a creed, that is, with the "things done in the church." Thus Islam, Judaism, Buddhism, etc. are simply religions like Christianity. That there is a genuine inner life, a communion with transcendental powers, a possibility of religious *experience* is mere hearsay. Nor are the churches over-sympathetic to the view that the alpha and omega of religion is the subjective individual experience, but put community in the first place, without paying attention to the fact that the more people there are the less individuality there is. To be alone with God is highly suspect, and, mind you, it is, because the will of God can be terrible and can isolate you from your family and your friends and, if you are courageous or foolish enough, you may end up in the lunatic asylum. And yet how can there be religion without the experience of the divine will? Things are comparatively easy as long as God wants nothing but the fulfilment of his laws, but what if he wants you to break them, as he may do equally well? Poor Hosea could believe in the symbolic nature of his awkward marriage, but what about the equally poor little doctor who has to swear his soul away to save a human life? He cannot even begin to point out what an affliction his act of lying is, although in his solitude with God he may feel justified.

[19] [The translation (1916) of the original (1912) version of *Symbols of Transformation*.]

But in case of discovery he has to face the ignominious consequences of his deed and nobody will believe him to be a witness for the divine will. To be God's voice is not a social function anymore. *Si parva licet componere magnis*—what did I get for my serious struggle over *Job,* which I had postponed for as long as possible? I am regarded as blasphemous, contemptible, a fiend, whose name is mud. It fell to my lot to collect the victims of the Summum Bonum and use my own poor means to help them. But I could not say that a church of any denomination has encouraged my endeavours. You are one of the *very few* who admit the *complexio oppositorum* in the Deity. (Cusanus does not seem to have really known what he was talking about, nor anybody else in those days, otherwise he would have been roasted long ago.) That is the reason why I don't identify religion with a creed. I can have a real communion only with those who have the same or similar religious experience, but not with the believers in the Word, who have never even taken the trouble to understand its implications and expose themselves to the divine will unreservedly. They use the Word to protect themselves against the will of God. Nothing shields you better against the solitude and forlornness of the divine experience than community. It is the best and safest substitute for individual responsibility.

1638 The self or Christ is present in everybody *a priori,* but as a rule in an *unconscious condition* to begin with. But it is a definite *experience* of later life, when this fact becomes *conscious.* It is not really understood by teaching or suggestion. It is only real when it *happens,* and it can happen only when you withdraw your projections from an *outward* historical or metaphysical Christ and thus *wake up* Christ within. This does not mean that the unconscious self is inactive, only that we do not understand it. The self (or Christ) cannot become conscious and real without the withdrawal of external projections. An act of *introjection* is needed, i.e., the realization that the self lives in you and not in an external figure separated and different from yourself. The self has always been, and will be, your innermost centre and periphery, your *scintilla* and *punctum solis.* It is even biologically the archetype of order and—dynamically—the source of life.

IV

Here the question is concerned with Jung's objections to the view that God is the Summum Bonum and sin is a privatio boni.

639 Well, I have noticed that it seems to be a major difficulty for the theological mind to accept the fact that (1) "good" and "evil" are man-made judgments. Somebody's "good" may be bad or evil for another *et vice versa.* (2) One cannot speak of "good" if one does not equally speak of "evil," any more than there can be an "above" without a "below," or "day" without "night." (3) The *privatio boni* appears to me a syllogism. If "good" and *οὐσία* are one without an equally valid counterpart, then "good" is also a *μὴ ὄν* because the term "good" has lost its meaning; it is just "being" and evil is just "not-being" and the term means "nothing." Of course you are free to call "nothing" evil, but nothing is just nothing and cannot bear another name, making it into "something." Something non-existing has no name and no quality. The *privatio boni* suggests that evil is *μὴ ὄν*, not-being or nothing. It is not even a shadow. There remains only the *ὄν*, but it is not good, since there is no "bad." Thus the epithet "good" is redundant. You can call God the Summum, but not the Bonum, since there is nothing else different from "being," from the Summum qua being! Although the *privatio boni* is not the invention of the Church Fathers, the syllogism was most welcome to them on account of the Manichaean danger of dualism. Yet without dualism there is no cognition at all, because discrimination is impossible.

640 I have never [as you state] understood from my study of the Fathers that God is the highest good *with reference to man,* no matter what he is in himself. This is certainly new to me. Obviously my critique of the Summum Bonum does not apply in this case. The Bonum then would be an anthropomorphic judgment, "God is good for me," leaving it an open question whether he is the same for other people. If one assumes him to be a *complexio oppositorum,* i.e., beyond good and evil, it is possible that he may appear equally well as the source of evil which you believe to be ultimately good for man. I am convinced, as I have seen it too often to doubt it, that an apparent evil is really no evil at all if you accept and obediently live it as far as possible, but I am equally convinced that an apparent good is in reality not always good at all but wholly destructive. If this were not the case, then everything would be ultimately good, i.e., good in its essence, and evil would not really exist, as it would be a merely transitory appearance. In other words: the term "good" has lost its meaning, and the only safe basis of cognition is our world of experience, in which the power of evil is very real and not at all a mere appearance. One can and does

cherish an optimistic hope that ultimately, in spite of grave doubts, "all will be well." As I am not making a metaphysical judgment, I cannot help remarking that at least in our empirical world the opposites are inexorably at work and that, without them, this world would not exist. We cannot even conceive of a thing that is not a form of energy, and energy is inevitably based upon opposites.

1641 I must however pay attention to the psychological fact that, so far as we can make out, *individuation* is a natural phenomenon, and in a way an inescapable goal, which we have reason to call *good for us,* because it liberates us from the otherwise insoluble conflict of opposites (at least to a noticeable degree). It is not invented by man, but Nature herself produces its archetypal image. Thus the credo "in the end all will be well" is not without its psychic foundation. But it is more than questionable whether this phenomenon is of any importance to the world in general, or only to the individual who has reached a more complete state of consciousness, to the "redeemed" man in accordance with our Christian tenet of eternal damnation. "Many are called, but few are chosen" is an authentic logion and not characteristic of Gnosticism alone.

V

Jung has been given the title "Gnostic" which he has rejected. This term has probably been used about him [and his system] because he appears to believe that salvation is for the few and that the many cannot and ought not to attempt individuation. Is it possible that he is a "Gnostic" in this sense?

1642 The designation of my "system" as "Gnostic" is an invention of my theological critics. Moreover I have no "system." I am not a philosopher, merely an empiricist. The Gnostics have the merit of having raised the problem of πόθεν τὸ κακόν; [whence evil?]. Valentinus as well as Basilides are in my view great theologians, who tried to cope with the problems raised by the inevitable influx of the collective unconscious, a fact clearly portrayed by the "gnostic" gospel of St. John and by St. Paul, not to mention the Book of Revelation, and even by Christ himself (unjust steward and Codex Bezae to Luke 6:4). In the style of their time they hypostatized their ideas as metaphysical entities. Psychology does not hypostatize, but considers such ideas as psychological statements about, or models of, essential unconscious factors inaccessible to immediate experience. This is about as far as scientific understanding can go. In our days there are plenty of people who are unable to believe a statement they cannot understand, and they appreciate the help psychology can give them by showing them that human behaviour is deeply influenced by numinous archetypes. That gives them some understanding of why and how the religious factor plays an important role. It also gives them ways and means of recognizing the operation of religious ideas in their own psyche.

43 I must confess that I myself could find access to religion only through the psychological understanding of inner experiences, whereas traditional religious interpretations left me high and dry. It was only psychology that helped me to overcome the fatal impressions of my youth that everything untrue, even immoral, in our ordinary empirical world *must* be believed to be the eternal truth in religion. Above all, the killing of a human victim to placate the senseless wrath of a God who had created imperfect beings unable to fulfil his expectations poisoned my whole religion. Nobody knew an answer. "With God all things are possible." Just so! As the perpetrator of incredible things he is himself incredible, and yet I was supposed to believe what every fibre of my body refused to admit! There are a great many questions which I could elucidate only by psychological understanding. I loved the Gnostics in spite of everything, because they recognized the necessity of some further *raisonnement,* entirely absent in the Christian cosmos. They were at least human and therefore understandable. But I have no *γνῶσις τοῦ θεοῦ*. I know the reality of religious experience and of psychological models which permit a limited understanding. I have Gnosis so far as I have immediate experience, and my models are greatly helped by the *représentations collectives* of all religions. But I cannot see why one creed should possess the unique and perfect truth. Each creed claims this prerogative, hence the general disagreement! This is not very helpful. Something must be wrong. I think it is the immodesty of the claim to god-almightiness of the believers, which compensates their inner doubt. Instead of basing themselves upon immediate experience they believe in words for want of something better. The *sacrificium intellectus* is a sweet drug for man's all-embracing spiritual laziness and inertia.

44 I owe you quite a number of apologies for the fact that my layman's mental attitude must be excruciatingly irritating to your point of view. But you know, as a psychologist I am not concerned with theology directly, but rather with the incompetent general pub-

lic and its erroneous and faulty convictions, which are however just as real to it as their competent views are to the theologians. I am continually asked "theological" questions by my patients, and when I say that I am only a doctor and they should ask the theologian, then the regular answer is, "Oh, yes, we have done so," or "we do not ask a priest because we get an answer we already know, which explains nothing."

1645 Well this is the reason why I have to try for better or worse to help my patients to some kind of understanding at least. It gives them a certain satisfaction as it has done to me, although it is admittedly inadequate. But to them it sounds as if somebody were speaking their language and understanding their questions which they take very seriously indeed. Once, for instance, it was a very important question to me to discover how far modern Protestantism considers that the God of the Old Testament is identical with the God of the New Testament. I asked two university professors. They did not answer my letter. The third (also a professor) said he didn't know. The fourth said, "Oh, that is quite easy. Yahweh is a somewhat more archaic conception contrasted with the more differentiated view of the New Testament." I said to him, "That is exactly the kind of psychologism you accuse me of." My question must have been singularly inadequate or foolish. But I do not know why. I am speaking for the layman's psychology. The layman is a reality and his questions do exist. My "Answer to Job" voices the questions of thousands, but the theologians don't answer, contenting themselves with dark allusions to my layman's ignorance of Hebrew, higher criticism, Old Testament exegesis, etc., but there is not a single answer. A Jesuit professor of theology asked me rather indignantly how I could suggest that the Incarnation has remained incomplete. I said, "The human being is born under the *macula peccati.* Neither Christ nor his mother suffers from original sin. They are therefore not human, but superhuman, a sort of God." What did he answer? Nothing.

1646 Why is that so? My layman's reasoning is certainly imperfect, and my theological knowledge regrettably meagre, but not as bad as all that, at least I hope not. But I do know something about the psychology of man now and in the past, and as a psychologist I raise the questions I have been asked a hundred times by my patients and other laymen. Theology would certainly not suffer by paying attention. I know you are too busy to do it. I am all the more anxious to prevent avoidable mistakes and I shall feel deeply obliged to you if you take the trouble of showing me where I am wrong.

647 Gnosis is characterized by the hypostatizing of psychological apperceptions, i.e., by the integration of archetypal contents beyond the revealed "truth" of the Gospels. Hippolytus still considered classical Greek philosophy along with Gnostic philosophies as perfectly possible views. Christian Gnosis to him was merely the best and superior to all of them. The people who call me a Gnostic cannot understand that I am a psychologist, describing modes of psychic behaviour precisely like a biologist studying the instinctual activities of insects. He does not *believe* in the tenets of the bee's philosophy. When I show the parallels between dreams and Gnostic fantasies I *believe* in neither. They are just facts one does not need to believe or to hypostatize. An alienist is not necessarily crazy because he describes and analyses the delusions of lunatics, nor is a scholar studying the *Tripitaka* necessarily a Buddhist.

4. Reply to a Letter from the Rev. David Cox[20]

648 The crux of this question is: 'Within your own personality." "Christ" can be an external reality (historical and metaphysical) or an archetypal image or idea in the collective unconscious pointing to an unknown background. I would understand the former mainly as a projection, but not the latter, because it is immediately evident. It is not projected upon anything, therefore there is no projection. Only, "faith" in Christ is different from faith in anyone else, since in this case, "Christ" being immediately evident, the word "faith," including or alluding to the possibility of doubt, seems too feeble a word to characterize that powerful presence from which there is no escape. A general can say to his soldiers, "You must have faith in me," because one might doubt him. But you cannot say to a man lying wounded on the battlefield, "You ought to *believe* that this is a real battle," or "Be sure that you are up against the enemy." It is just too obvious. Even the historical Jesus began to speak of "faith" because he saw that his disciples had no immediate evidence. Instead they had to believe, while he himself being identical with God had no need to "have faith in God."

649 As one habitually identifies the "psyche" with what one knows of it, it is assumed that one can call certain (supposed or believed)

[20] [Philp, pp. 239–50. (25 Sept. 1957.)]

metaphysical entities non-psychic. Being a responsible scientist I am unable to pass such a judgment, for all I know of regular religious phenomena seems to indicate that they are psychic events. Moreover I do not know the full reach of the psyche, because there is the limitless extent of the unconscious. "Christ" is definitely an archetypal image (I don't add "only") and that is all I actually know of him. As such he belongs to the (collective) foundations of the psyche. I identify him therefore with what I call the self. The self rules the whole of the psyche. I think our opinions do not differ essentially. You seem to have trouble only with the theological (and self-inflicted) devaluation of the psyche, which you apparently believe to be ultimately definable.

1650 If my identification of Christ with the archetype of the self is valid, he is, or ought to be, a *complexio oppositorum.* Historically this is not so. Therefore I was profoundly surprised by your statement that Christ contains the opposites. Between my contention and historical Christianity there stretches that deep abyss of Christian dualism—Christ and the Devil, good and evil, God and Creation.

1651 "Beyond good and evil" simply means: we pass no moral judgment. But in fact nothing is changed. The same is true when we state that whatever God is or does is *good.* Since God does everything (even man created by him is his instrument) everything is good, and the term "good" has lost its meaning. "Good" is a relative term. There is no good without bad.

1652 I am afraid that even revealed truth has to evolve. Everything living changes. We should not be satisfied with unchangeable traditions. The great battle that began with the dawn of consciousness has not reached its climax with any particular interpretation, apostolic, Catholic, Protestant, or otherwise. Even the highly conservative Catholic Church has overstepped its ancient rule of apostolic authenticity with the *Assumptio Beatae Virginis.* According to what I hear from Catholic theologians, the next step would be the Coredemptrix. This obvious recognition of the female element is a very important step foward. It means psychologically the recognition of the unconscious, since the representative of the collective unconscious is the *anima,* the archetype of all divine mothers (at least in the masculine psyche).

1653 The equivalent on the Protestant side would be a confrontation with the unconscious as the counterpart or consort of the masculine Logos. The hitherto valid symbol of the supreme spiritual structure was Trinity + Satan, the so-called 3 + 1 structure, corresponding to three conscious functions versus the one unconscious, so-called inferior function; or 1 + 3 if the conscious side is understood as one versus the co-called inferior or chthonic triad, mythologically characterized as three mother figures.[21] I suppose that the negative evaluation of the unconscious has something to do with the fact that it has been hitherto represented by Satan, while in reality it is the female aspect of man's psyche and thus not wholly evil in spite of the old saying: *Vir a Deo creatus, mulier a simia Dei.*

654 It seems to me of paramount importance that Protestantism should integrate psychological experience, as for instance Jacob Boehme did. With him God does not only contain love, but, on the other side and in the same measure, the fire of wrath, in which Lucifer himself dwells. Christ is a revelation of his love, but he can manifest his wrath in an Old Testament way just as well, i.e., in the form of evil. Inasmuch as out of evil good may come, and out of good evil, we do not know whether creation is ultimately good or a regrettable mistake and God's suffering. It is an ineffable mystery. At any rate we are not doing justice either to nature in general or to our own human nature when we deny the immensity of evil and suffering and turn our eyes from the cruel aspect of creation. Evil should be recognized and one should not attribute the existence of evil to man's sinfulness. Yahweh is not offended by being feared.

655 It is quite understandable why it was an Εὐαγγέλιον [evangel, "good tidings"] to learn of the *bonitas Dei* and of his son. It was known to the ancients that the *cognitio sui ipsius* [self-knowledge][22] was a prerequisite for this, not only in the Graeco-Roman world but also in the Far East. It is to the individual aptitude that the man Jesus owes his apotheosis: he became the symbol of the self under the aspect of the infinite goodness, which was certainly the symbol most needed in ancient civilization (as it is still needed today).

656 It can be considered a fact that the dogmatic figure of Christ is the result of a condensation process from various sources. One of the main origins is the age-old god-man of Egypt: Osiris-Horus and his four sons. It was a remodeling of the unconscious archetype

[21] [Cf. "The Phenomenology of the Spirit in Fairytales" (C.W., vol. 9, i), pars. 425f., 436ff.; *Aion,* par. 351; and "The Spirit Mercurius" (C.W., vol. 13), pars. 270ff.]

[22] [Cf. "The Spirit Mercurius," par. 301.]

hitherto projected upon a divine non-human being. By embodying itself in a historical man it came nearer to consciousness, but in keeping with the mental capacity of the time it remained as if suspended between God and man, between the need for good and the fear of evil. Any doubt about the absolute *bonitas Dei* would have led to an immediate regression to the former pagan state, i.e., to the amorality of the metaphysical principle.

1657 Since then two thousand years have passed. In this time we have learned that good and evil are categories of our moral judgment, therefore relative to man. Thus the way was opened for a new model of the self. Moral judgment is a necessity of the human mind. The Christ (ὁ Χριστός) is the Christian model that expresses the self, as the Ἄνθρωπος is the corresponding Egypto-Judaic formula. Moral qualification is withdrawn from the deity. The Catholic Church has almost succeeded in adding femininity to the masculine Trinity. Protestantism is confronted with the psychological problem of the unconscious.

1658 It is, as far as I can see, a peculiar process extending over at least four thousand years of mental evolution. It can be contemplated in a "euhemeristic" way as a development of man's understanding of the supreme powers beyond his control. [The process consists of the following stages:] (1) Gods. (2) A supreme Deity ruling the gods and demons. (3) God shares our human fate, is betrayed, killed or dies, and is resurrected again. There is a feminine counterpart dramatically involved in God's fate. (4) God becomes man in the flesh and thus historical. He is identified with the abstract idea of the Summum Bonum and loses the feminine counterpart. The female deity is degraded to an ancillary position (Church). Consciousness begins to prevail against the unconscious. This is an enormously important step forward in the emancipation of consciousness and in the liberation of thought from its involvement in things. Thus the foundation of science is laid, but on the other hand, that of atheism and materialism. Both are inevitable consequences of the basic split between spirit and matter in Christian philosophy, which proclaimed the redemption of the spirit from the body and its fetters. (5) The whole metaphysical world is understood as a psychic structure projected into the sphere of the unknown.

1659 The danger of this viewpoint is exaggerated scepticism and rationalism, since the original "supreme powers" are reduced to mere representations over which one assumes one has complete control. This leads to a complete negation of the supreme powers (scientific materialism).

560 The other way of looking at it is from the standpoint of the archetype. The original chaos of multiple gods evolves into a sort of monarchy, and the archetype of the self slowly asserts its central position as the archetype of order in chaos. One God rules supreme but apart from man. It begins to show a tendency to relate itself to consciousness through a process of penetration: the humanizing effect of a feminine intercession, expressed for instance by the Isis intrigue. In the Christian myth the Deity, the self, penetrates consciousness almost completely, without any visible loss of power and prestige. But in time it becomes obvious that the Incarnation has caused a loss among the supreme powers: the indispensable dark side has been left behind or stripped off, and the feminine aspect is missing. Thus a further act of incarnation becomes necessary. Through atheism, materialism, and agnosticism, the powerful yet one-sided aspect of the Summum Bonum is weakened, so that it cannot keep out the dark side, and incidentally the feminine factor, any more. "Antichrist" and "Devil" gain the ascendancy: God asserts his power through the revelation of his darkness and destructiveness. Man is merely instrumental in carrying out the divine plan. Obviously he does not want his own destruction but is forced to it by his own inventions. He is entirely unfree in his actions because he does not yet understand that he is a mere instrument of a destructive superior will. From this paradox he could learn that—*nolens volens*—he serves a supreme power, and that supreme powers exist in spite of his denial. As God lives in everybody in the form of the *scintilla* of the self, man could see his "daemonic," i.e., ambivalent, nature in himself and thus he could understand how he is penetrated by God or how God incarnates in man.

561 Through his further incarnation God becomes a fearful task for man, who must now find ways and means to unite the divine opposites in himself. He is summoned and can no longer leave his sorrows to somebody else, not even to Christ, because it was Christ that has left him the almost impossible task of his cross. Christ has shown how everybody will be crucified upon his destiny, i.e., upon his self, as he was. He did not carry his cross and suffer crucifixion so that we could escape. The bill of the Christian era is presented to us: we are living in a world rent in two from top to bottom; we are confronted with the H-bomb and we have to face our own shadows. Obviously God does not want us to remain little

children looking out for a parent who will do their job for them. We are cornered by the supreme power of the incarnating Will. God really wants to become man, even if he rends him asunder. This is so no matter what we say. One cannot talk the H-bomb or Communism out of the world. We are in the soup that is going to be cooked for us, whether we claim to have invented it or not. Christ said to his disciples "Ye are gods." This word becomes painfully true. If God incarnates in the empirical man, man is confronted with the divine problem. Being and remaining man he has to find an answer. It is the question of the opposites, raised at the moment when God was declared to be good only. Where then is his dark side? Christ is the model for the human answers and his symbol is the *cross,* the union of the opposites. This will be the fate of man, and this he must understand if he is to survive at all. We are threatened with universal genocide if we cannot work out the way of salvation by a symbolic death.

1662 In order to accomplish his task, man is inspired by the Holy Ghost in such a way that he is apt to identify him with his own mind. He even runs the grave risk of believing he has a Messianic mission, and forces tyrannous doctrines upon his fellow-beings. He would do better to dis-identify his mind from the small voice within, from dreams and fantasies through which the divine spirit manifests itself. One should listen to the inner voice attentively, intelligently and critically (*Probate spiritus!*), because the voice one hears is the *influxus divinus* consisting, as the *Acts of John* aptly state, of "right" and "left" streams, i.e., of opposites.[23] They have to be clearly separated so that their positive and negative aspects become visible. Only thus can we take up a middle position and discover a middle way. That is the task left to man, and that is the reason why man is so important to God that he decided to become a man himself.

1663 I must apologize for the length of this exposition. Please do not think that I am stating a truth. I am merely trying to present a hypothesis which might explain the bewildering conclusions resulting from the clash of traditional symbols and psychological experiences. I thought it best to put my cards on the table, so that you get a clear picture of my ideas.

1664 Although all this sounds as if it were a sort of theological speculation, it is in reality modern man's perplexity expressed in symbolic

23 [James, *The Apocryphal New Testament,* p. 255: "The Acts of Peter." Cf. "Transformation Symbolism in the Mass" (C.W., vol. 11), par. 429.]

terms. It is the problem I so often had to deal with in treating the neuroses of intelligent patients. It can be expressed in a more scientific, psychological language; for instance, instead of using the term God you say "unconscious," instead of Christ "self," instead of incarnation "integration of the unconscious," instead of salvation or redemption "individuation," instead of crucifixion or sacrifice on the Cross "realization of the four functions or of "wholeness." I think it is no disadvantage to religious tradition if we can see how far it coincides with psychological experience. On the contrary it seems to me a most welcome aid in understanding religious traditions.

665 A myth remains a myth even if certain people believe it to be the literal revelation of an eternal truth, but it becomes moribund if the living truth it contains ceases to be an object of belief. It is therefore necessary to renew its life from time to time through a *new interpretation.* This means re-adapting it to the changing spirit of the times. What the Church calls "prefigurations" refer to the original state of the myth, while the Christian doctrine represents a new interpretation and re-adaptation to a Hellenized world. A most interesting attempt at re-interpretation began in the eleventh century,[24] leading up to the schism in the sixteenth century. The Renaissance was no more a rejuvenation of antiquity than Protestantism was a return to the primitive Christianity: it was a new interpretation necessitated by the devitalization of the Catholic Church.

666 Today Christianity is devitalized by its remoteness from the spirit of the times. It stands in need of a new union with, or relation to, the atomic age, which is a unique novelty in history. The myth needs to be retold in a new spiritual language, for the new wine can no more be poured into the old bottles than it could in the Hellenistic age. Even conservative Jewry had to produce an entirely new version of the myth in its Cabalistic Gnosis. It is my practical experience that psychological understanding immediately revivifies the essential Christian ideas and fills them with the breath of life. This is because our worldly light, i.e., scientific knowledge and understanding, coincides with the symbolic statement of the myth, whereas previously we were unable to bridge the gulf between knowing and believing.

667 Coming back to your letter (pp. 2–3, 25 September) I must say that I could accept your definition of the Summum Bonum,

[24] [Cf. *Aion,* pars, 139ff.]

"Whatever God is, that is good," if it did not interfere with or twist our sense of good. In dealing with the moral nature of an act of God, we have either to suspend our moral judgment and blindly follow the dictates of this superior will, or we have to judge in a human fashion and call white white and black black. In spite of the fact that we sometimes obey the superior will blindly and almost heroically, I do not think that this is the usual thing, nor is it commendable on the whole to act blindly, because we are surely expected to act with conscious moral reflection. It is too dangerously easy to avoid responsibility by deluding ourselves that our will is the will of God. We can be forcibly overcome by the latter, but if we are not we must use our judgment, and then we are faced with the inexorable fact that humanly speaking some acts of God are good and some bad, so much so that the assumption of a Summum Bonum becomes almost an act of hubris.

1668 If God can be understood as the perfect *complexio oppositorum,* so can Christ. I can agree with your view about Christ completely, only it is not the traditional but a very modern conception which is on the way to the desired new interpretation. I also agree with your understanding of Tao and its contrast to Christ, who is indeed the paradigm of the reconciliation of the divine opposites in man brought about in the process of individuation. Thus Christ stands for the treasure and the supreme "good." (In German "good" = *gut,* but the noun *Gut* also means "property" and "treasure.")

1669 When theology makes metaphysical assertions the conscience of the scientist cannot back it up. Since Christ never meant more to me than what I could understand of him, and since this understanding coincides with my empirical knowledge of the self, I have to admit that I mean the self in dealing with the idea of Christ. As a matter of fact I have no other access to Christ but the self, and since I do not know anything beyond the self I cling to his archetype. I say, "Here is the living and perceptible archetype which has been projected upon the man Jesus or has historically manifested itself in him." If this collective archetype had not been associated with Jesus he would have remained a nameless Zaddik. I actually prefer the term "self" because I am talking to Hindus as well as Christians, and I do not want to divide but to unite.

1670 Since I am putting my cards on the table, I must confess that I cannot detach a certain feeling of dishonesty from any metaphysical assertion—one may speculate but not assert. One cannot reach beyond oneself, and if somebody assures you he can reach beyond himself and his natural limitations, he overreaches himself and becomes immodest and untrue.

671 This may be a *deformation professionelle,* the prejudice of a scientific conscience. Science is an honest-to-God attempt to get at the truth and its rule is never to assert more than one can prove within reasonable and defensible limits. This is my attitude in approaching the problem of religious experience.

672 I am unable to envisage anything beyond the self, since it is—by definition—a borderline concept designating the unknown totality of man: there are no known limits to the unconscious. There is no reason whatsoever why you should or should not call the beyond-self Christ or Buddha or Purusha or Tao or Khidr or Tifereth. All these terms are recognizable formulations of what I call the "self." Moreover I dislike the insistence upon a special name, since my human brethren are as good and as valid as I am. Why should their name-giving be less valid than mine?

673 It is not easy for a layman to get the desired theological information, because even the Church is not at one with herself in this respect. *Who* represents authentic Christianity? Thus the layman whether he likes it or not has to quote Protestant or Catholic statements *pêle-mêle* as Christian views because they are backed up by some authority. In my case I believe I have been careful in quoting my sources.

674 You as a theologian are naturally interested in the best possible view or explanation, while the psychologist is interested in all sorts of opinions because he wants to acquire some understanding of mental phenomenology and cares little for even the best possible metaphysical assertion, which is beyond human reach anyhow. The various creeds are just so many phenomena to him, and he has no means of deciding about the truth or the ultimate validity of any metaphysical statement. I cannot select the "best" or the "ultimate" opinions because I do not know which kind of opinion to choose from which Church. Also I do not care particularly where such opinions come from, and it is quite beyond my capacity to find out whether they are erroneous or not. I would be wrong only if I attributed, for instance, the idea of the *conceptio immaculata* to Protestantism or the *sola fide* standpoint to Catholicism. The many misunderstandings attributed to me come into this category. In either case it is plain to see that someone has been careless in his assumptions. But if I attribute Ritschl's christological views to

Protestantism, it is no error in spite of the fact that the Church of England does not subscribe to the opinions of Mr. Ritschl or of Mr. Barth.[24a] I hope I have not inadvertently been guilty of some misquotation.

1675 I can illustrate the problem by a typical instance. My little essay on Eastern Meditation[25] deals with the popular tract *Amitāyur Dhyāna Sūtra,* which is a relatively late and not very valuable Mahāyāna text. A critic objected to my choice: he could not see why I should take such an inconspicuous tract instead of a genuinely Buddhist and classical Pāli text in order to present Buddhist thought. He entirely overlooked the fact that I had no intention whatever of expounding classical Buddhism, but that my aim was to analyse the psychology of this particular text. Why should I not deal with Jacob Boehme or Angelus Silesius as Christian writers, even though they are not classical representatives either of Catholicism or of Protestantism?

1676 A similar misunderstanding appears in your view that I am not doing justice to the *ideal* of community. Whenever possible I avoid *ideals* and much prefer *realities.* I have never found a community which would allow "full expression to the individual within it." Suppose the individual is going to speak the truth regardless of the feelings of everybody else: he would not only be the most abominable enfant terrible but might equally well cause a major catastrophe. Edifying examples of this can be observed at the meetings of Buchman's so-called Oxford Group Movement. At the expense of truth the individual has to "behave," i.e., suppress his reaction merely for the sake of Christian charity. What if I should get up after a sermon about ideals and ask the parson how much he himself is able to live up to his admonitions? In my own case the mere fact that I am seriously interested in psychology has created a peculiar hostility or fear in certain circles. What has happened to those people in the Church, that is in a Christian community, who ventured to have a new idea? No community can escape the laws of mass psychology. I am critical of the community in the same way as I suspect the individual who builds his castles in Spain while anxiously avoiding the expression of his own convictions. I am shy of ideals which one preaches and never lives up to, simply because one cannot. I want to know rather what we

24a [Albrecht Ritschl (1822–1889) and Karl Barth (1886–1968), resp. German and Swiss Protestant theologians.]

25 ["The Psychology of Eastern Meditation" (C.W., vol. 11).]

can live. I want to build up a possible human life which carries through God's experiment and does not invent an ideal scheme knowing that it will *never* be fulfilled.

Later Letter[26]

1677 I am much obliged to you for telling me exactly what you think and for criticizing my blunt ways of thinking and writing (also of talking, I am afraid). It seems, however, to be the style of natural scientists: we simply state our proposition, assuming that nobody will think it to be more than a disputable hypothesis. We are so imbued with doubts concerning our assumptions that scepticism is taken for granted. We are therefore apt to omit the conventional *captatio benevolentiae lectoris* with its "With hesitation I submit . . . ," "I consider it a daring hypothesis . . . ," etc. We even forget the preamble: "This is the way I look at it . . . ."

1678 The case of the Jesuit[27] was that he put the direct question to me: "How on earth can you suggest that Christ was not human?" The discussion was naturally on the *dogmatic* level, as there is no other basis on which this question can be answered. It is not a question of *truth,* because the problem itself is far beyond human judgment. My "Answer to Job" is merely a reconstruction of the psychology discernible in this and other Old Testament texts for the interested layman. He knows very little of Higher Criticism, which is historical and philological in the main, and it is but little concerned with the layman's reactions to the paradoxes and moral horrors of the Old Testament. He knows his Bible and hears the sermons of his parson or priest. As a Catholic he has had a dogmatic education.

1679 When talking of "Job" you must always remember that I am dealing with the psychology of an archetypal and anthropomorphic image of God and not with a metaphysical entity. As far as we can see, the archetype is a psychic structure with a life of its own to a certain extent.

1680 God in the Old Testament is a guardian of law and morality, yet is himself unjust. He is a moral paradox, unreflecting in an ethical sense. We can perceive God in an infinite variety of images, yet all of them are anthropomorphic, otherwise they would not

[26] [Philp, pp. 250–54. (12 Nov. 1957.)]

[27] [Cf. supra, par. 1645.]

get into our heads. The divine paradox is the source of unending suffering to man. Job cannot avoid seeing it and thus he sees more than God himself. This explains why the God-image has to come down "into the flesh." The paradox, expressed of course with many hesitations in the particularities of the myth and in the Catholic dogma, is clearly discernible in the fact that the "Suffering Righteous man" is, historically speaking, an erroneous conception, not identical with the suffering God, because he is Jesus Christ, worshipped as a separate God (he is a mere prefiguration, painfully included in a triunity) and not an ordinary man who is forced to accept the suffering of intolerable opposites he has not invented. They were preordained. He is the victim, because he is capable of three-dimensional consciousness and ethical decision. (This is a bit condensed. Unlike Yahweh, man has self-reflection.)

1681 I don't know what Job is supposed to have seen. But it seems possible that he unconsciously anticipated the historical future, namely the evolution of the God-image. God had to become man. Man's suffering does not derive from his sins but from the maker of his imperfections, the paradoxical God. The righteous man is the instrument into which God enters in order to attain self-reflection and thus consciousness and rebirth as a divine child trusted to the care of adult man.

1682 Now this is not the statement of a truth, but the psychological reading of a mythological text—a model constructed for the purpose of establishing the psychological linking together of its contents. My aim is to show what the results are when you apply modern psychology to such a text. Higher Criticism and Hebrew philology are obviously superfluous, because it is simply a question of the text which the layman has under his eyes. The Christian religion has not been shaped by Higher Criticism.

1683 The trouble I have with my academic reader is that he cannot see a psychic structure as a relatively autonomous entity, because he is under the illusion that he is dealing with a concept. But in reality it is a living thing. The archetypes all have a life of their own which follows a biological pattern. A Church that has evolved a masculine Trinity will follow the old pattern: 3 + 1, where 1 is a female and, if 3 = good, 1 as a woman will mediate between good and evil, the latter being the devil and the shadow of the Trinity. The woman will inevitably be the Mother-Sister of the Son-God, with whom she will be united *in thalamo,* i.e., in the ἱερὸς γάμος, *quod est demonstratum* by the second Encyclical concerning the Assumption.[28]

684 A passionate discourse between the man Job and God will logically lead to a mutual rapprochement: God will be humanized, man will be "divinized." Thus Job will be followed by the idea of the Incarnation of God and the redemption and apotheosis of man. This development, however, is seriously impeded by the fact that the "woman," as always, inevitably brings in the problem of the shadow. Therefore *mulier taceat in ecclesia.* The arch-sin the Catholic Church is ever after is sexuality, and the ideal *par excellence* virginity, which puts a definite stop to life. But if life should insist on going on, the shadow steps in and sin becomes a serious problem, because the shadow cannot be left to eternal damnation any more. Consequently, at the end of the first millennium of the Christian aeon, as predicted in the Apocalypse, the world was suspected of being created by the devil.[29] The impressive and still living myth of the Holy Grail came to life with its two significant figures of Parsifal and Merlin. At the same time we observe an extraordinary development of alchemical philosophy with its central figure of the *filius macrocosmi,* a chthonic equivalent of Christ.

685 This was followed by the great and seemingly incurable schism of the Christian Church, and last but not least by the still greater and more formidable schism of the world towards the end of the second millennium.

686 A psychological reading of the dominant archetypal images reveals a continuous series of psychological transformations, depicting the autonomous life of archetypes behind the scenes of consciousness. This hypothesis has been worked out to clarify and make comprehensible our religious history. The treatment of psychological troubles and the inability of my patients to understand theological interpretations and terminology have given me my motive. The necessities of psychotherapy have proved to me the immense importance of a religious attitude, which cannot be achieved without a thorough understanding of religious tradition, just as an individual's troubles cannot be understood and cured without a basic knowledge of their biographical antecedents. I have applied to the

28 [*Apostolic Constitution* ("*Munificentissimus Deus*") *of Pius XII,* sec. 22: "The place of the bride whom the Father had espoused was in the heavenly courts." Sec. 33: ". . . on this day the Virgin Mother was taken up to her heavenly bridal-chamber."]

29 [*Aion,* pars. 225ff.]

God-image what I have learned from the reconstruction of so many human lives through a knowledge of their unconscious. All this is empirical and may have nothing to do with theology, if theology says so. But if theology should come to the conclusion that its tenets have something to do with the empirical human psyche, I establish a claim. I think that in those circumstances my opinion should be given a hearing. It cannot be argued on the level of metaphysical assertions. It can be criticized only on its own psychological level, regardless of whether it is a psychologically satisfactory interpretation of the facts or not. The "facts" are the documented historical manifestations of the archetype, however "erroneous" they may be.

1687 I have stated my point of view bluntly (for which I must ask your forgiveness!) in order to give you a fair chance to see it as clearly as possible. The end of your letter, where you deal with Christ, leaves me with a doubt. It looks to me as if you were trying to explain the empirical man Jesus, while I am envisaging the archetype of the Anthropos and its very general interpretation as a collective phenomenon and not as the best possible interpretation of an individual and historical person. Christianity as a whole is less concerned with the historical man Jesus and his somewhat doubtful biography than with the mythological Anthropos or God-Son figure. It would be rather hazardous to attempt to analyse the historical Jesus as a human person. "Christ" appears from a much safer (because mythological) background, which invites psychological elucidation. Moreover it is not the Jewish rabbi and reformer Jesus, but the archetypal Christ who touches upon the archetype of the Redeemer in everybody and carries conviction.

1688 My approach is certainly not theological and cannot be treated as a theologoumenon. It is essentially a psychological attempt based upon the archetypal, amoral God-image, which is not a concept but rather an irrational and phenomenal experience, an *Urbild*. But in so far as theologians are also concerned with the adult human psyche (perhaps not as much as medical psychology), I am convinced that it would be of advantage to them to become acquainted with the psychological aspects of the Christian religion. I will not conceal the fact that theological thinking is very difficult for me, from which I conclude that psychological thinking must be an equally laborious undertaking for the theologian. This may explain why I inundate you with such a long letter.

1689 When I see how China (and soon India) will lose her old culture under the impact of materialistic rationalism, I grow afraid that the Christian West will succumb to the same malady, simply because the old symbolic language is no longer understood and people cannot see any more where and how it applies. In Catholic countries anyone leaving the Church becomes frankly atheistic. In Protestant countries a small number become sectarians, and the others avoid the churches for their cruelly boring and empty sermons. Not a few begin to believe in the State—not even knowing that they themselves are the State. The recent broadcasts of the B.B.C.[30] give a good picture of the educated layman's mind with regard to religion. What an understanding! All due to the lack of a psychological standpoint, or so it seems to me.

690 I am sorry that I am apparently a *petra scandali*. I do not mean to offend. Please accept my apologies for my bluntness. I am sincerely grateful to you for giving me your attention.

Faithfully yours, C. G. JUNG

30 [Probably a series of five talks on "Religion and Philosophy," by Robert C. Walton, J. D. Mabbott, Alasdair MacIntyre, and the Rev. F. A. Cockin, broadcast in Sept.–Oct. 1957, according to information from the B.B.C.]

THE COLLECTED WORKS OF

C. G. JUNG

EDITORS: SIR HERBERT READ, MICHAEL FORDHAM, AND GERHARD ADLER; *EXECUTIVE EDITOR*, WILLIAM McGUIRE. *TRANSLATED BY* R.F.C. HULL, EXCEPT WHERE NOTED.

IN THE FOLLOWING LIST, dates of original publication are given in parentheses (of original composition, in brackets). Multiple dates indicate revisions.

1. PSYCHIATRIC STUDIES (1957; 2nd edn., 1970)
   On the Psychology and Pathology of So-Called Occult Phenomena (1902)
   On Hysterical Misreading (1904)
   Cryptomnesia (1905)
   On Manic Mood Disorder (1903)
   A Case of Hysterical Stupor in a Prisoner in Detention (1902)
   On Simulated Insanity (1903)
   A Medical Opinion on a Case of Simulated Insanity (1904)
   A Third and Final Opinion on Two Contradictory Psychiatric Diagnoses (1906)
   On the Psychological Diagnosis of Facts (1905)

2. EXPERIMENTAL RESEARCHES (1973)
   Translated by Leopold Stein in collaboration with Diana Riviere

   STUDIES IN WORD ASSOCIATION (1904–7, 1910)
   The Associations of Normal Subjects (by Jung and F. Riklin)
   An Analysis of the Associations of an Epileptic
   The Reaction-Time Ratio in the Association Experiment

(*continued*)

2. (*continued*)

Experimental Observations on the Faculty of Memory
Psychoanalysis and Association Experiments
The Psychological Diagnosis of Evidence
Association, Dream, and Hysterical Symptom
The Psychopathological Significance of the Association Experiment
Disturbances in Reproduction in the Association Experiment
The Association Method
The Family Constellation

PSYCHOPHYSICAL RESEARCHES (1907–8)

On the Psychophysical Relations of the Association Experiment
Psychophysical Investigations with the Galvanometer and Pneumograph in Normal and Insane Individuals (by F. Peterson and Jung)
Further Investigations on the Galvanic Phenomenon and Respiration in Normal and Insane Individuals (by C. Ricksher and Jung)
Appendix: Statistical Details of Enlistment (1906); New Aspects of Criminal Psychology (1908); The Psychological Methods of Investigation Used in the Psychiatric Clinic of the University of Zurich (1910); On the Doctrine of Complexes ([1911] 1913); On the Psychological Diagnosis of Evidence (1937)

3. THE PSYCHOGENESIS OF MENTAL DISEASE (1960)

The Psychology of Dementia Praecox (1907)
The Content of the Psychoses (1908/1914)
On Psychological Understanding (1914)
A Criticism of Bleuler's Theory of Schizophrenic Negativism (1911)
On the Importance of the Unconscious in Psychopathology (1914)
On the Problem of Psychogenesis in Mental Disease (1919)
Mental Disease and the Psyche (1928)
On the Psychogenesis of Schizophrenia (1939)
Recent Thoughts on Schizophrenia (1957)
Schizophrenia (1958)

4. FREUD AND PSYCHOANALYSIS (1967)

Freud's Theory of Hysteria: A Reply to Aschaffenburg (1906)
The Freudian Theory of Hysteria (1908)
The Analysis of Dreams (1909)
A Contribution to the Psychology of Rumour (1910–11)
On the Significance of Number Dreams (1910–11)
Morton Prince, "The Mechanism and Interpretation of Dreams": A Critical Review (1911)
On the Criticism of Psychoanalysis (1910)
Concerning Psychoanalysis (1912)

The Theory of Psychoanalysis (1913)
General Aspects of Psychoanalysis (1913)
Psychoanalysis and Neurosis (1916)
Some Crucial Points in Psychoanalysis: A Correspondence between Dr. Jung and Dr. Loÿ (1914)
Prefaces to "Collected Papers on Analytical Psychology" (1916, 1917)
The Significance of the Father in the Destiny of the Individual (1909/1949)
Introduction to Kranefeldt's "Secret Ways of the Mind" (1930)
Freud and Jung: Contrasts (1929)

5. SYMBOLS OF TRANSFORMATION ([1911–12/1952] 1956; 2nd edn., 1967)

PART I

Introduction
Two Kinds of Thinking
The Miller Fantasies: Anamnesis
The Hymn of Creation
The Song of the Moth

PART II

Introduction
The Concept of Libido
The Transformation of Libido
The Origin of the Hero
Symbols of the Mother and of Rebirth
The Battle for Deliverance from the Mother
The Dual Mother
The Sacrifice
Epilogue
Appendix: The Miller Fantasies

6. PSYCHOLOGICAL TYPES ([1921] 1971)

A revision by R.F.C. Hull of the translation by H. G. Baynes

Introduction
The Problem of Types in the History of Classical and Medieval Thought
Schiller's Ideas on the Type Problem
The Apollinian and the Dionysian
The Type Problem in Human Character
The Type Problem in Poetry
The Type Problem in Psychopathology

(*continued*)

6. (*continued*)

The Type Problem in Aesthetics
The Type Problem in Modern Philosophy
The Type Problem in Biography
General Description of the Types
Definitions
Epilogue
Four Papers on Psychological Typology (1913, 1925, 1931, 1936)

7. TWO ESSAYS ON ANALYTICAL PSYCHOLOGY (1953; 2nd edn., 1966)

On the Psychology of the Unconscious (1917/1926/1943)
The Relations between the Ego and the Unconscious (1928)
Appendix: New Paths in Psychology (1912); The Structure of the Unconscious (1916) (new versions, with variants, 1966)

8. THE STRUCTURE AND DYNAMICS OF THE PSYCHE (1960; 2nd edn., 1969)

On Psychic Energy (1928)
The Transcendent Function ([1916] 1957)
A Review of the Complex Theory (1934)
The Significance of Constitution and Heredity in Psychology (1929)
Psychological Factors Determining Human Behavior (1937)
Instinct and the Unconscious (1919)
The Structure of the Psyche (1927/1931)
On the Nature of the Psyche (1947/1954)
General Aspects of Dream Psychology (1916/1948)
On the Nature of Dreams (1945/1948)
The Psychological Foundations of Belief in Spirits (1920/1948)
Spirit and Life (1926)
Basic Postulates of Analytical Psychology (1931)
Analytical Psychology and *Weltanschauung* (1928/1931)
The Real and the Surreal (1933)
The Stages of Life (1930–1931)
The Soul and Death (1934)
Synchronicity: An Acausal Connecting Principle (1952)
Appendix: On Synchronicity (1951)

9. PART I. THE ARCHETYPES AND THE COLLECTIVE UNCONSCIOUS (1959; 2nd ed., 1968)

Archetypes of the Collective Unconscious (1934/1954)
The Concept of the Collective Unconscious (1936)
Concerning the Archetypes, with Special Reference to the Anima Concept (1936/1954)

Psychological Aspects of the Mother Archetype (1938/1954)
Concerning Rebirth (1940/1950)
The Psychology of the Child Archetype (1940)
The Psychological Aspects of the Kore (1941)
The Phenomenology of the Spirit in Fairytales (1945/1948)
On the Psychology of the Trickster-Figure (1954)
Conscious, Unconscious, and Individuation (1939)
A Study in the Process of Individuation (1934/1950)
Concerning Mandala Symbolism (1950)
Appendix: Mandalas (1955)

9. PART II. AION ([1951] 1959; 2nd ed., 1968)

RESEARCHES INTO THE PHENOMENOLOGY OF THE SELF

The Ego
The Shadow
The Syzygy: Anima and Animus
The Self
Christ, a Symbol of the Self
The Sign of the Fishes
The Prophecies of Nostradamus
The Historical Significance of the Fish
The Ambivalence of the Fish Symbol
The Fish in Alchemy
The Alchemical Interpretation of the Fish
Background to the Psychology of Christian Alchemical Symbolism
Gnostic Symbols of the Self
The Structure and Dynamics of the Self
Conclusion

10. CIVILIZATION IN TRANSITION (1964; 2nd edn., 1970)
The Role of the Unconscious (1918)
Mind and Earth (1927/1931)
Archaic Man (1931)
The Spiritual Problem of Modern Man (1928/1931)
The Love Problem of a Student (1928)
Woman in Europe (1927)
The Meaning of Psychology for Modern Man (1933/1934)
The State of Psychotherapy Today (1934)
Preface and Epilogue to "Essays on Contemporary Events" (1946)
Wotan (1936)
After the Catastrophe (1945)
The Fight with the Shadow (1946)

(continued)

10. (*continued*)

The Undiscovered Self (Present and Future) (1957)
Flying Saucers: A Modern Myth (1958)
A Psychological View of Conscience (1958)
Good and Evil in Analytical Psychology (1959)
Introduction to Wolff's "Studies in Jungian Psychology" (1959)
The Swiss Line in the European Spectrum (1928)
Reviews of Keyserling's "America Set Free" (1930) and "La Révolution Mondiale" (1934)
The Complications of American Psychology (1930)
The Dreamlike World of India (1939)
What India Can Teach Us (1939)
Appendix: Documents (1933–1938)

11. PSYCHOLOGY AND RELIGION: WEST AND EAST (1958; 2nd edn., 1969)

WESTERN RELIGION

Psychology and Religion (The Terry Lectures) (1938/1940)
A Psychological Approach to the Dogma of the Trinity (1942/1948)
Transformation Symbolism in the Mass (1942/1954)
Forewords to White's "God and the Unconscious" and Werblowsky's "Lucifer and Prometheus" (1952)
Brother Klaus (1933)
Psychotherapists or the Clergy (1932)
Psychoanalysis and the Cure of Souls (1928)
Answer to Job (1952)

EASTERN RELIGION

Psychological Commentaries on "The Tibetan Book of the Great Liberation" (1939/1954) and "The Tibetan Book of the Dead" (1935/1953)
Yoga and the West (1936)
Foreword to Suzuki's "Introduction to Zen Buddhism" (1939)
The Psychology of Eastern Meditation (1943)
The Holy Men of India: Introduction to Zimmer's "Der Weg zum Selbst" (1944)
Foreword to the "I Ching" (1950)

12. PSYCHOLOGY AND ALCHEMY ([1944] 1953; 2nd edn., 1968)
Prefatory note to the English Edition ([1951?] added 1967)
Introduction to the Religious and Psychological Problems of Alchemy
Individual Dream Symbolism in Relation to Alchemy (1936)
Religious Ideas in Alchemy (1937)
Epilogue

13. ALCHEMICAL STUDIES (1968)
Commentary on "The Secret of the Golden Flower" (1929)
The Visions of Zosimos (1938/1954)
Paracelsus as a Spiritual Phenomenon (1942)
The Spirit Mercurius (1943/1948)
The Philosophical Tree (1945/1954)

14. MYSTERIUM CONIUNCTIONIS ([1955–56] 1963; 2nd edn., 1970)

AN INQUIRY INTO THE SEPARATION AND
SYNTHESIS OF PSYCHIC OPPOSITES IN ALCHEMY

The Components of the Coniunctio
The Paradoxa
The Personification of the Opposites
Rex and Regina
Adam and Eve
The Conjunction

15. THE SPIRIT IN MAN, ART, AND LITERATURE (1966)
Paracelsus (1929)
Paracelsus the Physician (1941)
Sigmund Freud in His Historical Setting (1932)
In Memory of Sigmund Freud (1939)
Richard Wilhelm: In Memoriam (1930)
On the Relation of Analytical Psychology to Poetry (1922)
Psychology and Literature (1930/1950)
"Ulysses": A Monologue (1932)
Picasso (1932)

16. THE PRACTICE OF PSYCHOTHERAPY (1954; 2nd edn., 1966)

GENERAL PROBLEMS OF PSYCHOTHERAPY

Principles of Practical Psychotherapy (1935)
What Is Psychotherapy? (1935)
Some Aspects of Modern Psychotherapy (1930)
The Aims of Psychotherapy (1931)
Problems of Modern Psychotherapy (1929)
Psychotherapy and a Philosophy of Life (1943)
Medicine and Psychotherapy (1945)
Psychotherapy Today (1945)
Fundamental Questions of Psychotherapy (1951)

SPECIFIC PROBLEMS OF PSYCHOTHERAPY

The Therapeutic Value of Abreaction (1921/1928)
The Practical Use of Dream-Analysis (1934)

(*continued*)

16. (*continued*)

The Psychology of the Transference (1946)
Appendix: The Realities of Practical Psychotherapy ([1937] added 1966)

17. THE DEVELOPMENT OF PERSONALITY (1954)
Psychic Conflicts in a Child (1910/1946)
Introduction to Wickes's "Analyses der Kinderseele" (1927/1931)
Child Development and Education (1928)
Analytical Psychology and Education: Three Lectures (1926/1946)
The Gifted Child (1943)
The Significance of the Unconscious in Individual Education (1928)
The Development of Personality (1934)
Marriage as a Psychological Relationship (1925)

18. THE SYMBOLIC LIFE (1954)
Translated by R.F.C. Hull and others

Miscellaneous writings

19. COMPLETE BIBLIOGRAPHY OF C. G. JUNG'S WRITINGS (1976; 2nd edn., 1992)

20. GENERAL INDEX TO THE COLLECTED WORKS (1979)

THE ZOFINGIA LECTURES (1983)
Supplementary Volume A to The Collected Works. Edited by William McGuire, translated by Jan van Heurck, introduction by Marie-Louise von Franz

PSYCHOLOGY OF THE UNCONSCIOUS ([1912] 1992)

A STUDY OF THE TRANSFORMATIONS AND SYMBOLISMS OF THE LIBIDO. A CONTRIBUTION TO THE HISTORY OF THE EVOLUTION OF THOUGHT

Supplementary Volume B to the Collected Works. Translated by Beatrice M. Hinkle, introduction by William McGuire

Related publications:

THE BASIC WRITINGS OF C. G. JUNG
Selected and introduced by Violet S. de Laszlo

C. G. JUNG: LETTERS
Selected and edited by Gerhard Adler, in collaboration with Aniela Jaffé. Translations from the German by R.F.C. Hull.

VOL. 1: 1906–1950
VOL. 2: 1951–1961

C. G. JUNG SPEAKING: Interviews and Encounters
Edited by William McGuire and R.F.C. Hull

C. G. JUNG: Word and Image
Edited by Aniela Jaffé

THE ESSENTIAL JUNG
Selected and introduced by Anthony Storr

THE GNOSTIC JUNG
Selected and introduced by Robert A. Segal

PSYCHE AND SYMBOL
Selected and introduced by Violet S. de Laszlo

Notes of C. G. Jung's Seminars:

DREAM ANALYSIS ([1928–30] 1984)
Edited by William McGuire

NIETZSCHE'S *ZARATHUSTRA* ([1934–39] 1988)
Edited by James L. Jarrett (2 vols.)

ANALYTICAL PSYCHOLOGY ([1925] 1989)
Edited by William McGuire

PRINCETON / BOLLINGEN PAPERBACK EDITIONS
FROM THE COLLECTED WORKS OF C. G. JUNG

Aion (CW 9,ii)
Alchemical Studies (CW 13)
Analytical Psychology
Answer to Job
Archetypes and the Collective Unconscious (CW 9,i)
Aspects of the Feminine
Aspects of the Masculine
Basic Writings of C. G. Jung
The Development of Personality (CW 17)
Dreams
Essay on Contemporary Events
Essays on a Science of Mythology
The Essential Jung
Experimental Researches (CW 2)
Flying Saucers
Four Archetypes
Freud and Psychoanalysis (CW 4)
The Gnostic Jung
Mandala Symbolism
Mysterium Coniunctionis (CW 14)
On the Nature of the Psyche
The Practice of Psychotherapy (CW 16)
Psyche and Symbol
Psychiatric Studies (CW 1)
Psychogenesis of Mental Disease (CW 3)
Psychological Types (CW 6)
Psychology and Alchemy (CW 12)
Psychology and the East
Psychology and the Occult
Psychology and Western Religion
The Psychology of the Transference
The Spirit in Man, Art, and Literature (CW 15)
Symbols of Transformation (CW 5)
Synchronicity
Two Essays on Analytical Psychology (CW 7)
The Undiscovered Self

OTHER BOLLINGEN PAPERBACKS DEVOTED TO C. G. JUNG

C. G. Jung Speaking
Complex/Archetype/Symbol in the Psychology of C. G. Jung
Psychological Reflections
Selected Letters
C. G. Jung: Word & Image